Professionalism, Law, and the Ontario Educator

Julian Kitchen
B.A., B.Ed., Ph.D.
Brock University

Christopher Dean
M.A., M.Ed.
Brock University

Highland
press

Published in 2010 by
Highland Press
Box 496, St. Davids, ON L0S 1P0
Telephone (905) 685 5568
Fax (905) 685 4327
E-mail hldpress@cogeco.ca

Canadian Cataloguing in Publication Data

Kitchen, Julian D., 1960-
Professionalism, law, and the Ontario educator / Julian Kitchen, Christopher Dean.

Includes bibliographical references and index.

ISBN 978-0-9865873-0-6

1. Teachers--Legal status, laws, etc.—Ontario.
2. Educational law and legislation—Ontario.
I. Dean, Christopher, 1944– II. Title.

KEO781.K58 2010 344.713'078 C2010-902557-1
KF4175.K58 2010

Cover design: Gnibel
Text design and typesetting: Casey Hooper Design
Editor and project coordinator: Donald G. Bastian
Bastian Publishing Services Ltd. www.bastianpubserv.com

Printed and bound in Canada
2 3 4 5 14 13 12

CONTENTS

PREFACE

Effective classroom teachers act *in loco parentis* to ensure that students learn in safe and supportive school environments. A broad knowledge of education law helps new teachers understand their rights and responsibilities. The study of education law, however, should involve more than an understanding of "do's and don'ts" and correct procedures. It should address issues at the very heart of teaching as a profession grounded in an ethic of caring. Our aim here is to capture the reader's interest by linking education law and professionalism to the central concerns of classroom teachers.

Each chapter is designed to stimulate thinking and generate discussion about topics of practical importance to teachers. Legal terminology is clearly defined and illustrated with examples. Concepts are broken into manageable chunks, with cases used to illustrate how education law relates to the teaching context. Summaries of significant legal cases are used to illustrate education law in action. These cases serve both as stories from the field and guideposts to help new teachers become prudent and effective practitioners. Some chapters feature controversial issues facing teachers or practical advice on working well with stakeholders in the education system.

Because education is primarily a provincial responsibility, much attention is given to the *Education Act* and other provincial legislation. Also, the role of the Ontario College of Teachers is considered in each chapter, often with examples of College rulings on misconduct cases. Chapters end with a review of key information and a fictionalized case study.

Our perspective on the issues of this book is a reflection our experiences as teachers, principals, and teacher educators. Julian Kitchen was a classroom teacher for fourteen years and a summer school principal for three. He has been a teacher educator for eleven years, as an adjunct professor at the Ontario Institute for Studies in Education of the University of Toronto and now as an associate professor in the Faculty of Education of Brock University. Christopher Dean teaches education law in the Faculty of Education at Brock University. He was a classroom teacher for twenty years and a secondary school administrator for fourteen.

We thank teacher candidates at Brock University for helping us develop an accessible and practical book to serve the needs of professional educators in Ontario. Over the past three years, their positive feedback and constructive suggestions on draft chapters have motivated and sustained our efforts. The many fine resources developed by the Ontario Ministry of Education and the Ontario College of Teachers were also of great use.

Finally, we acknowledge editor Don Bastian and Highland Press for enhancing the clarity of this book.

We trust that our practical and theoretical backgrounds will serve to make the subject of professionalism and the law of interest and help to you.

Julian Kitchen
Christopher Dean

Chapter 1

Studying Education Law

After reading this chapter, you will understand the purpose of law, its sources and categories, and where education law fits within the Canadian constitutional framework. In addition, you will acquire a basic understanding of the structure of the educational system at the local and provincial levels.

Speed limit 100.

No parking without a permit.

No trespassing.

No smoking on school property.

All visitors must report to the main office.

No loitering in the hallways during classes.

Teachers must take attendance.

Students are required to attend school.

Teachers must teach the curriculum mandated by the school board and province.

Teachers may be disciplined for their words or actions outside school.

It would be easy to feel overwhelmed by the myriad laws, regulations, policies, and procedures that govern daily life in a society as complex as ours. Yet it would be virtually impossible for us to live and work without them.

The same is true of our schools. They are bound by laws that regulate the behaviour and relationships of the various members of the school community. Without them, it would be difficult if not impossible for schools to function as safe and supportive environments where students and teachers work together to achieve common purposes.

Many new teachers, while committed to making a difference in the lives of students, may not have considered in systematic fashion the professional, ethical, and legal dimensions of teaching. Yet the events and interactions that unfold in classrooms and schools are imbued with ethical implications. Educators need to develop sound judgment in order to properly exercise their duty of care to students. The legal framework and professional standards that govern the school system reflect the values and beliefs of our society concerning the welfare of children. By developing an understanding of education law and professional expectations, teachers can be guided by the basic principles underlying the law rather than become intimidated by the minutiae of specific rules and regulations.

The overview of law that follows in this chapter will give you a basic understanding of law, paving the way for you to understand all of the issues discussed in this book.

THE LEGAL SYSTEM IN CANADA

PURPOSE OF LAW

What would happen if there were no rules guiding human behaviour? How would you manage to drive safely from your home to the downtown core? How would we protect our homes and families? How would schools be run? How much learning would take place? Who would pay the teachers?

Whenever people form into groups, whether formally or informally, they soon develop rules. Why? To maintain order. Without clear rules that apply to everyone in the group, there would be chaos or rule by the strongest. Canada is a highly complex society in which our individual actions are bound by laws intended to guide our conduct, protect everyone's rights and freedoms, and keep us safe from crime.

In democratic societies such as ours, the actions of both citizens and governments are guided by the rule of law. This fundamental principle of justice affirms that laws are necessary to regulate society, apply equally to everyone, and cannot arbitrarily be changed or interpreted by those in authority.

LAW AND MORALITY

Although we often focus on the practical purpose of particular laws, it is important to keep in mind that the law is essentially the enactment of a moral code for guiding the behaviour of citizens. Individual laws are generally derived from larger moral principles that are widely accepted as collective community standards. In Canada, many of these standards are based on the Judeo-Christian values of our forebears. This is reflected in the *Canadian Charter of Rights and Freedoms*, which states that "Canada is founded upon principles that recognize the supremacy of God and the rule of law."

Today not everyone accepts the collective community standards that have guided lawmakers in the past. Traditional social norms that remain deeply held by many have been successfully challenged by others who regard them as no longer relevant or meaningful. Recently, the issue of same-sex marriage has proved very divisive. In our multicultural and multi-faith society, new communities of belief sometimes clash with both traditional norms and contemporary standards. Requests for the application of sharia law by some Islamic groups is one example of this moral debate. Schools, as important social institutions, sometimes become battlegrounds for these issues. Prayer in schools and sex education are two examples of moral issues that have caused considerable debate among people with widely differing viewpoints.

It may be useful to distinguish between the moral domain and social norms (Nucci, 2001). The moral domain is centred on foundational principles or virtues such as honesty, justice, integrity, respect, kindness, and trustworthiness. These are universally accepted and can act as guides for the behaviour of all citizens. Social norms are non-principle-based conventions or personal preferences of particular religious, cultural, and social groups. As will be shown later, the courts are often guided by foundational principles as they rule on controversial court cases.

CANADA'S LEGAL TRADITION

Canada's law originates from three distinct yet interconnected sources: common law, statute law, and constitutional law. Understanding these general sources will help you make sense of the specific laws that relate to education in Ontario.

Common Law

Most people in medieval Europe worked as serfs on the feudal estates of nobles and lords. Under feudalism, which was brought to England by William the Conqueror in 1066, serfs obtained the right to work farmland by swearing fealty (loyalty and service) to their lords. Lords, in turn, swore fealty to the monarch, who owned all of the land in the kingdom. Among the duties of lords was acting as a judge in disputes taking place on their land.

As England grew in size and complexity, monarchs appointed travelling judges to rule on controversial cases. These judges met regularly to establish consistent laws and punishments in criminal and civil cases. From these legal decisions emerged the English tradition of common law. *Common law*, which applied across England, was based on the principle of precedent. A *precedent* is a previous legal decision that serves as a rule or example. The rulings in some cases became known by members of the legal community as particularly significant, leading judges to make similar decisions in cases with similar facts. Over time, these decisions were written down, and later all cases were systematically documented.

When English colonists settled in North America, they brought the English common law tradition with them. Today it remains a critical part of the Canadian and American legal systems.

Common law is also known as case law because, as mentioned, significant past cases serve as precedents for present legal rulings. In this book, key cases are cited to explain how the law applies to the work of educators in schools. Studying legal cases may seem daunting to many readers because of the legal nomenclature and language used. Yet very often they are interesting stories that pose dilemmas for jurists and society. Understanding these cases, and the lessons offered in the legal judgments associated with them, can improve our understanding and practice as teachers. The case of *R. v. A.M.* is a good example.

Case: Should Police Sniffer Dogs Be Allowed in Schools?
R. v. A.M. (2008)

On November 7, 2002, three Sarnia police officers visited St. Patrick's High School with a sniffer dog. They were responding to an "open invitation" from the principal, who was enforcing a zero tolerance policy for possession of illegal drugs and alcohol. The principal gave them permission to conduct a search of the school premises even though there were no reports that drugs were present at the school that day.

After the principal informed students and teachers that they had to remain in their classrooms, the police and sniffer dog began their search of the premises. In the gym, the sniffer dog led police to a backpack containing ten bags of marijuana and ten magic mushrooms (psilocybin). The student identified by its contents as the owner of the bag was charged with possession for the purpose of trafficking marijuana and possession of psilocybin.

A lower court ruled that the search was unreasonable and violated the student's constitutional rights under the *Canadian Charter of Rights and Freedoms.* The police's actions were criticized as being unreasonable under criminal law and the *Education Act* since the "entire student body" was "held in detention" for a "warrantless random search."

The Crown appealed the lower court decision to the Supreme Court of Canada, where it was upheld by a majority of justices. They found that the police did not have the authority to conduct sniffer dog searches without an adequate basis. As for what constitutes an adequate basis, four justices set the bar high at "reasonable and probable grounds," while three were satisfied with "reasonable suspicion."

(1) What are the facts of the case?
(2) What important issues does this case raise?
(3) Why did the court rule in favour of the student?
(4) What are your thoughts on this case and the final court decision?

These issues are explored in more depth in chapter 6, Ensuring Safe Classrooms and Schools.

Studying Cases

Each legal case has a formal case *citation*, or reference heading, designed as an aid to locating legal cases. The citation begins with the name of the case, such as R. v. A.M. The letter "R" for Rex (King) or Regina (Queen) denotes that this is a criminal case in which the Crown or government is charging a member of the public. The other name is that of the defendant; in this case, the defendant was a minor (under the age of eighteen), so his name does not appear in full. In civil cases where one person or organization sues another, two names appear. In *Chamberlain v. Surrey School District*, for example, the first name indicates that Chamberlain is the plaintiff suing the local school district, which is the defendant.

The year of the case appears next, followed by a reference to one of the case-law reporters. In general, when cases are cited in this book they will be identified simply by name and year of case.

Statute Law

While common law is an important part of our legal system, most of our laws are now made by democratically elected representatives. *Statute law* consists of all the laws or acts passed by the Parliament of Canada and the provincial and territorial legislatures.

In order to make or change a law, the elected government must work through a stringent process that ensures careful consideration of the law and its effects. When, for example, the Ontario government decided that teachers should be regulated through a professional body, it introduced a bill in the Ontario Provincial Parliament. This *bill*, or draft of proposed legislation, was prepared by the Ministry of Education and introduced to the legislature for *first reading* by the Minister of Education.

Once the bill passed first reading, which meant that approval was given to consider the bill, it was introduced again in *second reading*, during which it was debated in general terms before a second vote was taken. The bill was then sent to a *committee* of the legislature for careful consideration. At the committee stage, experts were called as witnesses, and interest groups and members of the public were invited to make deputations. Committee members studied the bill in detail and proposed changes to it. Each section of the bill was voted on separately.

Once the bill passed through the committee stage, it was re-introduced to the legislature for *third reading*. After a brief debate, a third vote was taken and the bill was approved by the legislature. Later it was signed by the Lieutenant Governor of Ontario and proclaimed into law. The *Ontario College of Teachers Act* became law in 1996, and a year later the Ontario College of Teachers (OCT) came into being.

Federal legislation follows a similar process, with bills passing through the same stages in both the elected House of Commons and the appointed Senate before being signed by the Governor General of Canada.

In addition to passing new laws, legislatures also amend existing laws through the same stringent process to meet perceived new needs. One law that has been amended often is the *Criminal Code*, which is a federal statute containing the majority of criminal laws passed by Parliament. It consists of both criminal offences, sentences for crimes, and procedures to be followed in criminal court cases. This act was first passed in 1892 as a codification of rules that had emerged from common law. Since then, the code has been amended almost every year to respond to changing needs and beliefs. Not all crimes are listed in the *Criminal Code*, because criminal law has become more complex over the years. Laws such as the *Youth Criminal Justice Act* and *Controlled Drug and Substances Act* also outline criminal offences.

Studying Statutes

Legislation can sometimes look imposing and even confusing to anyone lacking a legal background, but statutes and regulations essentially contain rules and procedures written out in precise and detailed legal language. Teachers need to be able to read and understand the statutes and regulations that guide the education system and their work as educators.

Statutes are divided into parts so they can be easily referenced and found by lawyers and citizens. The name of the act is written in italics and then divided into sections, subsections, paragraphs, etc. For example, *Ontario*

College of Teachers Act, section 26(1) refers to section 26 of the act, which, in paragraph 1 states that any member of the public can launch a complaint against a member. Some acts, such as the *Criminal Code*, are divided into chapters before being divided into sections.

Statutes are revised periodically and bound into volumes. The most common abbreviation for these volumes is "R.S.", as in the Revised Statutes of Canada (R.S.C.) and the Revised Statutes of Ontario (R.S.O.). The *Ontario College of Teachers Act* is found in Statutes of Ontario, 1996. Generally, when common education legislation is cited in this book, no reference will be made to the revised statute volume in which the statute or regulations can be found.

Statutes are often supplemented by regulations, which typically elaborate on sections of the act under which they were created. *Regulations* are orders in council approved by the government without further legislation. No further legislation is needed since the statute under which the regulation is issued already gives the government the power to make regulations on a variety of topics. So, for example, section 11 of the *Education Act* gives the Minister the authority to make regulations on a wide range of issues, including the qualifications and duties of principals and teachers. In turn, *Regulation 298 (Operation of Schools—General)* adds considerable procedural detail about these two issues as well as other matters relating to the operation of schools that are not included in the *Education Act*. The advantage of a regulation is that, since it does not have to go through the same stringent process in the legislature as a statute, it can be amended much more easily.

Principals and other school administrators have books in their offices that contain most of the laws related to education. Two common volumes are the *Education Statutes and Regulations of Ontario Consolidation* and *Consolidated Ontario Education Statutes and Regulations*. These are useful reference tools for teachers and school administrators when they need to check on particular legal points.

Constitutional Law

A third source of Canadian law is the Constitution. A constitution is a body of law dealing with the division of powers between levels of government, and the relationship between a government and its people.

Canada's first constitution is actually a statute of the British Parliament. The *British North America Act* (*BNA Act*), which took effect on July 1, 1867, created the Dominion of Canada, which originally consisted of Ontario, Quebec, New Brunswick, and Nova Scotia. Other provinces would later join the federation. Canada was not a fully independent country at the time; Britain controlled our foreign policy and the Judicial Committee of the Privy Council in the U.K. was our highest court. Also, Canada could not change its constitution without requesting amendments by the British Parliament.

In 1931, the British Parliament passed the *Statute of Westminster*, which gave Canada control over its foreign affairs, and in 1949 the Supreme Court of Canada became the highest court of appeal for Canadian legal cases.

In 1982, after the majority of provinces (Quebec being the sole exception) agreed on a formula to amend the constitution, the *Constitution Act* was signed into law by Queen Elizabeth II. This new constitution guides the governments and courts of Canada on a wide range of important issues.

Constitution Act, 1867. The *BNA Act*, now renamed the *Constitution Act, 1867*, remains the main part of the new Constitution. The most significant sections of the 1867 act are the sections that outline the jurisdictions of the various levels of government. Section 91 outlines the powers of the federal government, while section 92 outlines the powers of provincial governments. Section 93 grants control over education to provincial governments.

DIVISION OF POWERS: CONSTITUTION ACT, 1867

Federal Powers (Section 91) include:	Provincial Powers (Sections 92 and 93) include:
• Peace, order, and good government • Criminal law • Banking and currency • Marriage and divorce • Aboriginal peoples and lands • Postal service • International trade	• Property rights • Civil rights • Police • Highways • Hospitals • Public schools • Separate schools

While the education of Canadian citizens may be of national interest, under the Constitution it lies (with the exception of First Nations education) within the exclusive jurisdiction of provincial governments. In Ontario, education is overseen by the Minister of Education, who through the *Education Act* has overarching control over nearly every aspect of the school system. The provincial government could if it so chose administer the whole system centrally, including, for example, hiring and firing teachers and paying their salaries. Traditionally, however, the government has delegated the day-to-day running of the system to locally elected school boards. It is important to remember that school boards, like municipal governments, are "creatures of the province," exercising powers and duties delegated to them by the provincial government. As such, their existence is not protected by the Constitution.

A major reason for designating education as a provincial area of jurisdiction in the *BNA Act* was the desire to protect religious and language rights. At the time of confederation, French-Canadian Roman Catholics believed that their educational interests could be served best if public education was administered by the government of Quebec rather than by a federal government dominated by English-speaking Protestants. They also believed that separate schools in Ontario would protect their religion and culture beyond the borders of Quebec. In return, they accepted constitutional guarantees for Protestant schools in Quebec.

Although section 93 of the *BNA Act* gave each province the exclusive right to make laws in relation to education, it went further to protect denominational rights in Canadian schools. It stated that no law "can prejudicially affect any Right or Privilege with respect to Denominational Schools which any Class of Persons have by Law in the Province at the Union" (the time of Confederation).

As a result, Roman Catholics in Ontario have a constitutional right that is not extended to members of other religious groups. The *Constitution Act, 1982* is explicit in guaranteeing that the *Charter of Rights and Freedoms* is not to abrogate these rights.

It is doubtful whether Confederation would have occurred if language and denominational concerns had not been addressed in the *BNA Act*, which had to be ratified by all the founding provinces. The implications for education in Ontario are outlined later in this chapter.

The Canadian Charter of Rights and Freedoms. The *Charter of Rights and Freedoms* is regarded by many as the most important part of the *Constitution Act, 1982*. The *Charter* also plays a critical role in education law. The *Charter* lists the civil rights and freedoms of all Canadians. These include:

- freedom of conscience and religion,
- freedom of thought and belief,
- the right to be secure from unreasonable search and seizure, and
- the right to equality without discrimination based on race, national or ethnic origin, colour, religion, sex, age or mental or physical disability.

Notwithstanding the various general rights and freedoms listed above, section 29 of the document makes clear that nothing in the *Charter* may interfere with the denominational rights of separate schools guaranteed under the original *Constitution Act, 1867*. In addition, section 23 establishes minority language educational rights for speakers of Canada's two national languages. In general terms, these rights guarantee citizens whose first language is that of the English or French linguistic minority population of the province in which they live the right to have their children educated in that language, numbers permitting.

The rights in the *Charter* are far more significant than any identified in common law or statute law, because not only the courts but all levels of government are required to abide by its guarantees. Furthermore, those who believe that their rights have been infringed may apply to the courts for a remedy. As a result, many groups have applied to the courts to protest laws or government policies that they perceive to be unconstitutional. The lawyers for the accused in *R. v. A.M.*, for example, argued that their client's constitutional right to be secure from unreasonable search and seizure had been violated. Other parties, as you will discover in subsequent chapters, have successfully appealed for remedies to perceived human and equality rights violations by teachers and school boards.

The *Charter*, like other common law and statute law, is subject to the interpretation of judges. Over the years, Supreme Court justices have had to rule on controversial issues such as abortion, corporal punishment of children, censorship of pornography, and same-sex marriage.

Since our education system is such an important public institution, events occurring in schools often lead to court cases, some of which have resulted in significant changes to our understanding of rights and freedoms in our society.

What happens when two rights or freedoms collide? The case below illustrates how the court works through such complex issues.

Case: Multani v. Commission Scolaire Marguerite-Bourgeoys (2006)

In 2001, twelve-year-old Gurbaj Singh Multani was playing in the school playground in Quebec when his kirpan fell to the ground. This playground incident led to a major constitutional case that will define human rights in Canada for decades to come.

The kirpan is a dagger worn by many devout Sikh men and boys. Although it once functioned as a dagger, it has become an important symbol of morality, justice, and faith.

The school administration, which permitted Sikh students to wear kirpans, regarded this as a safety issue. The parents were asked to safely secure the kirpan inside Gurbaj's clothing so it could not fall out again. The parents accepted this as a reasonable way to balance religious freedom and school safety.

When the school board learned of this incident, it revoked the agreement and determined that kirpans in schools constituted a potential threat to student safety and violated the school's code of conduct, which prohibited weapons. Since Gurbaj was forbidden from wearing a kirpan, his parents withdrew him from the public school system and filed a lawsuit against the school board.

In May 2002, the Superior Court of Quebec rejected the board's ban on the wearing of kirpans. It did, however, stipulate that Gurbaj was to be required to secure his kirpan by placing it in a wooden case, wrapped in fabric, and sewn into his clothes.

The Quebec Court of Appeal overturned this judgment in March 2004. It ruled that kirpans constituted a potential safety threat. The school board's duty to ensure safety for all students was deemed to outweigh protecting one student's religious rights.

This controversial case, which raised many important ethical and legal issues, was then appealed to the Supreme Court of Canada. In March 2006, the Supreme Court ruled that a complete ban on kirpans violated section 2(a) of the *Canadian Charter of Rights and Freedoms,* which protects freedom of religion. The court did not regard the curtailing of this right as reasonable or justifiable under section 1 of the *Charter.* While the Supreme Court acknowledged limits to freedom of religion, it did not find a total ban to be proportional to the threat posed by the kirpan. As a result, it affirmed the set of conditions designed by the Superior Court to address the safety concerns of the board.

The justices of the Supreme Court determined that mutual respect and tolerance are essential to living in a multicultural society. Students could learn to distinguish between a weapon and a religious artifact important to one group. Also, the withdrawal of Gurbaj from the school underlined the importance of kirpans to the Sikh community.

Currently, a number of school boards in Ontario have policies permitting kirpans in schools under specific conditions.

---

(1) Why was Gurbaj wearing a kirpan?

(2) Why did the school board decide to ban kirpans?

(3) Do you think the Supreme Court ruling was fair? Why or why not?

These issues are explored in more depth in chapter 7, The Rights and Responsibilities of Students and Parents.

Studying Constitutional Cases

Constitutional challenges move through the courts in the same fashion as common law cases. Judges at various levels make rulings based on both the merits of the cases and their interpretation of existing laws. Judges are expected to defer to the rulings of higher-level courts in cases with similar facts. Major constitutional cases, such as *Multani v. Commission Scolaire Marguerite-Bourgeoys*, often introduce new issues for the courts to consider. As these cases wind their way through the court system, individual judges— and later, panels of judges—weigh in on the constitutional and other issues at hand. By the time the Supreme Court hears the case, a significant body of legal thought already exists on the issues of the case.

The ruling of the Supreme Court is the final word on these issues, which makes it both an interpreter of the law and, in practical terms, a maker of the law. Courts often defer to the legislatures to make decisions. For example, the Supreme Court initially refused to make decisions on abortion cases until Parliament had debated the issue. The failure of Parliament to resolve the issue led the court to rule that women had the right to abortions, although the government could regulate conditions.

Constitutional cases can be difficult to understand because they are very complex and tightly argued. Making them all the more confusing is the fact that the Supreme Court ruling often involves detailed analyses of the decisions of various lower courts, many of which may have ruled on different sides of the issue. Nonetheless, studying these cases is worth the effort, because they define the society in which we live and the schools in which we work.

CATEGORIES OF LAW

There are many categories of law. Understanding these in broad terms helps us make sense of the laws that affect our practice as teachers. Unfortunately, they are not easily distinguished from each other. In many cases, several different categories of law apply to a single situation.

The first broad distinction is between international law and domestic law. *International law* includes treaty law and laws written by international bodies such as the United Nations. These international laws do not apply directly to education in Canada. *Domestic law* refers to the laws that govern life within a nation's borders. In Canada, these laws include ones deriving from case, statute, and constitutional sources.

Domestic law is further divided into procedural law and substantive law. *Procedural law* outlines the legal processes that must be followed in order to protect an individual's rights given under substantive law. For the most part, this book will not examine procedural law, except for the *Statutory Powers Procedures Act*, which outlines the processes that tribunals must follow in order to ensure that individuals are treated fairly under Ontario administrative law. (See the Disciplinary Investigations in Schools section in chapter 6, pp. 186–87).

Domestic substantive law comprises two broad categories: public law and private law. *Public law* addresses the relationship between the government and the people of a society. It is divided into constitutional law (discussed earlier), criminal law, and administrative law. *Criminal law* defines crimes and sets penalties for those crimes. Although criminal acts may be directed at individual citizens, the law regards these acts as violations of the public interest; thus, charges are laid by a Crown Attorney. In criminal cases, guilt must be proved beyond a reasonable doubt. *Administrative law* deals with the relationships between citizens and government agencies. The decisions of the Ministry of Education, school boards, and the Ontario College of Teachers, all based on principles of administrative law, have a profound impact on the lives of students and teachers.

DOMESTIC LAW IN CANADA

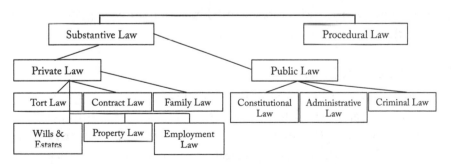

Private law, more generally known as *civil law*, deals with the relationships between individuals and/or organizations (e.g., companies and school

boards). Its primary purpose is to manage the behaviour of people and organizations in conflict and award damages to those who have been wronged.
There are no Crown Attorneys involved in civil cases. The filer of the lawsuit
is known as the *plaintiff*, while the person who is being sued is the *defendant*.
In civil cases, the standard of proof is "a balance of probabilities," rather than
"beyond a reasonable doubt."

Branches of civil law are tort law, contract law, family law, wills and
estates, property law, and employment law. The most significant of these for
educators are tort law and employment law. *Tort law*, which will be covered
in depth in later chapters, permits someone to sue an individual or organization for a wrong committed, whether intentional or unintentional. An
example of tort law would be a former student's suit against a teacher and the
school because s/he may have been sexually assaulted. A lawsuit could also be
launched by someone who alleges s/he was been injured due to negligence
(carelessness) on the part of a teacher. *Employment law* governs the relationship between employees and employers. In education, the *collective agreements* between teachers' federations and school districts govern issues such as
salaries, working conditions, and dismissal and grievance procedures.

As you will discover, more than one category of law can apply to a particular situation. For example, a teacher who is alleged to have assaulted a student
could be charged with assault or child abuse (criminal law), professionally disciplined by the Ontario College of Teachers (administrative law), suspended or
dismissed (employment law), and/or sued for damages (tort law).

By acquiring the knowledge and skills of an ethical and professional
practitioner who acts with care and prudence, you can avoid getting caught
up in the complex machinery of the law.

EDUCATION LAW

Education law, or school law, is a term that refers broadly to the wide range
of laws that apply to students, teachers, schools, and school boards. Some of
these laws (e.g., the *Education Act*, the *Ontario College of Teachers Act*, and the
Teaching Profession Act) relate specifically to schools. Other laws that apply
to all Canadians (e.g., the *Criminal Code*) or to all Ontario citizens (e.g., the
Child and Family Services Act) may have particular force within the educa-

tional context. For example, since teachers are responsible for the care of children, they are held to a higher standard of care than ordinary citizens. In addition, teachers as professionals are expected to adhere to standards of practice befitting professionals. School boards constantly require legal advice to ensure that they are complying with the specific and specialized statutes, regulations, and policies that apply to education. The collective agreements between school boards and teachers' federations also require specialized understandings. Furthermore, as custodians of children, educators need to have some awareness of privacy law, family law, and criminal law.

Teachers who understand ethics, professionalism, and education law are better able to make sound educational decisions. Here's how Justice Paul S. Rouleau (2006) of the Court of Appeal for Ontario put it in his speech "Education in Transition: A Delicate Balance":

> Taken independently or as a whole, these cases show a consistent approach by the courts in recognizing the professionalism, rights and, importantly, the judgment of educators ... I hope that the educators among you are able to take up my challenge and operate within the legal framework in a way that respects your ultimate professional goal or purpose: to be an effective educator. Know that courts show respect for decisions made by educators.

THE EDUCATION SYSTEM IN ONTARIO

In Canada, public education is primarily administered by local school boards working under the direction of provincial governments, which have jurisdiction according to the *Constitution Act, 1867*. The one significant exception is the education of First Nations students, which is the responsibility of Indian and Northern Affairs Canada (INAC). INAC funds band councils and First Nations education authorities for the education of 120,000 kindergarten to grade 12 students who attend schools on reserves or who attend provincially run schools off reserve.

The Ontario education system is extremely large and complex. As of 2007–2008, according to the Ministry of Education, there were 4,026 elementary and 897 secondary schools in Ontario serving the needs of over two million students. There were also 116,179 teachers (full-time equivalents) in Ontario, 72,207 of them elementary and 43,971 secondary. These schools were administered by 7,368 principals and vice-principals, 5,281 of them elementary and 1,887 secondary. Government funding for public education in Ontario for 2009–2010 was projected at $19.8 billion.

As mentioned, education is a provincial responsibility according to the *Constitution Act, 1867*. Publicly funded schools in Ontario, however, are administered by elected local school boards, public and separate. Who, then, is in charge of our schools?

The Constitution clearly identifies education as an area of provincial jurisdiction, even though schools are run locally. The courts have reinforced this through decisions in a number of cases in which public and separate school boards have sought constitutional status. As was made clear in *Ontario Public School Boards Association v. Ontario (Attorney General)* (1999):

> Municipal governments and special purpose municipal institutions such as school boards are creatures of the provincial government subject to the constitutional limits of s. 93 ... these institutions have no constitutional status or independent autonomy and the province has absolute and unfettered legal power to do with them as it wills.

The fact that school boards have sought more powers from the courts suggests that their relationship with the provincial government, while generally positive and sustainable, is not always easy.

How do the Ministry and the school boards work together? What roles do each play? What are some of the sources of tension between them?

ONTARIO MINISTRY OF EDUCATION

The government of Ontario, through the Ministry of Education, provides the statutory basis for education in Ontario's publicly funded schools. The *Education Act*, along with its attendant regulations, guidelines, and policies, establishes rules for how school boards and schools are administered. For example, it sets policies and guidelines for school trustees, directors of education, principals, and other school board officials.

The Minister of Education, who is an elected member of the Ontario Provincial Parliament and an appointed member of the provincial cabinet, is responsible for public policy and political direction. The Deputy Minister, an appointed official, is responsible for the day-to-day operations of the Ministry.

The Ministry of Education administers the system of publicly funded elementary and secondary school education in Ontario, in accordance with the directions set by the provincial government. Provincial curriculum documents determine the subjects that are covered in classrooms. Diploma and graduation requirements are also determined at the provincial level, as are the textbooks that may be used in Ontario schools.

Other legislation and policy documents outline both codes of conduct for students and discipline procedures that teachers and principals may apply. Finally, much of the funding for education is either provided or controlled by the provincial government.

Increasingly, the Ministry of Education has been demanding greater accountability from schools and school boards. The Education Quality and Accountability Office (EQAO) was established by the Ontario government in 1996 to evaluate the quality and effectiveness of elementary and secondary school education. EQAO is responsible for:

- developing and administering tests to evaluate the achievement of Ontario elementary and secondary school students;
- reporting test results to the Minister and to the public; and
- providing recommendations to improve test results.

This increased scrutiny, combined with strict financial constraints, has been a source of considerable tension in recent years.

SCHOOL BOARDS

While educational policy is set at the provincial level, the running of schools at the local level is the responsibility of publicly funded and locally elected school boards. They work, within the administrative constraints set by the provincial government, to meet the specific educational needs of students within their jurisdictions.

Ontario's schools are administered by seventy-two district school boards and eleven school authorities. There are thirty-one English-language public school boards, which are non-denominational and open to all school-age students in the province. There are twenty-nine English-language Roman Catholic school boards. These are operated according to Roman Catholic principles but are also accessible to all students. In addition, there are four French-language public school boards and eight French-language Catholic school boards. In all cases, the boards are overseen by locally elected school trustees. School authorities consist of geographically isolated boards and hospital school boards.

School boards are responsible for all of the details of running a local school board and individual schools. The following list of responsibilities under the *Education Act* conveys some of the complexities that school board trustees and administrators face:

- determining the number, size, and location of schools
- building, equipping, and furnishing schools
- providing education programs that meet the needs of the school community, including needs for special education
- prudent management of the funds allocated by the province to support all board activities, including education programs for elementary and secondary school students, and the building and maintaining of schools
- preparing an annual budget
- supervising the operation of schools and their teaching programs
- developing policy for safe arrival programs for elementary schools
- establishing a school council at each school
- hiring teachers and other staff
- helping teachers improve their teaching practices
- teacher performance
- approving schools' textbook and learning materials choices, based on the list of approved materials provided by the Ministry of Education

- enforcing the student attendance provisions of the *Education Act*
- ensuring that schools abide by the *Education Act* and its regulations.

These responsibilities can lead to heated debate in the community. Parents often attend meetings in large numbers to influence decisions concerning transportation to schools and the provision of special programs (e.g., French immersion). Opening new schools also tends to generate heated discussions about new school boundaries. Proposals to close existing schools usually face profound resistance.

School boards, in order to meet these demands, are very large and complex organizations. The Hamilton-Wentworth District School Board (HWDSB), for example, is led by a board of eleven trustees, one of whom is chair of the board. These trustees are elected for four-year terms. The school board must appoint a supervisory officer as Director of Education. The director runs the day-to-day operations of the school board, including implementing provincial and board policies and submitting an annual report (*Education Act*, section 283). Given the size of the HWDSB, the director is assisted by an Associate Director, eleven superintendents, and various departmental managers. According to the *Education Act*, a school board may employ "such other supervisory officers as it considers necessary to supervise all aspects of the programs under its jurisdiction" (section 279). The superintendents, according to regulation, must have successfully completed courses granting them Supervisory Officer papers; in the case of superintendents of education, these papers can be earned only after they have also completed principals' qualifications. A complex bureaucracy serves under them to keep the entire system running effectively. At the individual school level, the principal is the person with the authority and responsibility for the management and organization of the school.

Ontario school boards are funded through a "funding formula" developed by the provincial government. Initial funding is from local property taxes raised from businesses and residents in the local municipality. These funds are topped up by the province to the level allocated in the Foundation Grant. The Foundation Grant allocates money on a per pupil basis to cover salaries and benefits for educators, textbooks and materials, equipment, supplies, and local initiatives. Additional funding is provided for the repair, maintenance, and building of schools. Further funds are provided for boards with unique needs such as special education classes, English as Second Language, and remote schools.

School trustees, who are elected every four years, collectively establish policies for the board within the scope of their powers under the *Education Act*. Individually, they have no authority over the school system, because the day-to-day running of the system is guided by the director, with principals as managers of individual schools. Meetings of the board and its standing committees are open to the public, though the board may hold parts of a meeting *in camera* (behind closed doors) if it is dealing with sensitive matters such as the security of board property; acquisition or disposal of a school site; intimate personal or financial information; salary negotiations; or litigation affecting the board (section 207).

Legislation now requires boards to arrange for the election of at least one but no more than three student trustees as representatives of all of the students in the jurisdiction (*Regulation 7/07*). Hamilton, for example, has two student trustees, who may speak and vote on issues. They are not *members* of the board (their votes are recorded but do not count as part of the official tally), and they are not entitled to attend closed-door meetings.

If a school board does not follow the rules imposed by the province, the Minister of Education may take it over. This could occur, for example, if a board fails to follow prescribed courses of study and minimum teaching time, or applies funds contrary to the Legislative Grant Regulations (*Education Act*, section 230). In addition, the Minister has the authority to scrutinize the financial affairs of a board. This includes the power to direct the board to comply with Ministry policies, such as the requirement that boards maintain a balanced operating budget. Failure to comply could lead to the appointment by the Minister of a supervisor to run the board in place of the elected trustees. This occurred in 2007 when the Dufferin-Peel Catholic District School Board refused to balance its budget by raising taxes or reducing costs.

In 2010, the government increased its oversight authority by granting the Minister of Education the authority to review a board's performance and recommend measures for improvement. *Under Regulation 43/10: Provincial*

Interest in Education, the Minister may provide for a a review of a board's performance if the Minister has concerns about any of the following:

- the academic achievement of students
- the health and safety of students
- board governance
- the performance of the board or director of education in carrying out statutory duties
- the level of involvement by parents.

The Minister may then make recommendations based on the findings of the reviewer, and require the board to report back on its implementation of the recommendations.

CHECKING YOUR UNDERSTANDING

- The law is a set of rules a society develops to protect the rights and freedoms of its citizens.

- Much of our law is derived from common law developed by judges in England.

- A precedent is a legal decision that applies to future cases with similar circumstances.

- Case citations are a nomenclature designed to assist in finding court decisions in legal books.

- A provincial statute is an act passed by the legislature and proclaimed as law by the Lieutenant Governor.

- A regulation is an order in council that supplements laws enacted through statute.

- Education is a provincial responsibility under the *Constitution Act, 1867.*

- Denominational rights of Roman Catholics in Ontario are protected under the *Constitution Act, 1867.*

- The *Canadian Charter of Rights and Freedoms* is the part of the Constitution that protects human and equality rights for all Canadians.

- The *Charter* also grants minority language educational rights to the English and French linguistic minority population of a province.

- Public law is divided into the categories of constitutional, criminal, and administrative law.

- Tort law and employment law are types of civil law.

- Education law is a term that refers to a range of laws that apply directly or indirectly to students, teachers, schools, and school boards.

- Under the *Education Act*, the Minister of Education has broad statutory authority over education in Ontario.

- Education at the local level is delegated to school boards consisting of elected trustees who develop policies in accordance with the duties and powers listed in the *Education Act.*

- Each board must appoint a director of education as chief executive officer; this person is responsible for running the system in accordance with board policy.

Chapter 2

Teachers as Professionals

After reading this chapter, you will have a deeper understanding of teaching as a moral activity. You will also become aware of your professional rights and responsibilities as a member of the Ontario College of Teachers and the Ontario Teachers' Federation.

Why did you decide to become a teacher?

How do you view your main responsibilities as a teacher?

What do you hope to achieve over the course of your career?

You may have become a teacher for many reasons, but chances are that you are motivated primarily by moral reasons. As David Hansen (2001) puts it:

> The idea that teaching is a moral endeavor is at least as old as recorded knowledge of the practice. Plato, Confucius, Lao Tzu, Aristotle, the Buddha, the Bhagavad Gita—to name only a few of the well-known sources—all provide arguments and testimonials about the moral significance of teaching. (p. 826)

Perhaps you have chosen to become a teacher because you care about children or are passionate about your subject area. You may be committed to making a difference in the lives of students or dedicated to teaching for social justice. Such reasons are moral in nature.

Teaching as a caring profession is infused with moral significance. In their mundane daily activities and in dilemmas of practice, teachers are guided by an ethic of caring for the students they are charged to supervise and teach.

Since education law is guided by moral and ethical thinking, these dimensions of teaching need to be considered thoughtfully. It is also important to understand that teaching is a caring profession guided by professional standards and regulated by the Ontario College of Teachers.

TEACHING AS A MORAL ACTIVITY

The moral dimension of teaching has been the subject of much profound discussion. Educational philosophers, in particular, have grappled with fundamental questions about the nature of teaching. In this section, the moral dimensions of teaching have been divided into three broad categories:

(1) the teacher as guardian
(2) the teacher as educator
(3) the teacher as moral educator.

THE TEACHER AS GUARDIAN

Primum non nocere, or "Above all, do no harm," is identified with the Hippocratic oath taken by medical doctors. It is useful advice for teachers, too, because it is essential for teachers to ensure that all students in their care are kept safe from physical and psychological harm, and that their basic intellectual, emotional, and intellectual needs are satisfied.

In common law, teachers are deemed to be acting *in loco parentis* (in the place of the parent); they are expected to act as a careful or prudent parent would. Ontario's *Education Act* also makes it clear that teachers owe a legal duty of care to their students similar to that of parents. Students, for example, are required to accept such discipline as would be exercised by a "kind, firm, and judicious parent." The legal duties of teachers will be developed more fully in chapter 3, and their duty of care will be reinforced throughout this book.

As a result of these expectations, the courts have held that, depending on the circumstances, the relationship that exists between a teacher and a student could also be considered to involve the law of "fiduciary duty." This legal term based in common law describes the relationship of trust, power, and vulnerability that exists between two people; the party that has the power to affect the interests of the other has a fiduciary duty with respect to that party. The Supreme Court of Canada has defined it in the following way:

> Relationships in which a fiduciary obligation have [sic] been imposed seem to possess three general characteristics:
>
> (1) The fiduciary has scope for the exercise of some discretion or power.
> (2) The fiduciary can unilaterally exercise that power or discretion so as to affect the beneficiary's legal or practical interests.
> (3) The beneficiary is peculiarly vulnerable to or at the mercy of the fiduciary holding the discretion or power. (As quoted in Brown & Zuker, 2004, p. 166)

Generally, legal and professional bodies are most concerned with preventing careless behaviour or misconduct that puts students at risk.

THE TEACHER AS EDUCATOR

While safety is a baseline concern of students, parents, and society, the aim of the school system is to educate young people. Aristotle defines education as a systematic course of instruction designed to develop the character and mental powers of students.

Teaching, on one level, is an instrumental activity: a means to an end. Teachers have a moral obligation to ensure that students learn the prescribed curriculum. In doing so, they are to be guided by provincial and local guidelines and expectations.

In *A Good Teacher in Every Classroom*, the National Academy of Education (2005, p. 5) identifies three general areas of knowledge as being necessary for effective teaching.

(1) Knowledge of *learners* and how they learn and develop within social contexts;

(2) Understanding of the *subject matter* and skills to be taught in light of the social purposes of education;

(3) Understanding of *teaching* in light of the content and learners to be taught, as informed by assessment and supported by a productive learning environment.

This elaboration of general areas of knowledge makes it clear that teachers must do more than simply cover the curriculum. They must also fulfill their professional and moral obligation to adapt that curriculum to the specific learning needs of their students and the communities in which they live.

As John Dewey (1938) writes, "Teachers discriminate between experiences that are worthwhile educationally and those that are not" (p. 33). They select "experiences that lead to growth" (p. 40) by taking into account both the student and context. The school system and the courts trust the professional expertise of teachers, giving them considerable latitude so long as they operate within the legal framework and act in a manner consistent with that trust.

THE TEACHER AS MORAL EDUCATOR

Aristotle cautions that excessive academic and vocational specialization can render citizens "unfit for the pursuit and practice of goodness." Many educators and members of the public share this concern. They see the aims of education "as political (e.g., promoting democratic life), as cultural (e.g., promoting cultural awareness), or as religious (e.g., advancing a particular set of religious values)" (Hansen, 2001, p. 829). Aristotle and Dewey both argue that genuine intellectual development always implies moral development. As Hansen (2001) writes, "Learning encompasses the intellectual and the moral; it describes the emergence and formation of human being" (p. 833).

Alan Tom (1984) describes teaching as a "moral craft" involving "a subtle moral relationship between teacher and student" (p. 11). Teachers sensitively use their authority to bring important knowledge, skills, and ideas to the awareness of the student. "Teaching is moral," according to Tom, "in the sense that a curriculum plan selects certain objectives or pieces of content instead of others; this selective process either explicitly or implicitly reflects a conception of desirable ends" (p. 78). Furthermore, Tom continues, teaching should be regarded as moral because it requires the ability "to analyze situations and to use instruction skills appropriate to these situations" (p. 11).

Because of the vulnerability and potentiality of youth, society is concerned that teachers engage with students in a morally acceptable manner. This is why care, trust, respect, and integrity are emphasized in the Ontario College of Teachers document The Ethical Standards for the Teaching Profession. These standards will be examined more closely later in this chapter. It is also why the College emphasizes the boundaries that must exist between the teacher and student. Like all professionals, teachers have an obligation to maintain a boundary between themselves and their students. This is not to say that teachers should not be friendly and welcoming, but that they must always remain professional. It has been well said that teachers may be friendly with their students but are not their friends. Students have their own friends. Most cases of professional misconduct reported to the Ontario College of Teachers begin when teachers step over the invisible line separating them from their students and place their own needs and interests above those of the students in their care. Maintaining boundaries will be discussed more fully in chapter 4.

The four qualities outlined in the Ethical Standards are essential to making moral judgments that are in the best interest of students. For example, according to philosopher Nel Noddings (2001), "a caring teacher is someone who has demonstrated that she can establish, more or less regularly, relations of care in a wider variety of situations" (pp. 100–01). Noddings cautions that professionalism without caring can lead to aloofness in the teacher–student relationship. Instead, she argues, the means used by teachers must embody the ends of education, because the relationship between student and teacher is vital to learning and personal understanding.

Due to their special relationship with students, teachers are also regarded as role models. This has profound implications for the teaching profession, since, in addition to behaving appropriately in school, teachers are expected to embody moral qualities in their civic lives and even in their personal lives.

Indeed, teachers should expect to be scrutinized more than ordinary citizens are. The degree to which the off-duty behaviour of teachers is judged by professional and legislative bodies will be explored later in this chapter and in subsequent chapters.

ETHICAL JUDGMENT IN TEACHING

- Should I direct my lesson to the majority of students who are keeping up with the curriculum or devote extra class time to assisting students who are struggling?
- Should I teach the history unit on immigration as laid out in the course of study or adapt it to the needs of the immigrant students in my inner-city school?
- If I smell marijuana on a student, should I report her to the vice-principal?
- If a student bolts from the classroom, should I follow him or remain with the rest of the class?
- If I suspect plagiarism, but cannot prove it, should I confront the student?

Teachers are continually faced with dilemmas of practice. Many of these have moral or ethical dimensions. Often there is no ideal solution.

Ethical judgment is the ability to make sound decisions when addressing dilemmas of practice. These dilemmas could be everyday situations or periodic crises. Effective teachers work through these dilemmas thoughtfully in order to enhance the knowledge and well-being of students.

Whereas morality is essentially private, ethical judgments are inherently public. They lead to the actions through which our morality is made manifest to others. As Elizabeth Campbell (2003) writes:

On the one hand, ethics seems easy and straightforward, especially in the most extreme situations; on the other hand, it is fraught with tensions and uncertainties that have challenged us for centuries to think deeply about the contextual realities of our lives as they influence our ethical knowledge. (pp. 16–17)

Campbell argues that teacher education would benefit from analyzing case studies that provide snapshots of teachers using ethical knowledge in their daily work. In this book, the legal cases embedded in each chapter act as snapshots of situations that occur in classrooms. The rulings of the courts offer guidance to teachers as they develop their practice. Similarly, cases from the Ontario College of Teachers offer guidance concerning the standards of the profession. The cases at the end of the chapters in this book provide opportunities for teachers to apply ethical, professional, and legal judgments to authentic teaching situations.

Campbell states that "we must harness ethical knowledge as the new body of knowledge to define professionalism in teaching" (p. 114). While she values professional standards, she argues that

> ethical knowledge is fostered not by means of formalized codes and standards alone, but through a collective mission in which teachers become fully aware of their moral agency and of how their actions and beliefs have a profound ethical influence on students. (p. 114)

Teaching is a profession unique in its moral responsibilities. Reflecting on teaching as a profession, Strike & Ternansky (1993) argue:

> Teaching may seek the respect it deserves not by comparing itself to other vocations but by focusing on the role and importance of teachers' moral and intellectual commitments to the lives of students and in society. (p. 220)

The Ontario College of Teachers seeks to promote respect for the teaching profession both by focusing on the ethical dimensions of teaching and by demonstrating the rigour of the self-regulatory bodies of other professions.

TEACHING AS A PROFESSION

Doctors and lawyers have long been recognized as professionals. One of the characteristics of a profession is "the ability to set its own standards of practice" (McIntyre & Bloom, 2002, p. 3). As a patient, if you have concerns about the competence of a physician, you may file a complaint with the College of Physicians and Surgeons of Ontario. Similarly, if you have concerns about the professional conduct of a lawyer, you may complain to the Law Society of Upper Canada. In both cases, the regulatory body involved will investigate your complaints and, as appropriate, conduct hearings into the conduct of the professional in question.

Until 1998, Ontario teachers governed themselves through the Ontario Teachers' Federation, the membership of which consists of the various federations (or unions) representing teachers in publicly funded schools.

One of the recommendations of the Ontario Royal Commission on Learning (1994) was the establishment of a college of teachers. The commissioners argued that "teaching should be a self-governing profession, with greater responsibility and greater autonomy for teachers" (p. 17).

As a result, in 1996 the government of Ontario passed the *Ontario College of Teachers Act*, which established the Ontario College of Teachers. Since 1998, the College has acted as the professional standards and regulatory body for the teaching profession. Ontario is only the second Canadian province to establish self-regulation for teachers. This is part of a broader trend in the 1990s that has resulted in provincial government legislation establishing self-regulatory colleges or councils for professions such as nurses, social workers, social service workers, and real estate agents.

One of the reasons for this separation of tasks between OTF and OCT is the perception that professional standards need to be determined and maintained by an independent body. In medicine, for example, the Ontario Medical Association is the advocacy group for doctors, while the College of Physicians and Surgeons of Ontario remains at arm's-length. Another reason is that the profession can regulate itself more effectively than the government can. The government, however, does review the activities of various professional colleges, and the colleges must operate within the constraints imposed by the relevant acts and regulations.

TEACHING PROFESSION ACT

Teachers have been considered professionals in Ontario since the *Teaching Profession Act, 1944*, which established the Ontario Teachers' Federation as the umbrella organization for the various bodies representing teachers in publicly funded schools. OTF now consists of four affiliate member organizations: the Elementary Teachers Federation of Ontario (ETFO); the Ontario English Catholic Teachers' Association (OECTA); the Ontario Secondary School Teachers' Federation (OSSTF); and l'Association des enseignantes et des enseignants franco-ontariens (AEFO). Everyone employed by a board as a teacher is a member of the federation. This includes teacher librarians, guidance teachers, consultants, and teachers on special assignment. It does not include vice-principals, principals, supervisory officers, or instructors in a teacher training institution.

Before the creation of the College of Teachers, OTF had two related but somewhat conflicting goals. On the one hand, it was dedicated to maintaining standards of excellence for the teaching profession across the province; on the other, it was dedicated to protecting its members. Now that the College has assumed responsibility for licensing and discipline, OTF's major purpose, in practical terms, is protective. Nevertheless, as can be seen below, OTF still expects its members to maintain a high level of professionalism.

One of OTF's objectives, according to section 3(a), was to "promote and advance the cause of education." The legislation allowed the organization's board of governors to make regulations outlining a code of ethics for teachers. This code of ethics, in the Regulation Made Under the *Teaching Profession Act*, contains provisions with respect to the general duties of members, as well as duties of members to the public, educational authorities, their federation within OTF, and fellow members.

Regulation Made Under the *Teaching Profession Act*
General Duties of Members

13. A member shall strive at all times to achieve and maintain the highest degree of professional competence and to uphold the honour, dignity, and ethical standards of the teaching profession.

Duties of a Member to His or Her Pupils

14. A member shall,

(a) regard as his first duty the effective education of his pupils and the maintenance of a high degree of professional competence in his teaching;

(b) endeavour to develop in his pupils an appreciation of standards of excellence;

(c) endeavour to inculcate in his pupils an appreciation of the principles of democracy;

(d) show consistent justice and consideration in all his relations with pupils;

(e) refuse to divulge beyond his proper duty confidential information about a pupil; and

(f) concern himself with the welfare of his pupils while they are under his care.

Duties of a Member to Educational Authorities

15. (1) A member shall,

(a) comply with the Acts and regulations administered by the Minister;

(b) co-operate with his educational authorities to improve public education;

(c) respect the legal authority of the board of trustees in the management of the school and in the employment of teachers;

(d) make in the proper manner such reports concerning teachers under his authority as may be required by the board of trustees; and

(e) present in the proper manner to the proper authorities the consequences to be expected from policies or practices which in his professional opinion are seriously detrimental to the interests of pupils.

(2) A member shall not,

(a) break a contract of employment with a board of trustees;

(b) violate a written or oral agreement to enter into a contract of employment with a board of trustees; or

(c) while holding a contract of employment with a board of

trustees, make application for another position the acceptance of which would necessitate his seeking the termination of his contract by mutual consent of the teacher and the board of trustees, unless and until he has arranged with his board of trustees for such termination of contract if he obtains the other position.

Duties of a Member to the Public

16. A member shall,

   (a) endeavour at all times to extend the public knowledge of his profession and discourage untrue, unfair or exaggerated statements with respect to teaching; and

   (b) recognize a responsibility to promote respect for human rights.

Duties of a Member to the Federation

17. A member shall co-operate with the Federation to promote the welfare of the profession.

Duties of a Member to Fellow Members

18. (1) A member shall,

   (a) avoid interfering in an unwarranted manner between other teachers and pupils;

   (b) on making an adverse report on another member, furnish him with a written statement of the report at the earliest possible time and not later than three days after making the report;

   (c) notwithstanding section 18(1)(b), a member who makes an adverse report about another member respecting suspected sexual abuse of a student by that other member need not provide him or her with a copy of the report or with any information about the report. (WB02)

   (d) refuse to accept employment with a board of trustees whose relations with the Federation are unsatisfactory; and

   (e) where he is in an administrative or supervisory position,

> make an honest and determined effort to help and counsel a
> teacher before subscribing to the dismissal of that teacher.
> (2) Under clause (c) of subsection (1), the onus shall be on the mem-
> ber to ascertain personally from the Federation whether an unsat-
> isfactory relationship exists.
> (3) A member shall not attempt to gain an advantage over other mem-
> bers by knowingly underbidding another member, or knowingly
> applying for a position not properly declared vacant, or by negotiat-
> ing for salary independently of his local group of fellow-members.

The duties outlined in this regulation clearly convey the higher standards of conduct expected of teachers as professionals. Although, as noted
above, OTF is no longer responsible for disciplining professional misconduct, this regulation remains in force and serves as a guide to teachers. In
becoming a teacher, one commits to working within these ethical and professional standards. An important point to note in the regulation is that, as
a result of an amendment to the *Teaching Profession Act* in 2002, a member
who makes an adverse report about another member respecting suspected
sexual abuse of a student is not required to provide the other member with
a copy of the report or any information about it. This will be discussed
further in chapter 4.

THE ONTARIO COLLEGE OF TEACHERS

The government of Ontario passed the *Ontario College of Teachers Act* in
1996. This act, which took effect in 1998, established the Ontario College of
Teachers as a self-regulatory body for the teaching profession in Ontario. All
teachers working in provincially funded schools in Ontario must be certified
to teach in the province as a member of the College. According to its website
(http://www.oct.ca/about/), the College:

- ensures Ontario students are taught by skilled teachers who adhere
  to clear standards of practice and conduct;
- establishes standards of practice and conduct;

- issues teaching certificates and may suspend or revoke them;
- accredits teacher education programs and courses;
- provides for ongoing professional learning opportunities for members;
- investigates complaints of misconduct or incompetence made against members. Disciplinary hearings are open to the public and a summary of each hearing and the outcome is published in *Professionally Speaking*, the College magazine and Find a Teacher;
- investigates complaints that members are unfit to practise due to medical or other reasons. This process is not public due to the nature of the complaints.

The specific objectives (or "objects") of the College are listed in section 3 (1) of the act:

1. To regulate the profession of teaching and to govern its members.
2. To develop, establish and maintain qualifications for membership in the College.
3. To accredit professional teacher education programs offered by post-secondary educational institutions.
4. To accredit ongoing education programs for teachers offered by post-secondary educational institutions and other bodies.
5. To issue, renew, amend, suspend, cancel, revoke and reinstate certificates of qualification and registration.
6. To provide for the ongoing education of members of the College.
7. To establish and enforce professional standards and ethical standards applicable to members of the College.
8. To receive and investigate complaints against members of the College and to deal with discipline and fitness to practise issues.
9. To develop, provide and accredit educational programs leading to certificates of qualification additional to the certificate required for membership, including but not limited to certificates of qualification as a supervisory officer, and to issue, renew, amend, suspend, cancel, revoke and reinstate such additional certificates.

10. To communicate with the public on behalf of the members of the College.

11. To perform such additional functions as are prescribed by the regulations. 1996, c.12, s.3(1); 2001, c.14, Sched. B, s.2; 2004, c.26, s.2.

According to section 3(2), "in carrying out its objects, the College has a duty to serve and protect the public interest."

ORGANIZATION OF THE COLLEGE OF TEACHERS

The Ontario College of Teachers, like other self-regulatory professional bodies, has a board of directors and an administrative branch.

A Governing Council functions as the board of directors of the College. It has thirty-seven members, twenty-three of whom are elected by Ontario teachers and fourteen who are selected by the Ontario government (and appointed by the Lieutenant Governor in Council). The teacher positions include representatives of principals' organizations, private schools, and faculties of education. The council, which has an elected chair, establishes policy, develops regulations, and oversees the work of the administrative staff working under the registrar. Members of the council are active on a wide range of College committees including the Professional Learning Committee, the Accreditation Committee, and the Discipline Committee.

The registrar, the chief executive officer of the College, is directly accountable to the council. The registrar is responsible for the College's operational duties and, with the assistance of a management team, directly supervises the staff to ensure that they are fulfilling their duties with respect to the College's functions.

With over 112,000 members, OCT is a large, complex, and sophisticated operation.

Its staff is divided into five administrative departments:

(1) The Executive Department is responsible for communication, policy and research, library and archives, as well as a large number of internal operational functions.

(2) The Membership Services Department maintains membership records, evaluates credentials, and provides client services.

(3) The Professional Affairs Department is divided into two units.
- One, the Accreditation Unit, is responsible for the accreditation and accreditation review of teacher education programs and additional qualification courses.
- The other, the Standards of Practice and Education Unit, supports the development and implementation of professional standards, as well as ongoing professional development related to the standards.

(4) The Investigation and Hearings Department is responsible for the investigation of complaints of professional misconduct and incapacity.

(5) Finally, the French Language Services Department provides support for the provision of services to francophone members.

MEMBERSHIP

The *Ontario College of Teachers Act, 1996* states that anyone holding a certificate of qualification and registration is a member of the College, and since the *Education Act* defines "teacher" as a member of the College of Teachers, only persons who hold a certificate of qualification in some form from the College are legally permitted to teach in a publicly funded school in Ontario. Private schools are not bound by the *Education Act*, though many of them do prefer their teachers to be members of the College. In order to remain in good standing, members must pay an annual membership fee. Teachers in publicly funded schools pay their fees automatically through payroll deduction. Other members of the College not working in publicly funded schools may be billed annually. Administrative fees are charged to lapsed members who seek to reactivate their memberships.

The College maintains a registry of all past and present members. All teachers, including those whose membership has lapsed, can be found by going to Find a Teacher on the College website (www.oct.ca). This registry contains the names of members, as well as their professional qualifications. If there is a finding of professional misconduct against a member, this, too, is listed. As teachers take further qualifications (e.g., through another degree or an additional qualification course), they provide documentation to the College so that the registry can be updated. These additional qualifications may also be considered by school boards for determining suitability to teach particular subjects or grade levels and, in some cases, for advances in levels of pay.

REGISTRATION

A teacher who graduates from an Ontario teacher education program may apply for a Certificate of Registration. In addition, applicants receive a Certificate of Qualification, which lists their academic and professional qualifications. Out-of-province applicants who are accepted for College membership receive an Interim Certificate of Qualification (ICQ). Once ICQ holders have accumulated 194 days of successful teaching experience, they may submit an Application for Conversion of an Interim Certificate of Qualification. The more complicated application process for teachers educated outside of Canada is outlined in the booklet Registration Guide for Teachers Educated Outside Ontario. (Go to http://oct.ca for details.)

In 2007, an Iranian refugee won a thirteen-year battle to become qualified by the College of Teachers. Fatima Siadat had been unable to fulfill the requirement that her qualification papers must come directly from the issuing authorities, because she was a refugee from Iran. OCT was unwilling to develop an alternative way of evaluating her teaching qualifications and experience. In *Siadat v. Ontario College of Teachers* (2007), Justice John Brockenshire of the Ontario Superior Court of Justice wrote that the College had

> failed to meet both the obligation to properly interpret and apply the relevant law, and the obligation to provide adequate reasons for its decision, that its decision must be rescinded, and the application of Ms. Siadat must be referred back to the committee for re-hearing.

After the ruling, the College agreed to work with Siadat to develop an innovative way of assessing her teaching credentials.

FOUNDATIONS OF PROFESSIONAL PRACTICE

Teachers in Ontario are guided by the profession's standards of practice. These standards, initially approved in 1999, outline in broad terms the knowledge, skills, and values inherent in the teaching profession. The standards were revised in 2006 following an extensive consultation with teachers and members of the public. Now formally known as the *Foundations of Professional Practice* (2006), they outline the principles of ethical behaviour, professional practice, and ongoing learning for the teaching profession in Ontario. The entire document may be found at the Ontario College of Teachers' website www.oct.on.ca.

According to the introduction of this document:

> The standards describe what it means to be a member of the teaching profession in Ontario and reflect widely shared beliefs within the profession. They articulate the goals and aspirations of a teaching profession dedicated to fostering student learning and preparing Ontario students to participate in a democratic society. College members use the standards to reflect on their own development as teaching professionals and inform their practice and ongoing learning choices. (p. 4)

The foundations of professional practice do not have the force of law. Rather, they are intended to act as guidelines for teachers in their classroom practice and ongoing professional development. Nonetheless, according to some experts, "it is reasonable to expect that they will be considered and applied" (McIntyre & Bloom, 2002, p. 74) in professional misconduct cases. Moreover, the five standards of practice described below are reflected in the sixteen competency statements used by principals and other school board officials to evaluate teachers. (The performance appraisal of new and experienced teachers is examined in more detail in chapter 9.)

The Ethical Standards for the Teaching Profession

The Ethical Standards for the Teaching Profession convey the professional beliefs and values that should guide all teachers in their professional practice and decision making. The four ethical standards—care, respect, trust, and integrity—establish the core ethics that inform all parts of the *Foundations of Professional Practice.*

The introduction to this section of the document states that the form standards "represent a vision of professional practice" centred on "a commitment to students and their learning" and responsibility to "students, parents, guardians, colleagues, educational partners, other professionals, the environment and the public" (p. 7).

The four ethical standards for the teaching profession are:

Care
The ethical standard of *Care* includes compassion, acceptance, interest and insight for developing students' potential. Members express their commitment to students' well-being and learning through positive influence, professional judgment and empathy in practice.

Trust
The ethical standard of *Trust* embodies fairness, openness and honesty. Members' professional relationships with students, colleagues, parents, guardians and the public are based on trust.

Respect
Intrinsic to the ethical standard of *Respect* is trust and fair-mindedness. Members honour human dignity, emotional wellness and cognitive development. In their professional practice, they model respect for spiritual and cultural values, social justice, confidentiality, freedom, democracy and the environment.

Integrity
Honesty, reliability and moral action are embodied in the ethical standard of *Integrity.* Continual reflection assists members in exercising integrity in their professional commitments and responsibilities.

The Standards of Practice for the Teaching Profession
The Standards of Practice for the Teaching Profession:

provide a framework of principles that describes the knowledge, skills, and values inherent in Ontario's teaching profession. These standards articulate the goals and aspirations of the profession. These standards convey a collective vision of professionalism that guides the daily practices of members of the Ontario College of Teachers. (Introduction, p. 11)

The standards are intended to guide "professional judgment" and "promote a common language that fosters an understanding of what it means to be a member of the teaching profession" (p. 12).

The five standards are:

Commitment to Students and Student Learning
Members are dedicated in their care and commitment to students. They treat students equitably and with respect and are sensitive to factors that influence individual student learning. Members facilitate the development of students as contributing citizens of Canadian society.

Leadership in Learning Communities
Members promote and participate in the creation of collaborative, safe and supportive learning communities. They recognize their shared responsibilities and their leadership roles in order to facilitate student success. Members maintain and uphold the principles of the ethical standards in these learning communities.

Ongoing Professional Learning
Members recognize that a commitment to ongoing professional learning is integral to effective practice and to student learning. Professional practice and self-directed learning are informed by experience, research, collaboration and knowledge.

Professional Knowledge
Members strive to be current in their professional knowledge and recognize its relationship to practice. They understand and reflect on student development, learning theory, pedagogy, curriculum, ethics, educational

research and related policies and legislation to inform professional judgment in practice.

Professional Practice
Members apply professional knowledge and experience to promote student learning. They use appropriate pedagogy, assessment and evaluation, resources and technology in planning for and responding to the needs of individual students and learning communities. Members refine their professional practice through ongoing inquiry, dialogue and reflection.

The Professional Learning Framework for the Teaching Profession
The final section of the document is the Professional Learning Framework for the Teaching Profession. This is designed to encourage ongoing professional learning. It identifies ways in which teachers can continuously develop their practice, through formal professional development and other learning opportunities.

Formal professional development includes *additional qualification courses* listed in *Regulation 184/97, Teachers' Qualifications.* The completion of such courses, taken through accredited providers such as universities, expands the formal qualifications of teachers and is recorded by the College on a teacher's Certificate of Qualification.

One of the most significant aspects of the revised standards is that the framework now recognizes that school-based professional development, mentoring, professional networks, teacher research, and even independent professional reading are valuable forms of professional development.

The framework identifies "the goal of professional learning as the ongoing improvement of practice" (p. 23):

Teacher learning is directly correlated to student learning.
The professional learning framework encourages learning activities based on provincial legislation and policy, system needs, personal growth needs and student learning needs. The framework also encourages members of the College to identify and pursue their strengths and personal interests to further their professional learning.

Standards–based professional learning provides for an integrated approach to teacher education.
All programs and professional learning activities accredited by the College must be designed to support The Standards of Practice for the Teaching Profession and The Ethical Standards for the Teaching Profession.

Exemplary professional learning opportunities are based on the principles of effective learning.
The framework takes into account individual career and personal priorities. It outlines professional learning activities that are varied, flexible and accessible to members of the College.

Teachers plan for and reflect on their professional learning.
Responsible lifelong learning is continuous learning that is initiated by members of the College and directed and reviewed by them on an ongoing basis.

Learning communities enhance professional learning.
The professional learning framework encourages collaboration. It supports ongoing commitment to the improvement and currency of teaching practice as an individual and collective responsibility.

In response to concerns expressed by teachers' federations, the College insists that the Professional Learning Framework and the standards as a whole are not guidelines for the evaluation of teachers. *Foundations of Professional Practice* states:

The standards are not intended to be the criteria for the ongoing performance appraisal of individual College members. Performance appraisal remains the responsibility of employers, who apply the criteria by which teaching performance is assessed. In publicly funded systems, this responsibility is outlined in the *Education Act* and *Regulation 99/02, Teacher Performance Appraisal* under this Act.

Nevertheless, as noted above, the five standards of practice do form the basis of the sixteen competency statements that together are one of the key components of teacher performance appraisal.

Standards in Practice: Fostering Professional Inquiry

The back page of *Foundations of Professional Practice* states:

> College members use the ethical standards and the standards of practice to reflect on their own development as teaching professionals and inform their practice and ongoing learning choices. (p. 30)

The OCT's Standards of Practice and Education Department is committed to making this a reality through its professional development resources and activities.

The College created the *Standards in Practice: Fostering Professional Inquiry* resource kit to support professional reflection and discussion. It provides practical inquiry-based resources for professional development at all career stages. The activities in the kit (available online at www.oct.ca/standards/) help teachers to reflect on their practice in relation to the ethical standards and standards of practice. Many of the activities are case-based and involve teachers in examining problem-based case studies in order to reflect on their practices.

The following activity, taken from Booklet Two, Exploring Ethical Knowledge Through Inquiry, illustrates the College's commitment to embedding ethics into teaching standards and grounding the standards in classroom practice.*

Dilemmas from Practice
The brief scenarios below provide examples of dilemmas that emerged from the experience of educators. Use or adapt these

---

* This activity has been adapted from Exploring Ethical Knowledge Through Inquiry (2006), a resource developed by the Ontario College of Teachers. The booklet, which includes additional activities, is available from the OCT website (www.oct.ca). The authors thank the Ontario College of Teachers for making this resource available for use.

dilemmas, or generate ethical dilemmas and issues from the experiences of group members as a focus for the discussion of and inquiry into ethics.

Experiences as Curriculum for Inquiry

Ethical dilemmas and issues from practice provide authentic experiences for integrating ethical knowledge and understanding through engagement in professional inquiry processes. Educators encounter ethical dilemmas within their practice on a daily basis. These dilemmas may emerge in areas such as:

- curriculum planning
- assessment and evaluation
- relationships with others
- special education
- leadership
- policy development.

Scenario 1

You are newly appointed to your professional position. At a meeting with an educational leader, your supervisor makes what you perceive to be a biased comment. What do you do?

Scenario 2

You and your colleagues from the intermediate division have agreed that the consequence for not completing assigned homework is an after-school detention the following day. All parents have been notified of this policy. A student informs you that his homework is not completed because he went to a hockey game with his father, whom he rarely sees. What do you do?

Scenario 3

The past practice in your school has allowed the students to elect the president of their student council. You and a colleague are the staff advisers. During the tabulation of the results, a student whom both you and your colleague perceive as inappropriate for student council president wins the election by three votes. The second-place candidate is perceived by both of you as a better choice for student council president. Your colleague destroys four of the ballots, giving the student council presidency to the runner-up. What do you do?

For each example, answer the following questions:
(1) Which ethical standards apply to this case?
(2) Which standards of practice apply to this case?
(3) What course of action would you take as a member of the teaching profession?

PROFESSIONAL MISCONDUCT

One of the characteristics of a professional self-regulatory body is the power it has to set out standards of professional conduct for its members. This also entails responsibility for identifying what constitutes professional misconduct. *Regulation 437/97* under the *Ontario College of Teachers Act* identifies an extensive list of acts that constitute professional misconduct by members:

ONTARIO REGULATION 437/97
PROFESSIONAL MISCONDUCT
(Last amendment: O. Reg. 134/08.)

1. The following acts are defined as professional misconduct for the purposes of subsection 30 (2) of the Act:
    1. Providing false information or documents to the College or any other person with respect to the member's professional qualifications.
    2. Inappropriately using a term, title or designation indicating a specialization in the profession which is not specified on the member's certificate of qualification and registration.

3. Permitting, counselling or assisting any person who is not a member to represent himself or herself as a member of the College.

4. Using a name other than the member's name, as set out in the register, in the course of his or her professional duties.

5. Failing to maintain the standards of the profession.

6. Releasing or disclosing information about a student to a person other than the student or, if the student is a minor, the student's parent or guardian. The release or disclosure of information is not an act of professional misconduct if,

   i. the student (or if the student is a minor, the student's parent or guardian) consents to the release or disclosure, or

   ii. if the release or disclosure is required or allowed by law.

7. Abusing a student verbally.

7.1 Abusing a student physically.

7.2 Abusing a student psychologically or emotionally.

7.3 Abusing a student sexually.

8. Practising or purporting to practise the profession while under the influence of any substance or while adversely affected by any dysfunction,

   i. which the member knows or ought to know impairs the member's ability to practise, and

   ii. in respect of which treatment has previously been recommended, ordered or prescribed but the member has failed to follow the treatment.

9. Contravening a term, condition or limitation imposed on the member's certificate of qualification and registration.

10. Failing to keep records as required by his or her professional duties.

11. Failing to supervise adequately a person who is under the professional supervision of the member.

12. Signing or issuing, in the member's professional capacity, a document that the member knows or ought to know contains a false, improper or misleading statement.

13. Falsifying a record relating to the member's professional responsibilities.

14. Failing to comply with the Act or the regulations or the by-laws.

15. Failing to comply with the *Education Act* or the regulations made under that Act, if the member is subject to that Act.

16. Contravening a law if the contravention is relevant to the member's suitability to hold a certificate of qualification and registration.

17. Contravening a law if the contravention has caused or may cause a student who is under the member's professional supervision to be put at or to remain at risk.

18. An act or omission that, having regard to all the circumstances, would reasonably be regarded by members as disgraceful, dishonourable or unprofessional.

19. Conduct unbecoming a member.

20. Failing to appear before a panel of the Investigation Committee to be cautioned or admonished, if the Investigation Committee has required the member to appear under clause 26 (5) (c) of the Act.

21. Failing to comply with an order of a panel of the Discipline Committee or an order of a panel of the Fitness to Practise Committee.

22. Failing to co-operate in a College investigation.

23. Failing to take reasonable steps to ensure that the requested information is provided in a complete and accurate manner if the member is required to provide information to the College under the Act and the regulations.

24. Failing to abide by a written undertaking given by the member to the College or by an agreement entered into by the member with the College.

25. Failing to respond adequately or within a reasonable time to a written inquiry from the College.

26. Practising the profession while the member is in a conflict of interest.

27. Failing to comply with the member's duties under the *Child and Family Services Act*, O. Reg. 437/97, s. 1; O. Reg. 134/08, s. 1.

2. A finding of incompetence, professional misconduct or a similar finding against a member by a governing authority of the teaching profession in a jurisdiction other than Ontario that is based on facts that would, in the opinion of the Discipline Committee, constitute professional misconduct as defined in section 1, is defined as professional misconduct for the purposes of subsection 30 (2) of the Act. O. Reg. 437/97, s. 2.

Investigating Complaints Against Members

It is in the public interest for all certified teachers to be held accountable for their professional activities and for any complaint of professional misconduct to be investigated in a manner befitting their professional status. As a result, the OCT's Investigation Committee investigates all complaints of alleged professional misconduct, incompetence, or incapacity made by:

- a member of the public
- a member of the College
- the Registrar
- the Minister.

In cases involving a member of the public, the process begins with a person inquiring whether a complaint should be filed. At this stage, College staff assists the member of the public in determining the best jurisdiction for resolving the complaint. In Steps to Take If You Have Concerns About a Member, the College encourages members of the public to consider resolving disputes in other jurisdictions before pursuing a formal complaint:

If you have concerns about a teacher, you should speak to the teacher, if appropriate, or go to the principal of the school and discuss your concerns. You may wish to contact your school board and speak to the superintendent who has responsibility for the school where the teacher works.

In certain circumstances, the College staff may be able to assist in the resolution of the matter. If not, you may wish to file a formal complaint with the College. (p. 1)

A member of the public who does decide to file a formal complaint must do so in writing and include his/her name, address, and telephone number. The complaint must provide the name of the member and provide specific detail concerning the nature of the allegation. The member is notified of the complaint and is given the opportunity to respond. A College investigator will ask the complainant and the member for details about the incident, and may contact witnesses identified by either party.

School boards are required to inform the College in writing if a teacher has been charged with or convicted of a criminal act involving sexual misconduct with a minor, or charged with or convicted of a criminal offence that indicates the teacher may be a risk to students. Also, if boards are aware of professional misconduct that should be reviewed by the College, they have a duty to report (*Ontario College of Teachers Act*, section 43.3(1)).

Members who are notified that a complaint has been filed about them should contact their local federation affiliate for support and guidance during the investigation process. The federation may also refer members to lawyers for advice on legal rights.

The Investigation Committee considers the information collected and decides how to proceed. The committee may elect to:

(1) dismiss the case
(2) suggest voluntary dispute resolution
(3) take other action as appropriate
(4) refer the complaint to the Discipline Committee or Fitness to Practice Committee for a hearing.

Eighty percent of cases are not referred for a hearing. Approximately four out of five complaints are not referred to the Discipline Committee but are dismissed or resolved by other means.

While cases that do not proceed to investigation are generally not published, a sample of such cases is published without identifying information, for illustrative purposes, in *Professionally Speaking*, a magazine published by the College and available online (www.oct.ca). The summaries below illustrate two cases from June 2007 that did not proceed to a hearing, and one from September 2009 that did.

Case #1

Complaint: Unwarranted, unfair punishment of student and using "scare tactic"

Outcome of investigation: No investigation

Parents of a Grade 6 student complained about their child's teacher, who they said had "centred out [their child] for unwarranted punishment" and had "belittled" the student in a number of ways, including: not allowing the student to return to class to pick up a forgotten backpack; not allowing the student to go to the washroom; giving a detention for talking after their child said "excuse me" for bumping into another student; making the student stand by an outside wall as punishment; making the student redo an assignment, which the member could not find; sending the student to the hall after someone threw something at the teacher; etc.

The parents also alleged that the teacher used a "scare tactic" by having a lawyer write to them to cease and desist the false allegations being made against the member.

The Investigation Committee panel considering the complaint directed that the allegations not be investigated because they do not relate to professional misconduct, incompetence or incapacity.

Case #2

Member: Not identified

Decision: Admonished by the Investigation Committee

Following notification by an employer, the Registrar initiated a complaint against a member of the College. The Registrar alleged that the member, an elementary teacher:

- hugged one or more students
- held hands with one or more students
- accessed inappropriate Internet sites on the classroom computer.

On January 26, 2006, the Investigation Committee ratified an MOA [memorandum of agreement] between the member and the College, in which the member:

- admitted the alleged conduct
- agreed to be admonished, in writing, by the Investigation Committee
- agreed to complete a course of instruction, pre-approved by the Registrar, regarding maintaining appropriate boundaries with students
- agreed to provide the Registrar with a written report, prepared by the course practitioner, indicating whether the member recognized the need for teachers to establish and maintain appropriate student/teacher boundaries
- agreed to notify the Registrar of any complaints of a similar nature made to his employer
- agreed to a notation being placed on the public register.

Case #3

Member: Not identified

Decision: Counselling and conditions

A Discipline Committee panel held a public hearing on August 20, 2009 into a complaint against a member for inappropriately disciplining students.

The member and his counsel attended the hearing.

In an agreed statement of facts, the elementary teacher with the Dufferin-Peel Catholic DSB admitted to encouraging two boys who had been fighting to continue fighting as a demonstration during a class discussion on bullying. When the students didn't continue, the member placed his hands on the shoulders of one of the boys and feigned punching motions. Afterwards, he apologized for possibly embarrassing the student.

In December 2008 the Ontario Court of Justice dismissed a charge against the member of assaulting the student.

Having considered the evidence, an agreed statement of facts, a plea of no contest, joint submission on penalty and the submissions of counsel, the panel found the member guilty of professional misconduct. The panel recognized that the member's intent was educative and agreed that his behaviour was an error in judgment. It directed the member to appear before the panel to be counselled and to complete within six months, at his own expense, a course regarding disciplinary techniques involving intermediate students.

Discipline for Professional Misconduct or Incompetence

In a case of alleged professional misconduct or incompetence, the Investigation Committee may refer the matter to a hearing by the Discipline Committee. An allegation is heard by a panel of discipline committee members, who, after weighing the evidence presented, render a decision on the case. The hearing, which is generally open to the public, is conducted in a manner very similar to a court trial.

According to section 30(3), in cases of incompetence:

The Discipline Committee may, after a hearing, find a member to be incompetent if, in its opinion, the member has displayed in his or her professional responsibilities a lack of knowledge, skill or judgment or disregard for the welfare of a student of a nature or extent that demonstrates that the member is unfit to continue to carry out his or her professional responsibilities or that a certificate held by the member under this Act should be made subject to terms, conditions or limitations.

According to section 30(2), in cases of professional misconduct:

A member may be found guilty of professional misconduct by the Discipline Committee, after a hearing, if the member has been guilty, in the opinion of the Committee, of professional misconduct as defined in the regulations.

There is a wide range of possible penalties under the act, including:

   (a) revoking the member's teaching certificate;

   (b) suspending the member's teaching certificate for up to 24 months;

   (c) imposing specific terms, conditions or limitations on the certificate;

   (d) reprimanding, admonishing and/or counselling the member;

   (e) fines of up to $5,000;

   (f) publishing the findings, including the member's name;

   (g) fixing costs to be paid by the member.

In sentencing and assessing penalties, the committee may take into account mitigating factors (e.g., cooperation, guilty plea, or remorse) and aggravating factors (e.g., lack of remorse, degree of exploitation, or efforts to cover up). Also, all decisions are subject to appeal through the courts.

In cases in which members are found guilty of professional misconduct, the summaries are generally published in *Professionally Speaking* and on the College website. Summaries of relevant Discipline Committee rulings are featured throughout this book. Full decisions are available from the College's library, in Toronto. In cases of incompetence the member's name is not published, and there are no fines or fixed costs.

Fitness to Practice

The Fitness to Practice Committee conducts hearings into whether a member is physically or mentally incapacitated. Because incapacity does not involve culpable conduct, the committee seeks to balance protection of the public interest and the rehabilitation of the member.

The hearing procedures are similar to those employed in discipline cases. Also, the penalties are similar to those applied in incompetency cases, with the exception that the hearings are closed to the public. Cases in which the facts are disputed can involve complex medical testimony. Also, in its rulings, the committee must be careful not to violate the human rights of the member, which are protected under Ontario's *Human Rights Code* and the *Canadian Charter of Rights and Freedoms*.

Because the hearings are closed, the results of the Fitness to Practice Committee hearings are generally unknown. A case in which the member appealed the College's decision to the courts provides a useful glimpse into the workings of the committee. In *Sclater v. the Ontario College of Teachers* (2000), the member challenged the decision of the committee, which rejected a joint submission from the member and the Investigation Committee on the disposition of the case. The committee determined that the joint submission did not attend sufficiently either to the "boundary violations" committed by the teacher in her relations with students or to the concerns about her ability to "act in a position of trust." The committee decided that the member must pay for twenty therapy sessions, followed by a psychiatric evaluation, before it would consider her application for reinstatement. Ultimately, the courts sided with the College, ruling that the teachers on the panel had sufficient knowledge of teaching to make this decision based on the evidence presented (McIntyre & Bloom, 2002, pp. 106–07).

It is important to keep in mind that making a complaint to the Ontario College of Teachers is only one process for dealing with allegations of professional misconduct or incompetence. Complaints may also be pursued through internal school board disciplinary procedures, which are covered in board policy and the collective agreements made with the local affiliate of the teachers' federation (see chapter 9, below). Allegations of professional misconduct may also result in civil or criminal court action.

CHECKING YOUR UNDERSTANDING

- In Ontario, the teaching profession is grounded in a legal framework based on an ethic of caring and is regulated by the professional standards established by the Ontario College of Teachers.

- As a caring profession, teaching is infused with moral significance; teachers may be thought of as guardians, educators, and moral educators.

- As "guardians," teachers are expected by the courts to act *in loco parentis* (in place of the parent) and as such are considered to owe their students a fiduciary duty.

- As "educators," teachers not only should cover the curriculum; they also should adapt it to the needs of their students and the communities in which they live.

- As "moral educators," teachers must engage with students in a morally acceptable manner and embody the qualities of care, trust, respect, and integrity identified in the OCT's Ethical Standards for the Teaching Profession.

- Teachers have been considered professionals in Ontario since 1944, with the passage of the *Teaching Profession Act*, which established the Ontario Teachers' Federation. OTF now consists of four affiliates: AEFO, ETFO, OECTA, and OSSTF.

- The Regulation Made Under the *Teaching Profession Act* outlines a code of ethics for teachers. Included in the code is a requirement that a member making an adverse report about a fellow member provide that member with a written copy of the report within three days, except in cases of suspected sexual abuse of a student.

- Although OTF still has a strong professional emphasis, its major purpose now is to protect and promote the interests of teachers. Only persons employed by a board as teachers are members of OTF. Principals and vice-principals, for example, are not members.

- In 1998, teachers in Ontario became fully self-regulating with the creation of the Ontario College of Teachers, which has the power to issue, suspend, and revoke certificates.

- OCT has one overriding duty: to serve and protect the public interest.

- Since the *Education Act* defines "teacher" as a member of the Ontario College of Teachers, only persons who hold a certificate of qualification in some form from OCT are permitted to teach in a publicly funded school in Ontario.

- In *Foundations of Professional Practice*, OCT identifies *four* ethical standards (care, trust, respect, and integrity) and *five* standards of practice (commitment to students and students' learning, leadership in learning communities, ongoing professional learning, professional knowledge, and professional practice). It also outlines its Professional Learning Framework for the Teaching Profession.

- Acts by a member of the College of Teachers considered to be professional misconduct are defined in *Professional Misconduct Regulation 437/97*.

- Complaints of professional misconduct or incompetence are now directed to the Investigation Committee of OCT, which may direct the complaint to the Discipline Committee or the Fitness to Practice Committee. A wide range of penalties is available under the act.

APPLYING YOUR UNDERSTANDING

Reflection from Practice #1[*]

I familiarize myself with the curriculum and the expectations of a particular subject for my Grade class. I also make sure I know the curriculum and the expectations for the previous grade so that the flow of learning is continuous and that I'm aware of the concepts and skills the students have acquired before coming into my class. Once I have taught a lesson and the expectations for that lesson have been established, I observe students to make sure they have clearly understood what was taught. If students are having difficulty, I review the lesson with small groups using different teaching strategies. I also provide individual reinforcement to help clarify a concept or skill.

Assessment takes place on a daily basis—through my own observations

---

[*]   These reflections and questions are from *Teachers' Reflections on the Standards* (2006), a resource developed by the Ontario College of Teachers. The booklet is available from the College website (www.oct.ca). The authors thank the Ontario College of Teachers for making this resource available for use.

and my anecdotal records, use of checklists and through reading student notebooks and journals.

Professional Inquiry: Which standards are illuminated in this reflection?

Reflection from Practice #2

I remember with gratitude the help and advice that I received in my early years of teaching from more experienced peers. From others, I have learned how to effectively deal with discipline issues, develop programs and interact with students. My professional growth has been a never-ending process. I feel that I can always learn to be a more effective teacher by observing and talking to others. I am aware that my years of experience have provided me with a different perspective and that I can now be helpful to beginning teachers. I realize that I can offer them support and advice that can help ease the pressures of being new in this profession.

Professional Inquiry: Which standards are illuminated in this reflection?

Reflection from Practice #3

I try to be involved in many aspects of school life and supportive of a variety of activities. My main area of involvement is through coaching and organizing house leagues. Seeing students come together and progress towards a common goal in sports, drama or academic ventures are some of the most positive aspects of my career. These experiences are also the most successful at building a strong sense of community. This year we had a 10-year-old visually challenged boy participate with the school cross-country running team. He ended up competing in a Special Olympics race. It was very rewarding to watch the Grade 8 students acting as his guide runner and teaching him to stretch and prepare for practice each day. There was a group of them waiting to "high five" him at the finish line. Several were sincerely moved and as excited about his race as they were about their own.

Professional Inquiry: Which standards are illuminated in this reflection?

Reflection from Practice #4

Always reach out to the community. Make those calls. Just talk to people. Half the time, parents of students just want to feel that their concerns have been heard. It's not that they are expecting miracles. They know their sons and daughters. They just want to have an open line of communication. We really encourage that communication. I think that communication with parents is part of our role in education as principals and teachers. I also believe in collaboratively setting goals for the school. I like mission statements and graduate outcomes. When we wanted to be able to describe the kind of student growth that we hoped to develop in this school, we went through a consultation process involving the students and the community.

Professional Inquiry: Which standards are illuminated in this reflection?

Reflection from Practice #5

One of my goals is to make sure that the school makes everyone feel welcome. It should be a place where students can come in and feel quite at home. That is really important to me. The school should also be part of the community. We highlight community events and try to become aware of the local customs. Our community holds mid-winter ceremonies and our school honours this practice as well

Professional Inquiry: Which standards are illuminated in this reflection?

Chapter 3

The Legal Duties and Rights of Teachers

After reading this chapter you will understand in broad terms the duties of teachers and principals under the Education Act *and its regulations. The implications of these duties are explored by examining legal cases and complaints before the Ontario College of Teachers. The rights of teachers are also delineated in relation to their duties. (Subsequent chapters address duties and rights in specific areas of practice.)*

A teacher was disciplined by the Ontario College of Teachers for making inappropriate jokes with sexual innuendo.

A teacher was suspended for insubordination by her school board for refusing to accept additional yard duty.

A teacher, Malcolm Ross, was fired for publishing anti-Semitic comments while off-duty. This happened even though Mr. Ross was careful not to present his views at school.

What do you think?

   What factors may have led to these decisions?

   Do you agree with these decisions?

Educators are held to a higher standard than other citizens. This is evident in the *Education Act* and its regulations, which outline the duties of teachers, principals, and school boards. It is also evident in the ways courts have ruled on cases concerning school personnel. As citizens and educational professionals, however, teachers and principals also enjoy rights that must be protected.

DUTY OF CARE IN COMMON LAW

It is important to keep in mind that school boards, teachers, and principals have a special relationship with students and the parents who entrust their children to the school system. As a result of being held *in loco parentis* by the courts, those responsible for providing educational services have a legal obligation to conduct themselves in a manner consistent with this trust. The courts have also held that the relationship between teachers and students could involve the law of "fiduciary duty" (see chapter 2), the term used to describe the relationship of trust, power, and vulnerability existing, for example, between a parent and child.

In Ontario, the duties of principals and teachers are set out in legislation. This legislation reflects the high ethical, professional, and legal standards set by society for educators. Teaching in a manner consistent with these duties will ensure that students learn in safe classrooms and schools.

STATUTORY DUTIES UNDER THE EDUCATION ACT

The *Education Act* and its accompanying regulations provide the statutory basis for public education in Ontario. This comprehensive piece of legislation, which has been added to in an *ad hoc* manner for decades, covers, among other things, school board governance, provincial funding, curriculum, special education, discipline codes, and the duties of various education professionals. In what follows, the focus is on the duties of principals and teachers under provisional legislation.

DUTIES OF PRINCIPALS
Although the school board has the overall responsibility for providing instruction and adequate accommodation (*Education Act*, section 170(1)), it is the school principal who is specifically charged with the instruction and

discipline of students, and for ensuring that each school is a safe and healthy place for students to learn. Section 265(1) of the act includes the following obligations for principals:

> It is the duty of a principal of a school, in addition to the principal's duties as a teacher,
>> (a) to maintain proper order and discipline in the school; ...
>> (j) to give assiduous attention to the health and comfort of the pupils, to the cleanliness, temperature and ventilation of the school, to the care of all teaching materials and other school property, and to the condition and appearance of the school buildings and grounds; ...
>> (m) subject to an appeal to the board, to refuse to admit to the school or classroom a person whose presence in the school or classroom would in the principal's judgment be detrimental to the physical or mental well-being of the pupils ...

The duties of the principal are elaborated in *Regulation 298*, a regulation made under the *Education Act*.

> 11(1) The principal of a school, subject to the authority of the appropriate supervisory officer, is in charge of,
>> (a) the instruction and the discipline of pupils in the school;
>> (b) the organization and management of the school.
> 11(3) In addition to the duties under the Act and those assigned by the board, the principal of a school shall, except where the principal has arranged otherwise under subsection 26(3),
>> (a) supervise the instruction in the school and advise and assist any teacher in co-operation with the teacher in charge of an organizational unit or program;
>> (b) assign duties to vice-principals and to teachers in charge of organizational units or programs; ...
>> (e) provide for the supervision of pupils during the period of time during each school day when the school buildings and playgrounds are open to pupils;

(f) provide for the supervision of and the conducting of any school activity authorized by the board; ...

(k) provide for instruction of pupils in the care of the school premises;

(l) inspect the school premises at least weekly and report forthwith to the board,

(i) any repairs to the school that are required, in the opinion of the principal,

(ii) any lack of attention on the part of the building maintenance staff of the school ...

As the "principal teacher" and the person charged with the management and organization of the school, the principal assumes wide-ranging authority and obligations. Recognizing the broad scope of the principal's duties, the act requires teachers to assist the principal in various ways.

DUTIES OF TEACHERS

Teachers employed by school boards assume statutory and regulatory duties as outlined in the *Education Act* and *Regulation 298*. These broad duties may be further defined—narrowed or expanded—in the collective agreement between a board and a teachers' federation.

In addition, the duties outlined in the regulations made under the *Teaching Profession Act* and *Ontario College of Teachers Act* apply to teachers by virtue of their membership in the Ontario Teachers' Federation and the Ontario College of Teachers. (See chapter 2.)

Teachers are charged with the duty of maintaining a safe and supportive learning environment within their classrooms. This responsibility also extends to their duties in other parts of school.

Section 264(1) of the *Education Act* states:

It is the duty of a teacher and a temporary teacher:

teach

(a) to teach diligently and faithfully the classes or subjects assigned to the teacher by the principal;

learning

(b) to encourage the pupils in the pursuit of learning;

religion and morals

(c) to inculcate by precept and example respect for religion and the principles of Judaeo-Christian morality and the highest regard for truth, justice, loyalty, love of country, humanity, benevolence, sobriety, industry, frugality, purity, temperance and all other virtues;

co-operation

(d) to assist in developing co-operation and co-ordination of effort among the members of the staff of the school;

discipline

(e) to maintain, under the direction of the principal, proper order and discipline in the teacher's classroom and while on duty in the school and on the school ground;

language of instruction

(f) in instruction and in all communications with the pupils in regard to discipline and the management of the school,
  (i) to use the English language, except where it is impractical to do so by reason of the pupil not understanding English, and except in respect of instruction in a language other than English when such other language is being taught as one of the subjects in the course of study, or
  (ii) to use the French language in schools or classes in which French is the language of instruction except where it is impractical to do so by reason of the pupil not understanding French, and except in respect of instruction in a language other than French when such other language is being taught as one of the subjects in the course of study;

timetable

(g) to conduct the teacher's class in accordance with a timetable which shall be accessible to pupils and to the principal and supervisory officers;

professional activity days

(h) to participate in professional activity days as designated by the board under the regulations;

absence from school

(i) to notify such person as is designated by the board if the teacher is to be absent from school and the reason therefor;

school property

(j) to deliver the register, the school key and other school property in the teacher's possession to the board on demand, or when the teacher's agreement with the board has expired, or when for any reason the teacher's employment has ceased; and

textbooks

(k) to use and permit to be used as a textbook in a class that he or she teaches in an elementary or a secondary school,

(i) in a subject area for which textbooks are approved by the Minister, only textbooks that are approved by the Minister, and

(ii) in all subject areas, only textbooks that are approved by the board;

duties assigned

(l) to perform all duties assigned in accordance with this Act and the regulations.

Section 20 of *Regulation 298* supplements the duties under the *Education Act* by indicating that teachers shall also:

(a) be responsible for effective instruction, training and evaluation of the progress of pupils in the subjects assigned to the teacher and for the management of the class or classes, and report to the principal on the progress of pupils on request;

(b) carry out the supervisory duties and instructional program assigned to the teacher by the principal and supply such information related thereto as the principal may require;

(c) where the board has appointed teachers under section 14 or 17, co-operate fully with such teachers and with the principal in all matters related to the instruction of pupils;

(d) unless otherwise assigned by the principal, be present in the class-room or teaching area and ensure that the classroom or teaching area is ready for the reception of pupils at least fifteen minutes before the commencement of classes in the school in the morning and, where applicable, five minutes before the commencement of classes in the school in the afternoon;

(e) assist the principal in maintaining close co-operation with the community;

(f) prepare for use in the teacher's class or classes such teaching plans and outlines as are required by the principal and the appropriate supervi-sory officer and submit the plans and outlines to the principal or the appropriate supervisory officer, as the case may be, on request;

(g) ensure that all reasonable safety procedures are carried out in courses and activities for which the teacher is responsible;

(h) co-operate with the principal and other teachers to establish and maintain consistent disciplinary practices in the school;

(i) ensure that report cards are fully and properly completed and pro-cessed in accordance with the guides known in English as Guide to the Provincial Report Card, Grades 1-8 and Guide to the Provincial Report Card, Grades 9-12, and in French as Guide d'utilisation du bulletin scolaire de l'Ontario de la 1ère à la 8e année and Guide du bulletin scolaire de l'Ontario de la 9e à la 12e année, as the case may be, both available electronically through a link in the document known in English as Ontario School Record (OSR) Guideline, 2000 and in French as Dossier scolaire de l'Ontario: Guide, 2000, online at www.edu.gov.on.ca/eng/document/curricul/osr/osr.html or www.edu.gov.on.ca/fre/document/curricul/osr/osrf.html;

(j) co-operate and assist in the administration of tests under the Education Quality and Accountability Office Act, 1996;

(k) participate in regular meetings with pupils' parents or guardians;

(l) perform duties as assigned by the principal in relation to co-operative placements of pupils; and

(m) perform duties normally associated with the graduation of pupils.
R.R.O. 1990, Reg. 298, s. 20; O. Reg. 95/96, s. 2; O. Reg. 209/03, s. 1.

The *Education Act, Regulation 298*, and other legislation make it clear that teachers and principals owe a duty of care to their students due to their special relationship of trust. Since parents are required to send their children to school, they are entitled to expect that their children will receive excellent teaching in orderly and welcoming classrooms, in a safe and supportive school environment.

(1) What are the duties of the principal?
(2) What are the duties of the teacher in the classroom?
(3) What are the duties of the teacher outside the classroom?
(4) Did any of these duties surprise you? If so, why?

A Judge's Perspective

Justice Paul S. Rouleau (2006) assures educators that their duties need not be onerous and that their professionalism is respected by the courts. Following are some excerpts from his speech "Education in Transition: A Delicate Balance."

Education is very much like a sonnet. The law has imposed many rules and regulations on the education system. Educators have to follow them, but if their objective is to simply comply with all the rules, the art of expression, the beauty, is lost. Compliance with the laws is necessary but should not be the educator's primary objective. It is possible to work within the rules and still to be fully expressive, to be an artist that is a true educator. Having now become a judge [after being a lawyer who had worked for school boards], I can tell you that courts, in their decisions, have recognized the important mission of educators.

I hope that the educators among you are able to take up my challenge and operate within the legal framework in a way that respects your ultimate professional goal or purpose: to be an effective educator. Know that courts show respect for decisions made by educators. Turning back to my example of sonnets, rules can be either a hindrance or helpful. Don't lose your focus on educating. Be mindful of the rules but don't let them consume you. Compliance alone does not ensure excellence.

TEACHERS' INSTRUCTIONAL DUTIES

The primary classroom duties of the teacher are to to "teach diligently and faithfully the classes or subjects assigned to the teacher by the principal," "encourage the pupils in the pursuit of learning," and instill core values through both words and actions (*Education Act,* section 264).

What do these broad statements mean in practice?

TEACH DILIGENTLY AND FAITHFULLY

Teachers are expected to be diligent and faithful in caring for students and promoting learning in their classrooms. As professionals charged with great social responsibilities, teachers are responsible for developing effective instructional resources, adapting them to the needs of their students, and evaluating the achievement of learning outcomes. This diligence and faithfulness is directed two ways. First, teachers are to show due care for the well-being and learning of students put into their charge by parents/guardians in a particular community. Second, they are to teach within the constraints of board and provincial curriculum guidelines and assess student achievement in relation to determined standards.

As professionals, teachers are charged with the task of adapting the curriculum to meet the needs of the students in their classes. This means that they have academic freedom in making judgments concerning the best ways to deliver the curriculum in particular teaching and learning contexts.

So long as they can demonstrate that their conduct is professional and their intentions thoughtful, most teachers are not likely to run into trouble for the decisions they make in their classroom teaching.

The effectiveness of teachers is being increasingly scrutinized. The appraisal processes for new and experienced teachers, which are outlined in chapter 9, identify competencies that teachers should demonstrate. Teachers who fail to meet minimal standards on the various competencies are given opportunities to improve their performance.

Case #1*
Ontario College of Teachers
(From the March 2006 edition of **Professionally Speaking**)
Decision: Suspended

A panel of the Discipline Committee held a public hearing on January 13, 2005 into allegations of professional misconduct against NM. NM was certified to teach in 1983 and was employed as a teacher by the Simcoe County District School Board. NM did not attend the hearing nor was she represented by counsel.

The member faced nine allegations of professional misconduct related to failing to maintain the standards of the profession, such as not marking or returning students' work assignments, failing to adequately supervise students, and engaging in acts that would reasonably be regarded as disgraceful, dishonourable or unprofessional.

College counsel advised the panel that the College withdrew allegations of abuse and conduct unbecoming a member.

In NM's absence, the chair of the panel entered a plea of not guilty on her behalf.

The panel heard that between September 1999 and April 2002 NM was a probationary teacher with the Simcoe board and that she was on sick leave for

---

*   The Discipline Committee often identifies by name members found guilty of professional misconduct. In OCT cases cited in this book, initials are used in place of names.

much of the time she was employed. When she was present, there were many complaints from students and parents about her failure to mark and return assignments and from colleagues about her unco-operative working relationships.

The principal of the first school NM was assigned to — a facility for students with mental health issues where treatment took precedence over educational issues — testified that NM had been responsible for setting back a student's progress by giving the student a heavy assignment in direct contravention of an established treatment plan.

The principal of the second high school to which NM was assigned told the panel that the member did not supply appropriate lesson plans during her absences. Many students and parents had complained of the teacher's numerous absences and unmarked assignments and that she distracted students with topics unrelated to the work they were trying to complete.

The panel was told that NM displayed a confrontational and antagonistic demeanour towards students, returned students' work only days before the end of the school year, and used the absence reporting system or voice mail in an unprofessional manner.

The principal recommended to the school board that NM's probationary contract be terminated.

The panel found NM guilty of professional misconduct and ordered that her teaching certificate be suspended for 12 months.

NM may not return to teaching until she has been reprimanded and has provided the Registrar with proof that she has successfully completed, at her own expense, a course on curriculum planning and a course on classroom management.

---

(1) What evidence is there that this teacher was not diligent or faithful in her practice?

(2) What other duties of teachers under the *Education Act*, section 264(1) or *Regulation 298*, section 20 did she fail to meet?

(3) Do you think the penalty imposed by the Discipline Committee was appropriate?

ENCOURAGE PUPILS IN THE PURSUIT OF LEARNING

Effective instruction should also lead to evidence of student learning. The wording of this duty stresses *encouragement* in the *pursuit* of learning. It does not require concrete evidence of learning. Implicit in this phrasing is a recognition that there is not a clear causal relationship between diligent or competent instruction and student learning. Indeed, much depends on the individual student, other students in the class, and the leaarning community.

Teacher competence, then, is not judged simply on the basis of student achievement, though students' success in meeting learning expectations may certainly be taken into account. Teachers are accountable to the principal to report on the progress of pupils. They are also required to report to parents or guardians at regular intervals. These reporting requirements point to teachers as professionals accountable for their actions. The teacher in the OCT case above, in addition to her other professional lapses, failed to meet standards of accountability for monitoring and reporting student learning.

In this era of increased accountability, which has been accompanied by increased assessment of students and use of standardized tests, teachers should maintain an effective system for recording student progress and should keep samples of student work. Teachers should also be able to demonstrate to administrators and parents, particularly in schools performing poorly on standardized tests, how they are working to improve student learning.

The professional misconduct case listed below lists some ways in which teachers may fail to encourage learning, and how they can go about improving their practice.

Case #2
Ontario College of Teachers
(From the March 2006 edition of **Professionally Speaking**)
Member: Not identified
Decision: Undertaking

A member of the public initiated a complaint against a member of the College alleging that she lacked the skills for effective delivery and evaluation of the required curriculum and for effective classroom management.

On May 27, 2005, the Investigation Committee ratified an MOA [Memorandum of Agreement] between the member and the College, in which:

- the parties acknowledged that the member had successfully completed a course of instruction regarding classroom programs and planning;
- the member agreed to complete a course of instruction, pre-approved by the Registrar, regarding positive classroom management strategies;
- the member agreed to provide the Registrar with written confirmation of completion of the courses of instruction;
- the member agreed to provide the Registrar with copies of her next two Teacher Performance Appraisals within 30 days of their completion;
- the member agreed that the College would provide her employer with a copy of the Investigation Committee's written decision, including the MOA.

INSTILL CORE VALUES THROUGH BOTH WORDS AND ACTIONS

Education is an ethical enterprise in which teachers play a major role in developing the character of students and, by extension, contribute to the development of good democratic citizens.

Even though they are no longer expected to adhere to the Judeo-Christian religious belief system, teachers should demonstrate in their classroom conduct that they respect the ethical principles and virtues conveyed in section 264. The language may be old-fashioned, but the call to be virtuous in one's classroom conduct is clear both from the law itself and from cases that arise from it.

Case: R. v. Keegstra (1990)

James Keegstra, a teacher in rural Alberta, was charged with criminally promoting hate in his classroom. In class, he used terms like "manipulative" and "deceptive" to identify Jews. He also insisted that students accept his claims of Jewish international banking conspiracies and his denials of the Holocaust, unless they were able to contradict him. He also expressed his views publicly in his role as a teacher. This case, which went before the Supreme Court, focused on the criminalization of hate speech rather than education. Nonetheless, Keegstra was found guilty and was removed from the classroom.

This case illustrates that the right to freedom of speech must be exercised responsibly. Teachers need to think carefully before entering into controversial topics and be aware that the classroom is not a soapbox for their views.

They also need to be careful about off-hand statements that are completely inappropriate. For example, a teacher was admonished by the Discipline Committee of OCT for saying to a complaining student, "If you really believe everything is as bad as that, you might as well go home, get a gun and shoot yourself" or "end it all" (*Professionally Speaking*, June 2004).

Rather than worry about specific scenarios, teachers can save themselves and their students' grief by recognizing the power of their words and actions and conducting themselves with appropriate prudence and care. Even the most sincere of teachers make mistakes in judgment, so be ready to apologize and make amends before an incident develops into a crisis.

The professional misconduct case described below is a particularly egregious example.

Case #3
Ontario College of Teachers
(From the March 2006 edition of **Professionally Speaking**)
Decision: Reprimand, suspension and TCL (Terms, Conditions and Limits)

A panel of the Discipline Committee held a public hearing on January 10 and 11, 2006 and March 20, 21 and 29, 2006 into allegations of professional misconduct against SM.

SM was certified to teach in 1995 and was employed as a teacher by the St. Clair Catholic DSB. The member was present for part of the hearing on March 20 and 21, 2006 and was not represented by counsel.

SM faced six allegations of professional misconduct related to inappropriate behaviour in the classroom and inappropriate comments to and about students.

In the member's absence on the first day of the hearing, the Chair of the panel entered a plea of not guilty on his behalf.

The panel heard evidence from CH, a social worker with experience working with the Children's Aid Society, who testified that she had interviewed 68 students from the school. Only two students, she said, did not report inappropriate statements or actions by SM.

The panel also heard evidence from two students who testified that in September 2002 SM made an offensive and derogatory remark about a female student. The Superintendent of Schools for the board testified that he had interviewed six students who all reported the same inappropriate comment.

The student about whom the comment was made also testified. She told the panel that she had been upset by the situation and was subsequently removed from SM's class because she was so uncomfortable.

SM attended the hearing on March 21 when he testified in his own defence. He admitted making the statement, but said he was repeating what a student had said the previous day. He acknowledged that repeating the comment was a mistake in judgment.

SM denied all other allegations, saying that students had attributed to him comments or actions made by other students.

The panel found SM guilty of professional misconduct with respect to the comment he admitted making, which humiliated and embarrassed the student. However, the panel expressed concerns about the evidence presented regarding other comments and said in its written decision that it gave that evidence little weight.

The panel ordered SM to be reprimanded and directed the Registrar to suspend his Certificates of Qualification and Registration for one month. The panel also ordered that prior to returning to the classroom SM undertake a program of study and/or counselling, at his own expense, regarding appropriate teacher-student boundaries and provide evidence of its successful completion.

(1) Identify examples of SM's failure to be a good teacher and role model.
(2) How might he have modified his behaviour in each example?
(3) Do you agree with the decision and penalty of the Discipline Committee?

This case and other discipline cases of a similar nature make it clear that the language and behaviour of teachers in the classroom should be consistent with their professional status and their duty to act as an appropriate role model for impressionable students.

Profane or vulgar language may be protected if it is used for clear instructional purposes. This means that a teacher would be protected if using an article or story containing swearing or sexual references (Brown & Zuker, 2007). Much depends, of course, on the maturity and sophistication of the students. It is still wise to consult with the principal before using such materials, particularly if you have any qualms about their appropriateness

Similarly, the physical appearance of teachers can sometimes engender controversy. There was a time when teachers could be reprimanded for their grooming or choice of clothing. In the 1970s, for example, many schools expected male teachers to wear jackets and ties, and female teachers were sometimes reprimanded for wearing pantsuits. There seems to be a more *laissez-faire* attitude toward dress today. There have been no cases before the courts or the College recently concerning physical appearance. Nonetheless, teachers are advised to dress in a manner appropriate for a professional. It is worth bearing in mind, for example, that an unkempt beard, torn jeans, miniskirts, or low-cut blouses may diminish the respect accorded the teacher by students, parents, and colleagues.

UNDER THE AUTHORITY OF THE PRINCIPAL AND THE SCHOOL BOARD

The teacher is in charge of the classroom, but this authority is subject to the authority of the principal, who in turn is under the authority of a supervisory officer and the Director of Education. The principal, as principal-teacher, is in charge of "the instruction and the discipline of pupils in the school" and the "organization and management of the school" (*Regulation 298*, section 11(1)(a)(b)).

Teachers are not islands unto themselves but members of a school community dedicated to teaching and learning within the jurisdiction of the local school board. They have considerable autonomy within their own classroom to implement the curriculum in ways that best meet the needs of their own students, and there are no "curriculum police" monitoring their performance to ensure that all are using the same methodologies and resources. Nonetheless, teachers have a clear professional and legal obligation to be consistent with school expectations, and to follow board policies and provincial guidelines. Teachers are usually most effective when working collegially with other professionals as part of a learning community to develop effective educational programs for students.

The case below illustrates some of the complexities regarding the academic freedom of teachers.

Case: Morin v. Prince Edward Island Regional Administrative Unit No. 3 (2002)

Morin was a junior high language arts teacher in his second year as a probationary teacher. He showed his grade 9 class a documentary exploring the influence of Christian fundamentalism on American politics. This video was related to a class project he was about to begin on the meaning of religion in different societies.

This documentary upset some students and parents, who complained to the principal. The principal told Morin not to show the video again and cancelled the class project.

While the curriculum committee of the board determined that the project itself was appropriate, it criticized Morin for not giving sufficient forethought before commencing with it.

Morin was placed on an involuntary paid leave of absence for the remainder of the school year. At the end of the year, his probationary contract was not renewed.

Morin believed that the decision to forbid the film and the subsequent hiring decision constituted violations of his human rights and filed a court action claiming that the principal had violated his right to freedom of expression by not renewing his contract. Morin lost at trial but appealed the case to the Supreme Court, which agreed that his *Charter* right to freedom of expression had been violated and ordered the school district to provide financial compensation for wrongful dismissal.

(1) What are some good reasons for protecting a teacher's freedom of expression in the classroom?

(2) What are some good reasons for limiting a teacher's freedom of expression in the classroom?

(3) Why do you think the Supreme Court ruled in Morin's favour and ordered the school board to pay him compensation?

(4) How might Morin have approached this controversial topic more effectively?

The judges in this case affirmed teachers' freedom of speech, arguing that access to such expression encourages diversity, critical thinking, and healthy debate. The majority in this split decision were critical of the principal for rushing to judgment in response to complaints. They did concede, however, that the principal had authority over the school and that free expression by teachers could lead to disruption.

The academic freedom of teachers must be weighed in the balance with school and societal issues. In similar circumstances, especially if the principal were to act rather more prudently and thoughtfully, it is possible that a teacher's academic freedom would be curtailed.

Kevin A. Kindred (2006), in "Teachers in Dissent: Freedom of Expression in the Classroom," concludes his study of this and similar cases with these comments:

> The decision makers in these cases recognized that teachers are entrusted with a captive and impressionable audience, and yet they were still willing to entrust the teacher with some degree of personal control over the subject being taught. This level of trust is consistent with the notion of a professional. As well, the recognition of the degree of independent control exercised by a teacher within the classroom is relevant to other potentially significant questions in education law ... (*Education Law Journal* 15(3), p. 231)

While teachers enjoy a degree of academic freedom in curriculum and instruction, this freedom does not generally apply to supervisory or administrative duties.

TEACHERS' SUPERVISORY DUTIES

Section 265(1) of the *Education Act* clearly identifies the principal as the head teacher and manager of the school. In addition to their duties as teachers, principals are required "to maintain proper order and discipline in the school" and "to give assiduous attention to the health and comfort of the pupils ..." This also entails a duty to ensure that students are properly supervised at school and in school activities (*Regulation 298*, section 11(3) (e)(f)).

These duties of the principal, and the attendant powers, are reinforced by the duties of the teacher listed in section 264(1) of the *Education Act*, which call on teachers to obey the principal's directions in the maintenance of safety, order, and discipline. Supervisory duties have often been an area of contention between school boards and teachers' federations. Federations have worked hard to negotiate limits on the number of hours teachers are required to supervise students. Recently, they negotiated a provincial framework agreement that limits assigned supervision to seventy-five minutes per week, with exceptions in cases of emergency. Some federations are seeking a supervision cap of sixty minutes in the next round of contract negotiations. The Ontario Principals' Council, on the other hand, has expressed concerns about the current level of supervision. Principals maintain that an adequate supervisory presence by teachers prevents problems. They suggest that supervision is spread too thin in some schools, which places students at greater risk of harm and school boards at greater risk of safety-related lawsuits.

In Ontario today, principals make every effort to comply with the supervisory limit of seventy-five minutes a week. There may be emergency situations in which the principal has to assign additional supervision. If asked or ordered to provide additional supervisions in order to ensure student safety, teachers should keep in mind that their professional and statutory duties and responsibilities extend beyond the terms negotiated in collective agreements. This principle was affirmed in the case of *Winnipeg Teachers' Association v. Winnipeg School Division No. 1* (1976), when the Supreme Court ruled that professional contracts should be read so that principals are able to discharge their legal and professional duties to ensure safety in schools. The Court applied the following test for determining whether the assignment of supervisory duties beyond explicit collective agreement provisions was reasonable:

(a) it must be related to the enterprise of education;

(b) it must be fair to the teacher;

(c) it must be in furtherance of the principal's duties.

The length of the school day has been a particularly contentious supervision issue, particularly as it relates to when teachers must be "present in the classroom or teaching area ... at least fifteen minutes before the commencement of classes in the school in the morning" (*Regulation 298*, section 20(d)). Arbitration cases have made it clear that teachers are required not just to be present in schools (e.g., the staffroom) but in their classrooms or other areas where they may be required to supervise students. The term "instructional day" in legislation is student focused and does not define the work day for teachers. Less well defined is what constitutes instructional duties (which are covered by contractual agreements on the number of "instructional minutes" teachers are expected to work each week) versus supervisory or administrative duties. Arbitration board rulings on cases between school boards and federations are not clear on this point, because they often hinge on the precise wording of each collective agreement.

Teachers are well advised to avoid insubordination or even the impression of insubordination, because these could lead to complex grievance procedures and even dismissal. (See chapter 9 for further discussion of employer–employee relations in schools.)

TEACHERS' ADMINISTRATIVE DUTIES

As employees and professionals, teachers also have administrative duties. While this principle is widely accepted, there have been disputes regarding the nature and amount of additional work that teachers are *required* to perform.

PROFESSIONAL DEVELOPMENT

Case: St. Clair Catholic District School Board and OECTA (2001)

Many issues between school boards and teachers' federations are heard by arbitrators under provisions in collective agreements. Generally, the decisions of arbitrators resolve the issues, though decisions could be appealed to the courts. Arbitrators' decisions, which are based on points of law, often set important precedents concerning the professional lives of teachers.

In this case, the school board directed that teachers must attend an asbestos awareness training session "... after the regular business day of the teachers." The teachers sought additional pay for attending the workshops. The training sessions were offered either before or after school, or during the teachers' lunch break.

Arbitrator Watters found that the school board was entitled to schedule asbestos training sessions outside the instructional day and that the teachers were obliged to attend them as part of their professional duties, without additional compensation. Watters, citing the Winnipeg Teachers' case (1976), wrote:

I am satisfied that the Asbestos Awareness Training was in "furtherance of [one of] the principal duties" to which the teacher is committed ... [T]he Association did not seriously challenge the fact the training had to occur. Its complaint, rather, was that it was scheduled outside of the instructional day and that teachers were not provided with additional compensation for their attendance. It is, therefore, necessary to determine whether the Employer could properly schedule the training outside of the instructional day and, if so, whether it was obligated to pay the teachers for their attendance. I can find nothing in the collective agreements, the Education Act, or the Regulations that would obligate the Employer to schedule the training within the hours of the instructional day ...

Under the terms of their collective agreements, teachers in both the Elementary and Secondary Units receive an annual salary. It is clear that this salary encompasses the performance of certain duties outside of the instructional day, such as staff meetings after school and parent-teacher interviews after school or in the evenings. I consider it significant that health and safety issues are addressed in the after school staff meetings and that teachers do not receive extra compensation for their attendance at same. In the final analysis, I have not been persuaded that good reason exists to treat the training sessions in a different fashion for purposes of compensation. I think that the training sessions were analogous to a single issue staff meeting. The only difference is that, instead of providing a forum for discussion of, or reporting on, issues, the meeting focused on the delivery of formal training ...

Given the nature of the latter group's [teachers'] professional obligations, it is difficult to speak in terms of a regular or clearly defined workday.

Mr. Watters did, however, rule that it was unreasonable to require teachers to participate in professional development during their lunch period.

---

(1) What was the statutory basis for the arbitrator's decision?
(2) How would you interpret the last sentence of the quotation in relation to teaching as a profession?
(3) What are the implications of this decision for teachers?

The above case affirms that teachers are expected to participate in a range of professional development activities as part of their responsibilities as employees and professionals.

Legislation also clearly states that teachers must "participate in professional development days" (*Education Act*, section 264(1)(h)) in their school boards. It is also expected that teachers will volunteer to participate in additional training without compensation, because annual salaries denote flexibility and professionalism involves a commitment to ongoing professional development.

OTHER ADMINISTRATIVE DUTIES

Preparation Time

Teachers are provided with paid preparation time during the school day. While they are afforded considerable flexibility in how they use this time, they are generally expected to be available in the school in case they are asked to assist the principal by performing supervisory duties.

Parent–Teacher Interviews

Teachers are expected to "participate in regular meeting with [pupils'] parents or guardians" (*Regulation 298*, section 20(j)). This was confirmed in an arbitration case, *Durham Catholic District School Board and Ontario English Catholic Teachers' Association* (1999). The arbitration board found that the school board had the right to require teachers "to report to parents by attending evening parent-teacher interviews." The arbitration board reached this decision despite the fact that neither statute law nor contracts expressly state that teachers must participate in evening interviews.

Attending Graduation

Teachers are also obliged to attend graduation. *Regulation 298*, section 20(m) requires teachers to engage in "duties normally associated with the graduation of pupils." This duty, like parent–teacher interviews, has a long history in Ontario education. It is also a duty that most teachers assume gladly.

Delegation by Principals

The principal may delegate to a teacher in the school any of his powers and duties under Part XIII of the act, dealing with student discipline. This delegation may occur only in the absence of both principal and vice-principal and must be in accordance with board policy.

RESPECTING COPYRIGHT

Educators often supplement board-approved textbooks with materials and resources drawn from other books and periodicals. All educators should be aware of their obligation to respect the *Copyright Act* and the extent of their right to use copyrighted material under the Access Copyright agreement.

The school board's Access Copyright licence preauthorizes educators and students to copy within certain limits from millions of copyright-protected newspapers, magazines, journals, and books from around the world. This authorization complements what is allowed under the concept of "fair dealing," educational exceptions made under the *Copyright Act,* and the right to freely copy materials that are in the public domain. A comprehensive licence ensures

(1) advance clearance, so educators do not have to obtain permission every time they use material that is not considered fair dealing or that is not in the public domain

(2) payment for copyright owners when their work is copied

(3) respect for Canada's creative community and support for the continued creation of Canadian content.

For copying beyond the comprehensive agreement, Access Copyright also offers pay-per-use licences for both copying and digital uses.

CONCLUSION

Teachers need to be aware of their legal duties with regard to instruction, supervision, and administrative tasks. Legislation and legal cases also make it clear that teachers as professionals are held to a higher standard than non-professional employees.

While collective agreements limit the additional work principals may assign teachers, teachers are advised to comply with their principal's directions. If they feel the directions are excessive, they can confer with their federation representatives and, if necessary, grieve the principal's order. Employer–employee relations are examined further in chapter 9.

CHECKING YOUR UNDERSTANDING

- As a result of being *in loco parentis*, educators are considered under common law to owe their students a "fiduciary duty."
- The *Education Act* and its attendant regulations provide the statutory basis for public education in Ontario.
- The principal is responsible for the organization and management of the school and the instruction and discipline of students.
- The principal is also the person charged with ensuring that the school is a safe and healthy learning environment.
- Teachers have a number of duties outlined in the *Education Act* and *Regulation 298*. These duties may be further defined in collective agreements.
- Teachers' instructional duties include: teaching the classes assigned by the principal; encouraging students in the pursuit of learning; and acting as an appropriate role model for students both on and off duty.
- Teachers have considerable autonomy in their own classroom but are expected to teach in a manner consistent with school expectations, board policy, and provincial guidelines.
- Teachers must carry out the supervisory duties assigned by the principal within the limitations established by their collective agreement.
- Teachers' administrative duties include: attending workshops and training sessions; participating in professional activity days; attending parent–teacher meetings; and assisting with graduation ceremonies. These duties could be scheduled outside the regular school day.
- Educators should be aware of their obligations under the *Copyright Act* and the provisions of the board's Access Copyright licence.

APPLYING YOUR UNDERSTANDING

Too Cool for School

Joe looked forward to his first day of teaching. He had been assigned a group
of grade 8 students as a home room class, and was sure that he would be able
to make friends with the students. He looked forward to being "Mr. Cool"
and "hanging out" with the kids.

Joe drove into the parking lot ten minutes before the beginning of the
school day, leaving himself just enough time to pick up his register, class list,
and room key. He smiled, pleased with his time-management skills. Because
he had not read the information package from the principal, he did not
realize that he had missed his scheduled supervision of students entering
through the south doors of the school.

Arriving at the classroom just as opening exercises were starting, he
greeted his students, who were crowded around the door waiting to get in.
He invited them to enter and decide where they would like to sit. A number
of boys jostled one another in friendly competition for the most coveted
seats at the back. Most of the students stood by their desks and began singing *O Canada*, which was being played over the intercom, but the boys at
the back continued to argue over where they were going to sit. Joe, who was
writing some notes on the board, did not intervene. He was not going to be
like the old-fashioned, uptight teachers he had endured growing up!

Joe told the students that they were going to have a fun year. While
they would cover the curriculum in broad terms, he was going to let their
interests guide class discussion and activities. They would not use textbooks
or maintain notebooks. Instead, he planned to make copies for the students
of all sorts of materials that he knew would really interest them. Testing and
assignments would be kept to a minimum.

As Joe outlined the year ahead, he gently tapped a kid on the head with
a rolled up sheet of paper. He got a good laugh from the boys at the back by
teasing a "nerd" who asked what he needed to do to get an A+. His language
was colloquial, with the occasional scatological or sexual reference. Joe was
energized by the students' laughter at his jokes and his iconoclastic manner.

On his way to get a mug of coffee from the staffroom at recess, Joe forgot to ensure that his students left class in single file and to accompany them to the door to the playground. Climbing the stairs, he noticed two students wrestling on the landing. "Nice headlock!" he called out.

At lunch, Joe went to the beer store to pick up a case to drink at home. This would save him a trip after work, he thought. He was puzzled by the stares of students and teachers when he re-entered the school.

As he looked over the flurry of activity in the class that afternoon, Joe was confident that he had been doing a good job. Just before afternoon recess, there was an announcement reminding students that school would end early that day so teachers could attend a staff meeting. Joe, who was feeling tired and hated meetings, decided to head home for a well-deserved brew.

The next morning, the principal took Joe aside as he entered the school. She had received a number of complaints from parents about his classroom manner and his interactions with the students, and asked Joe for an explanation. She had also noticed that he had missed his morning supervision duty and was not at the staff meeting.

Joe did not attempt to deny any of the allegations. He explained that he firmly believed in his own professional autonomy and student freedom. He also thought that time outside the classroom was his own. He was not going to change his ways.

The principal then informed Joe that she would be asking the superintendent to carry forward a recommendation to the board for immediate termination of his contract, with the Minister of Education's approval. Joe would be asked to leave immediately and would receive a cheque equivalent to one-tenth of his annual salary.

As he left, Joe shrugged his shoulders. He was just too cool for the rules of school.

---

(1) In what ways did Joe fail to fulfill his instructional, supervisory, and administrative duties?

(2) In what ways did he fail to act as an appropriate role model?

(3) Do you think he should have been terminated?

(4) What lessons does this case offer to new teachers?

CHAPTER 4

The Conduct of Teachers at School and in the Community

After reading this chapter, you will have a deeper understanding of the professional and legal expectations for teacher conduct in the following areas: (1) classroom management, (2) sexual conduct, (3) contact with students outside school, (4) use of technology, and (5) teachers as role models.

"Be a wonderful role model because you will be the window through which many children will see their future."
–Thomas McKinnon

"In their position of trust, teachers must teach by example as well as by lesson, and that example is set just as much by their conduct outside the classroom as by their performance within it. The misconduct which occurs outside regular teaching hours can be the basis for discipline proceedings."
–Ontario Court of Appeal, *Toronto (City) Board of Education v. O.S.S.T.F., District 15*

The legal rights and duties of teachers have implications for teachers' conduct both in school and in the community. The behaviour of teachers, as professionals, should be appropriate, even exemplary, in school and in society. Teachers who exercise poor judgment or behave inappropriately either in school or in the public realm risk losing the respect of students and parents, and may also face professional or legal sanctions.

CLASSROOM MANAGEMENT AND DISCIPLINE

According to the *Ontario Schools Code of Conduct* (p. 5):

> Teachers and school staff, under the leadership of their principals, maintain order in the school and are expected to hold everyone to the highest standards of respectful and responsible behaviour. As role models, staff uphold these high standards when they:
>
> * Help students work to their full potential and develop their self-worth;
> * Communicate regularly and meaningfully with parents;
> * Maintain consistent standards of behaviour for all students;
> * Demonstrate respect for all students, staff and parents;
> * Prepare students for the full responsibilities of citizenship.

Teachers have a special role at schools and in society. This is evident in the duties of teachers in educational legislation, the high standards to which they are held in criminal and civil law, and the professional standards established by the Ontario College of Teachers. All of these have implications for how teachers manage their classrooms and discipline students.

CORRECTIVE FORCE AND PHYSICAL RESTRAINT

Section 43 of the *Criminal Code* states:

> Every school teacher, parent or person standing in the place of a parent is justified in using force by way of correction toward a pupil or child, as the case may be, who is under his care, if the force does not exceed what is reasonable under the circumstances.

This provision in the *Criminal Code* protects parents, teachers, and other caregivers from criminal sanction for using force when correcting a child's behaviour.

The Canadian Foundation for Children, Youth and the Law asked the courts to repeal this section of the *Criminal Code*, arguing that it violated the best interests and constitutional rights of children. Among those defending the law were representatives of parents who were proponents of corporal punishment and representatives of teachers who believed they might need to apply corrective force or physical restraint in the course of their duties. Those in favour of maintaining section 43 argued that it protects teachers from charges of criminal assault for using physical restraint to break up a fight, manage a student with behavioural/development issues, guide a child by the arm to the office, or defend themselves. The parents involved argued that a parent who mildly spanks a child on the leg was protected by section 43 from criminal assault charges.

Section 43 and Corrective Force
R. v. Wetmore (1996)

Mr. Wetmore, a teacher in New Brunswick who did not believe that suspension was an effective form of punishment, demonstrated his karate skills as a means of disciplining four students in his Grade 10 class. He struck the students about the shoulders, hitting one student's face and another's hands, which were covering the student's face. This was in order to discuss and reduce disruptive behaviour among middle school students. A complaint from parents led to charges. After several appeals, the Supreme Court ruled the teacher not guilty of assault, because the use of force was for the purpose of correction. The judge concluded that although the method of discipline was unorthodox, it was not unreasonable. The students did not suffer any injuries and their disruptive behaviour was effectively controlled.

R. v. Park (S.M.) (1999)

Ms. Park of Newfoundland slapped the leg of a kindergarten girl who

---

was kicking and screaming while she was attempting to put her in a snowsuit. Parents, noticing the bruising, reported the incident to the police, who filed criminal charges of assault on the grounds of excessive force. Ultimately, the courts ruled that "apparent good faith in administering mild corporal punishment" is reasonable.

(1) Do you think the corrective force used by these teachers was appropriate?

(2) Do you agree with the courts' decisions in these cases? Why or why not?

(3) Do you think section 43 is a necessary protection for teachers?

Section 43 provides teachers with a special defence against charges of criminal assault. The Canadian Teachers' Federation, while supportive of the Canadian Foundation for Children, Youth and the Law's desire to protect children from abuse, opposed the foundation's argument for the elimination of this special defence for teachers against assault charges. Removal of this section, the federation argued, would result in a dramatic increase in the number of assault charges filed and prosecuted. As a result, the federation continued, teachers would hesitate to respond to innapropriate student behaviour that might require the use of reasonable force, and students most likely to disrupt may interpret the removal of section 43 as freedom to do so without consequences.

The Ontario Court of Appeal in *Canadian Foundation for Children, Youth and the Law v. Canada* (Attorney General) (2002) rejected the claim that this section constituted cruel and unusual punishment for children. It concluded that Parliament had enacted this provision so "parents and teachers have a protected sphere of authority within which to fulfil their responsibilities" for nurturing and educating children. It also saw no benefit to criminalizing non-abusive corporal punishment used by parents and others for purposes of discipline and instruction.

The Court disagreed that section 43 was inconsistent with the principle of "best interests of the child," saying that this is a principle that informs legal and policy initiatives rather than a principle of fundamental justice under the *Charter.*

The Supreme Court in 2004 upheld this ruling in a split decision. Justice Arbour, in her dissent, argued that judicial attitudes toward discipline had evolved significantly over time and that section 43 was no longer appropriate. The majority, while upholding the section, made it clear that "the substantial social consensus on what is reasonable correction, supported by comprehensive and consistent expert evidence on what is reasonable presented in this appeal, gives clear content to s. 43." The list provided of harmful corporal punishment situations made it clear that the courts are unlikely to tolerate severe corporal punishment.

The Supreme Court decision also established clear directions for teachers:

> Contemporary social consensus is that, while teachers may sometimes use corrective force to remove children from classrooms or to secure compliance with instructions, the use of corporal punishment by teachers is not acceptable. Many school boards forbid the use of corporal punishment, and some provinces and territories have legislatively prohibited its use by teachers ... This consensus is consistent with Canada's international obligations, given the findings of the Human Rights Committee of the United Nations ... Section 43 will protect a teacher who uses reasonable, corrective force to restrain or remove a child in appropriate circumstances.

PROFESSIONALISM IN CLASSROOM MANAGEMENT

Section 43 offers special protection for teachers who may need to use corrective force or physical restraint in managing student behaviour. The court rulings on the constitutionality of section 43 also offer insights into types of teacher conduct that are considered unreasonable, such as the use of corporal punishment or force that results from the teacher's anger or frustration.

The *Ontario Schools Code of Conduct* outlines broad standards for respectful and responsible classroom management and discipline by teachers.

The recent amendments to the safe schools provisions in the *Education Act* emphasize prevention, progressive discipline, and early intervention. Many books and manuals are available to guide teachers in developing positive classroom management practices.

Recent rulings by the Discipline Committee of the Ontario College of Teachers also help educators to determine what constitutes effective professional conduct in managing students and classrooms. The following cases, which were published in *Professionally Speaking*, illustrate conduct to be avoided by teaching professionals. As the cases make clear, despite the legal protection provided by section 43 of the *Criminal Code* from charges of criminal assault, society increasingly expects teachers to manage conflict situations without resorting to physical force.

Case #1
(From the March 2006 issue of **Professionally Speaking**)
Decision: Cautioned

Following notification by a school board, the registrar initiated a complaint against a member of the College alleging that she had inappropriately disciplined an elementary school student by pushing him into the hallway.

On September 28, 2005, the Investigation Committee ratified a memorandum of agreement between the member and the College, in which the member:
- acknowledged that she engaged in the alleged conduct
- agreed to be cautioned by the Investigation Committee, in writing, regarding her conduct
- agreed to successfully complete a course of instruction regarding positive classroom management strategies
- agreed to provide the Registrar with written confirmation of successful completion of the course of instruction.

(1) What was the nature of the misconduct?
(2) What would have been a better course of action by the teacher?

Case #2

(From the June 2007 issue of **Professionally Speaking**)

Decision: Reprimand

A panel of the Discipline Committee held a public hearing on January 30 into an allegation of professional misconduct against a member, related to interacting improperly with a student. The member attended the hearing and was represented by counsel.

The panel heard evidence that the member failed to adhere to the school and board's "hands off" policy when interacting with a four-year-old male student in her class who was crying. To stop him from crying, the member yelled at the student, held his wrists and pulled him to her. Consequently, further upset and frightened, the child became physically ill and vomited. For a short period the student was inconsolable. Another teacher and a parent volunteer witnessed the incident.

The member acknowledged that the actions constituted professional misconduct and pleaded no contest to the allegation.

Based on an agreed statement of facts, a plea of no contest and a joint submission on penalty, the panel reprimanded the member for professional misconduct and directed that the decision appear in summary in *Professionally Speaking* as a general deterrent.

---

(1) What was the nature of the misconduct?

(2) What would have been a better course of action by the teacher?

Case #3

(From the September 2006 issue of **Professionally Speaking**)

Decision: Reprimand

A panel of the Discipline Committee held a public hearing April 25, 2006 into allegations of professional misconduct against WJ. WJ was certified to teach in 1978 and was employed as a teacher by the Ottawa-Carleton District School Board. The member attended the hearing and was represented by counsel.

WJ faced six allegations of professional misconduct related to behaving in an unprofessional and inappropriate manner towards a male student.

The panel received an agreed statement of facts, guilty plea and joint submission on penalty in which WJ admitted that during the 2002-03 school year he acted in an unprofessional and inappropriate manner towards a male Grade 7 student in his class. The member placed his hands on the student's shoulders and used his hands to square the student's shoulders while admonishing him for his behaviour.

In a review of his conduct by his board the member admitted that he had suffered a lapse in judgment in making physical contact with the student. In a letter to him the board said that WJ demonstrated poor judgment, warned against such future interactions with students and urged him to attend a workshop in non-violent crisis intervention.

The panel concluded that the facts support a finding of professional misconduct. The panel ordered that WJ appear before them to be reprimanded. The panel directed the member to provide the Registrar with proof within 60 days that he has successfully completed a course in non-violent crisis intervention.

(1) What was the nature of the misconduct?
(2) What would have been a better course of action by the teacher?

MAINTAINING BOUNDARIES IN SCHOOL AND BEYOND

MAINTAINING BOUNDARIES IN SCHOOL

The student–teacher relationship is critical to classroom learning. Students are more likely to learn when they have a positive rapport with teachers and teachers are genuinely interested in making learning personally meaningful for them. In order to personalize and promote effective learning, teachers will sometimes use colloquial language, make references to popular culture, tell jokes, gently tease students, ask personal questions, or share their own personal stories. Teachers as professionals must exercise great caution in their efforts to develop positive relationships with students. A remark or strategy that seems appropriate from the teacher's adult perspective may be interpreted quite differently by students, who are both younger and less sophisticated. Irony, for example, is frequently misunderstood by children, who not only tend to have a literal view of the world but also are used to respecting what their teacher tells them.

It is important, then, for teachers to stand back and consider beforehand the implications and appearance of what they say and do in the classroom. Teachers are advised to err on the side of caution. Like teachers in the previous section who were too severe in their classroom management practices, teachers who become too familiar with their students risk transgressing the professional boundaries established to protect students. Understanding these boundaries enables teachers to maintain positive and educative relationships with students that are free from inadvertent or intentional harm.

One area of concern is verbal and non-verbal communication in the classroom. Although the use of colloquial language by teachers in the classroom may not be inappropriate, it may well seem contrived to students or cause them to lose respect. It is also important to remember that as role models teachers should help their students develop proficiency in the conventions and standards of language usage. Teachers should never swear or make sexually suggestive comments. Not only is such language entirely inappropriate for a teacher, it is likely to be offensive to many students and could well lead to disciplinary action by the Ontario College of Teachers. Teachers should also avoid making personal comments about students even if they are intended in jest. The College cautioned a teacher who made personal and inappropriate comments about a student and the student's family and ordered the teacher to complete a course of instruction on appropriate boundaries. The College also reprimanded a teacher who gently stroked a student's arm while praising the student's clothing.

Teachers are expected to establish positive relationships with students but must maintain the highest standards of respectful and responsible behaviour at all times. Novice teachers should exercise discretion in communicating with students. Observing master teachers who effectively establish rapport while respecting boundaries will help them.

MAINTAINING BOUNDARIES OUTSIDE SCHOOL

Teachers and students typically interact within the milieu of the school and school-related activities. Teachers who exercise good judgment will generally avoid contact with students outside this milieu. Those who live in the same community as their students are likely to meet students in other settings. While this should be no cause for alarm, they should keep these interchanges pleasant yet short, particularly if other people are not present.

In *Professional Advisory: Professional Misconduct Related to Sexual Abuse and Sexual Misconduct* (2002), the Ontario College of Teachers encourages teachers to avoid:

- inviting students into their homes;
- seeing students in private and isolated situations;
- exchanging personal notes, comments, or e-mails;
- personally becoming involved in students' affairs;
- giving personal gifts to students;
- sharing personal information about themselves;
- making physical contact of a sexual nature.

By knowing and understanding the reasons for these limits, teachers protect the interests of students and demonstrate sound professional judgment.

Case #4

(From the March 2008 issue of **Professionally Speaking**)
Decision: Reprimanded with conditions

A Discipline Committee panel held a public hearing on September 18, 2007 into two allegations of professional misconduct against LR for engaging in an inappropriate relationship with a 17-year-old female student.

LR, who was certified to teach in August 1991 and taught at the secondary level for the Conseil scolaire catholique de district du Grand Nord de l'Ontario, attended the hearing and was represented by counsel.

The panel heard evidence that LR held telephone conversations of a personal nature with the student, met her after school off campus and drove her to and from a Harvey's restaurant where they had a soft drink and talked.

Based on the evidence, an agreed statement of facts, a guilty plea and a joint submission on penalty, the panel reprimanded LR for professional misconduct.

The panel further directed the Registrar to suspend LR's teaching certificates for a month if he failed to complete a course on appropriate teacher-student boundaries at his own expense within eight months of the decision.

The panel said that LR "showed a lack of judgment" and "acted unwisely" in his behaviour with the student, which could have been misconstrued as a sign of friendship or as a personal relationship.

"Specifically, the fact that he had discussions and telephone conversations of a personal nature with her constitutes conduct unbecoming a member of the profession," the Discipline Committee panel wrote.

---

(1) What was the nature of the misconduct?
(2) What does this case tell you about the professional boundary
   between student and teachers?

LR was ruled to have demonstrated conduct that was unbecoming of a member of the teaching profession. Socializing with a student over a hamburger, while perhaps innocent enough, raised reasonable concerns about propriety. Driving the student to and from the restaurant showed even worse judgment, because the teacher was alone with a student in a private space. The telephone calls of a personal nature further transgressed professional boundaries. The College, taking all of these acts together, determined that they constituted serious professional misconduct according to the Ontario College of Teachers. Adults who abuse children often begin to *groom* their victims through such interactions. Teachers are expected to maintain a professional relationship with students outside the classroom and school setting.

THE SEXUAL CONDUCT OF TEACHERS

While most people take sexual misconduct seriously, many are unaware of the prevalence of unwanted or inappropriate sexual activity in the lives of school-aged children. Sexual abuse, according to conservative research estimates, affects more than twenty-five percent of girls and ten percent of boys by the age of eighteen. Sexual harassment, which includes objectionable comments, is even more prevalent. Cook & Truscott (2007) put it well when they say:

> There are *no* circumstances in which sexual activity between a teacher and a student is acceptable. Sexual activity between a student and teacher is always detrimental to the student's best interest, regardless of what rationale or belief system a teacher might choose to excuse it. (p. 87)

Sexual activity between teachers and students is deemed particularly unacceptable due to the duty of care teachers owe parents and students, and the position of authority they hold as professional educators. According to *Protecting Our Children* (2000), a report by Justice Robbins, such a betrayal of trust by a teacher can be particularly harmful to students:

> The impact is often less correlated with the severity or intrusiveness of the sexual behaviour than with the pre-abuse relationship to the abuser, the vulnerability of the victim or the way in which the disclosure of the abuse was responded to. Accordingly, a seemingly minor incident of sexual touching by a close and trusted adult can have a profound and lasting impact. (chapter 3)

Teachers who violate this trust through non-consensual or consensual sexual contact with students risk severe criminal and professional consequences. Teachers who engage in sexual harassment may also face disciplinary action from their employer or the Ontario College of Teachers.

THE CRIMINAL CODE

The *Criminal Code* sets out several sexual offences that are particularly relevant to sexual misconduct in the school context:

Sexual Interference (Section 151)

Every person who, for a sexual purpose, touches, directly or indirectly, with a part of the body or with an object, any part of the body of a person under the age of 16 years is guilty of an indictable offence and is liable to imprisonment for a term not exceeding ten years ... or is guilty of an offence punishable on summary conviction ...

Invitation to Sexual Touching (Section 152)

Every person who, for a sexual purpose, invites, counsels or incites a person under the age of 16 years to touch, directly or indirectly, with a part of the body or with an object, the body of any person, including the body of the person who so invites, counsels or incites and the body of the person under the age of 16 years, is guilty of an indictable offence and is liable to imprisonment for a term not exceeding ten years ... or is guilty of an offence punishable on summary conviction ...

Sexual Exploitation (Section 153)

Every person commits an offence who is in a position of trust or authority towards a young person [defined as "a person 16 years of age or more but under the age of eighteen years"], who is a person with whom the young person is in a relationship of dependency or who is in a relationship with a young person that is exploitative of the young person, and who

> (a) for a sexual purpose, touches, directly or indirectly, with a part of the body or with an object, any part of the body of the young person; or
>
> (b) for a sexual purpose, invites, counsels or incites a young person to touch, directly or indirectly, with a part of the body or with an object, the body of any person, including the body of the person who invites, counsels or incites and the body of the young person.

Every person who commits an offence under subsection (1) [Sexual Exploitation described above] is guilty of an indictable offence and liable to imprisonment for a term not exceeding ten years ... or is guilty of an offence punishable on summary conviction ...

Simply put, teachers should never engage in sexual activities with students. "Sexual interference" applies to the activity of any adult who touches a child under the age of sixteen for sexual purposes. "Invitation to sexual touching" occurs when an adult invites a victim under the age of sixteen to touch a part of the body with a sexual purpose. The sentences for these offences involving children under the age of sixteen are severe, since young children are considered vulnerable and dependent on the protection of adults, particularly their teachers. Avoiding "sexual exploitation" is particularly important for secondary schools: This clause provides young adults over the age of sixteen but under the age of eighteen with the same protection from sexual misconduct by their teachers and others who may be in a position of trust or authority.

It should be noted that consent is no defence in all three of these offences. Although students over the age of eighteen are not covered by the preceding sections of the *Criminal Code*, the general charge of sexual assault (section 271) could still apply, particularly if the consent of the student is judged to have been given "by reason of the exercise of authority" of the teacher (section 265). In addition, as will be discussed later in this chapter, sexual misconduct with a student of any age is considered by the Ontario College of Teachers to be professional misconduct.

The following case suggests that the scope of a teacher's position of trust and authority extends beyond his or her own students.

R. v. Audet (1996)

Mr. Audet, a twenty-two-year-old physical education teacher, had sex with a fourteen-year-old female former grade 8 student whom he encountered by chance during the summer vacation. The teacher accompanied the former student and her two cousins to a party where the girls consumed alcohol. The teacher left the party and lay down in a bedroom of the cottage in which the party took place. His former student subsequently joined him and they engaged in oral sex; when the former student became uncomfortable, the teacher stopped immediately.

At the trial level, the court acquitted Audet, noting that the incident took place during the holidays and that the teacher did nothing to instigate the sexual encounter. This decision was upheld by the New Brunswick Court of Appeal.

The Supreme Court of Canada upheld the appeal made by the Crown in a split decision. Whereas the lower courts viewed the circumstances as mitigating the actions of the teacher, the Supreme Court interpreted section 153 of the *Criminal Code* on sexual exploitation literally. Because Audet was in a position of trust and authority and did engage in sex with a former student who had just turned fourteen, he was ultimately held responsible for the sexual activity that took place and guilty of sexual exploitation. (It should be noted that at the time of this case, "sexual exploitation" applied to young people over the age of fourteen but under the age of eighteen.)

Justice LaForest, writing for the majority, emphasized the responsibility of the teacher: "I am of the view that in the vast majority of cases teachers will indeed be in a position of trust and authority towards their students."

While some teachers who engage in sexual conduct with students are sexually aggressive or predatory, most appear to have personal problems, poor judgment, or an inability to understand the professional boundaries that exist between teachers and students. The majority of these teachers are male; an Ontario study (Dolmage, 1995) of sexual assault charges over five years found that forty-six males and one female were charged. There are, however, a number of high-profile instances of female teachers becoming romantically involved with male or female students.

An accusation of sexual abuse can be very damaging for teachers, even if the accusation is subsequently proven false. Michael Hanson of St. Andrew's College waited fifteen months to have his name cleared after a false accusation of sexual abuse that was publicized in the media. Mr. Hanson suffered the stress of not knowing about his future, even though he was on paid leave and enjoyed the support of former students, parents, and colleagues. Teachers should conduct themselves professionally at all times and avoid placing themselves in situations that could lead to false allegations of sexual misconduct. The Elementary Teachers' Federation of Ontario reported that the union receives about five calls a day from teachers who have been accused of physical abuse, but few calls concerning sexual abuse.

Students are more likely to be victims of sexual harassment by peers. Nonetheless, sexual harassment by teachers—objectionable comments or conduct of a sexual nature—can be particularly harmful to the security and sense of integrity of students. Such behaviour may be overtly sexual or be based on gender, sexual orientation, or perceptions about gender-appropriate behaviour.

ADVICE FROM THE ONTARIO COLLEGE OF TEACHERS

The Ontario College of Teachers' publication *Professional Advisory: Professional Misconduct Related to Sexual Abuse and Sexual Misconduct* (2002) advises teachers to avoid sexual relations, touching of a sexual nature, and "behaviour or remarks of a sexual nature by the member towards students" (p. 2) since these constitute sexual abuse as defined in the *Ontario College of Teachers' Act* and the *Teaching Profession Act*.

Note that this definition of "sexual abuse" is much broader than the sexual offences described in sections 151–53 of the *Criminal Code* discussed above. First, "sexual abuse" covers inappropriate language as well as behaviour; second, it can involve the teachers' own students, other students, or even adult students. Misconduct of a sexual nature may also be viewed as a violation of other professional responsibilities such as maintaining the standards of the profession, refraining from conduct unbecoming of a member, and upholding the *Education Act*. The standard of proof at a College disciplinary hearing is lower than that of a court of criminal law. The suspension or revocation of one's teaching certification obviously would have significant implications for the individual involved.

The College also urges members to exercise caution about both the implications and the appearance of their actions: "Members have an additional responsibility to avoid activities that may reasonably raise concerns as to their propriety." This applies to any interaction with students of a sexual nature and to crossing the professional boundary that should be maintained between teachers and students.

REPORTING SUSPICIONS OF SEXUAL MISCONDUCT BY TEACHERS

A teacher who has reasonable grounds to suspect another teacher of sexual misconduct with a student under the age of sixteen, even in the absence of concrete evidence, is legally obligated to report the suspicion directly to the Children's Aid Society or the Catholic Children's Aid Society, since such behaviour could qualify as child abuse (sexual molestation or exploitation) under the *Child and Family Services Act*. It would also be prudent for the teacher to inform the principal of the suspicions and action taken. If the student is over the age of sixteen, the teacher who suspects possible sexual abuse should report the matter to the principal or other school board personnel.

When suspicions are reported, the appropriate authority is to collect information, ensure the student's safety (possibly by removing him/her from the classroom), and then inform the teacher of the accusation. The teacher will likely be suspended with pay until the complaint has been fully investigated. The teacher should contact the appropriate teachers' federation immediately to obtain legal advice and, possibly, retain a lawyer. Depending on the circumstances and outcome of the investigation, the matter could also be referred to the police and the Ontario College of Teachers.

There have been concerns that teachers are reluctant to report suspicions of colleagues due to section 18 of the *Teaching Profession Act*, which warns against "interfering in an unwarranted manner between other teachers and pupils" and requires that the teacher making such an "adverse report on another member, furnish him with a written statement of the report at the earliest possible time and not later than three days after making the report." (See chapter 2 for further information on adverse reports.)

In *Protecting Our Children* (2000), Justice Robbins recommended that teachers be able to make an anonymous adverse report of another teacher if sexual abuse of a student is suspected. Since the passage of the *Student Protection Act* in 2002, this exception has been permitted.

REPORTING SUSPICIONS OF ABUSE BY PARENTS OR GUARDIANS

Teachers in Ontario, as part of their duty of care, also have a statutory obligation to report suspicions of child abuse that may occur in the home or elsewhere. This is because the *Child and Family Services Act* gives primacy at all times to the child's best interests, protection, and well-being. This protection is viewed as more important than the protection of parental freedom from state intervention and the awkwardness for teachers and other caregivers who may be required to report suspicions of abuse to the proper authorities. It is worth noting, as well, that teachers cannot stop at reporting these suspicions to the principal, although it is wise to notify principals in advance.

Child abuse occurs when someone under the age of sixteen suffers physical harm, sexual molestation or exploitation, emotional harm, or neglect, caused by an act or omission by the person in charge of the child. Teachers, particularly elementary teachers, are often well positioned to notice physical and behavioural signs of abuse.

For example, signs of physical abuse include bruises, cuts, fractures, burns, and malnutrition. While one bruise or one fall down the stairs may not be the basis of a reasonable suspicion of physical abuse, the regular appearance of these signs should lead to suspicion, especially if they are accompanied by changes in behaviour.

Signs of sexual abuse—crying, changes in behaviour, inappropriate sexual knowledge, fear of physical contact—are harder to discern but may become apparent to teachers who know their students well.

Similarly, signs of emotional abuse—decline in self-confidence and over-aggression—may be difficult to detect.

Signs of neglect—the failure to adequately care for or protect a child—may include fatigue, lack of sleep, and malnutrition.

Note also that students often confide information to teachers that may lead the teachers to suspect abuse. Even if students offer information to teacher in confidence, a teacher's duty to report overrides confidentiality. Some teachers, with this in mind, advise students that they cannot promise confidentiality.

As caregivers who work closely with children, teachers are well placed to notice child abuse and, by reporting suspicions, to help children live safer and happier lives. Teachers who suspect abuse may wish to review school board resources or reputable websites that can help them better identify the signs of abuse. They are also advised to record their observations. It is important to remember that teachers are only reporting suspicions, not rendering judgment. The teacher's duty to report overrides the potential for strained relationships with parents.

THE ONTARIO COLLEGE OF TEACHERS ON REPORTING SUSPICIONS OF ABUSE

In the summer of 2005, two female teachers took two female students they had coached on an overnight shopping trip in another city. Although parental permission had been received, the parents did not know that the husband of one of the teachers would be accompanying them. Later, one of the students, who was under sixteen at the time, informed both teachers that she had been touched sexually at the hotel by the husband. The teachers did not report the allegation to the parents, school board, or the Children's Aid Society.

Both teachers were charged under the *Child and Family Services Act*, but the courts dismissed the charge. The Discipline Committee of the College found both teachers guilty of professional misconduct. In the summary of its ruling against KAR in *Professionally Speaking* (March 2010), the Discipline Committee panel wrote:

> The member had a duty to report allegations of child abuse and this did not occur. On two separate occasions, over a period of approximately 10 days, the student disclosed to the member that she had been sexually touched by the colleague's husband. By failing to report the disclosure, the member did not follow the written policy of the Durham DSB to report a case of suspected child abuse.
>
> Teachers are expected to protect students in their care at all time. By not reporting allegations of sexual abuse, the member failed to maintain the standards of the profession and failed to comply with the *Education Act*. Her conduct was unprofessional and unbecoming a member. (pp. 69-70)

KAR was reprimanded and ordered to complete a course in professional ethics at her own expense. The other teacher who was involved, the wife of the alleged abuser, faced further penalties, because she was also found guilty of fostering an inappropriate relationship with the student. Not only was she reprimanded and required to take the same course in professional ethics, but her certificate was suspended for three months.

These two cases suggest that the College of Teachers expects teachers to take allegations of sexual abuse very seriously. It is significant that the College took action even though the courts dismissed the case.

TEACHERS AND TECHNOLOGY

We live in an increasingly wired world. Many teachers now rely on cyberspace for information, entertainment, communication, and social networking. Because information technology is largely benign, many people are unaware of potential problems associated with it. Because of their public profiles and duty of care to students, teachers need to be particularly mindful of the ethical and legal dimensions of new technologies.

R. v. Cole (2009)

A sixteen-year-old female grade 10 student sent nude photographs of herself to another student. Cole, a computer science teacher and supervisor of his school's computer network, found the file on the school computer network and copied the photographs to the laptop computer that had been assigned to him by the Rainbow District School Board.

In the course of his duties, another information technology specialist monitoring the school system discovered a hidden file on the teacher's E-drive that contained the nude photographs. The principal then notified the police. The police, however, did not obtain a search warrant because the school authorities indicated that they were the owners of the materials.

After he was charged with possession of child pornography, Cole argued that his *Charter* right to be protected from unreasonable search and seizure had been violated when the police searched the laptop and its contents.

A lower court sided with Cole's claim to a reasonable expectation of privacy, comparing the password-protected computer files to a locked office credenza containing personal items.

On appeal, the court concluded that Cole had no reasonable expectation of privacy and ruled that the laptop and its files were admissible as evidence. The court concluded that the teacher's expectation of privacy was unreasonable because (a) the school board provided the laptop, (b) the user agreement he had signed stated that files stored in the system should not be considered private, (c) the teacher knew that accounts were accessible by other IT personnel, and (d) school board policy stated that school board employees were prohibited from using the equipment provided to post or access sexually explicit material.

This court decision reminds teachers that they need to exercise prudence when using technology in schools or storing information on school networks. Employment law and the professional standards of the College make it clear that viewing inappropriate materials in the workplace is problematic and that those who do so may be subject to sanction. This particular case also draws attention to the fact that teachers do not have a reasonable expectation of privacy while using technology in a school setting. While this case does not address wireless access, it is our opinion that it would also be unreasonable to expect privacy when using a school board wireless system. Finally, regardless of the circumstances, the possession of child pornography is a criminal offence that is always viewed as a serious violation of professional standards—and even more so when the images are of students.

Teachers should also exercise care in their personal use of the Internet. Jiri Tlusty of the Toronto Maple Leafs suffered public embarrassment when nude photos of himself that he had included on his Facebook page were posted on a public website and received considerable media attention. Tlusty's experience should serve as a caution to all people in the public eye, including teachers, who have a particular responsibility to model positive behaviour and to maintain appropriate boundaries on social networking sites. Teachers are advised to maintain high-privacy settings on their social networking accounts and to avoid posting images or words that could prove embarrassing or unprofessional. In British Columbia, a parent launched a professional complaint against a teacher after finding a nude photo of the teacher among thousands of photos posted on a personal website. While this incident blew over after brief media scrutiny, it does illustrate that teachers need to exercise greater discretion than other members of the public. Even if they avoid professional sanction, teachers who lack discretion may still have to deal with the judgment and mockery of students and parents.

Teachers should also avoid contact with students on the Internet, save for communication on approved board sites and e-mail accounts. This is consistent with the College's recommendation that teachers avoid social contact with students outside school.

Teachers should also be aware of the prevalence of cyberbullying. According to research conducted for the Ontario College of Teachers (Browne, 2007), "Cyberbullying students have targeted the vast majority of Ontario's 210,000 certified teachers, seeking to embarrass and intimidate them with criticism of their appearance and their grading skills, malicious gossip, and threats of physical harm" (p. 51). While the majority of teachers did not regard the impact as serious, teachers should be aware that they have the legal right to be protected from such abuse.

TEACHERS AS ROLE MODELS

In the 1870s a female teacher who married or engaged in unseemly conduct could be dismissed. In addition, a teacher who smoked, used liquor, frequented pool halls, or got shaved in a barber shop gave "good reason to suspect his worth, intention, and honesty."

In the 1920s, female teachers were not permitted to enter ice-cream parlours or to be courted by a man without a chaperone. Married women in the 1950s were able to teach but were dismissed once they became pregnant.

---

(1) Why do you think these rules were put in place?
(2) What do these rules reveal about society's views of teachers as role models?
(3) Do you think it was fair to deny teachers rights that were held by other citizens?

Ontario has changed considerably since those days, yet there remains a tension between the individual rights of teachers and the higher expectations that society holds for professionals entrusted to take care of children. This is reflected in the admittedly somewhat old-fashioned wording of section 264(1)(c) of the *Education Act*, which states that it is the teacher's duty "to inculcate by precept and example" respect for religion and the principles of Judeo-Christian morality and the "highest regard" for truth, justice, and other virtues.

The Supreme Court of Canada is unequivocal in recognizing teachers as role models. In the 1997 case of *Toronto (City) Board of Education v. O.S.S.T.F., District 15*, the Court stated:

> The language [of section 264(1)(c) of the *Education Act*] is that of another era. The requirements it sets for teachers reflect the ideal and not the minimal standard ... However, the section does indicate that teachers are very properly expected to maintain a higher standard of conduct than other employees because they occupy such an extremely important position in society.

The Supreme Court went on to elaborate its reasoning:

> In their position of trust, teachers must teach by example as well as by lesson, and that example is set just as much by their conduct outside the classroom as by their performance within it. Thus misconduct which occurs outside regular teaching hours can be the basis for discipline proceedings.

Clearly, then, the professional responsibilities of teachers do not end once they leave the school, as has been made clear in a number of cases. For example, in *R. v. Audet* (1996), discussed earlier in this chapter, the Supreme Court ruled that sexual activity with a former student during the summer holidays constituted sexual exploitation and was therefore just cause for a teacher to be discharged. The Court made it clear that the teacher "seriously prejudiced his status as a role model." Similarly, other acts of misconduct by teachers could serve as a basis for discipline or dismissal, depending on factors such as the likelihood of recurrence, the impairment of the teacher's relations with students, and extenuating circumstances.

At the same time, the courts are reluctant to encroach on the human rights of teachers, given the *Canadian Charter of Rights and Freedoms* as well as changing social norms. Judges' decisions attempt to strike a delicate balance between the individual rights of teachers and the expectation that they be role models in their actions in school and beyond.

In what follows, court decisions and professional misconduct cases are used to examine this balance between teachers' individual rights and the higher professional standard to which they must adhere.

LIFESTYLES OF TEACHERS

The challenge of striking a delicate balance between individual rights and social expectations is particularly evident in situations concerning the lifestyles of teachers.

Abbotsford School District 34 v. Shewan (1987)

In 1984, John Shewan submitted three pictures of his wife as part of an entry to *Gallery* magazine's Girl Next Door Amateur Erotic Photo Contest. These semi-nude pictures were subsequently published in February 1985. The entry identifying Ilze S as a teacher in Clearbrook, B.C., caught the attention of a radio reporter, who made inquiries with the superintendent of education. After an investigation and hearing, both Ilze and John Shewan were suspended without pay for six weeks. Newspaper reports of the school board decision sparked controversy regarding teachers as role models in the community.

The Shewans appealed their suspension to a board of reference. This administrative tribunal determined that the couple's behaviour fell within reasonable standards. In making this determination, members of the board decided that the standard to be applied was not whether "the Shewans' conduct fell below some of the community's standards but whether it was within the accepted standards of tolerance in contemporary Canadian society."

The B.C. Supreme Court and, subsequently, the B.C. Court of Appeal, found the Shewans guilty of misconduct and upheld suspensions of one month. The Court of Appeal found in part that "the publication of such a photograph of a teacher in such a magazine will have an adverse effect upon the educational system to which the teacher owes a duty to act responsibly." The obligation of teachers, the court explained, extends beyond the school to the profession and the community.

---

(1) What actions on the part of the Shewans caused them to be accused of misconduct?

(2) Why did the board of reference rule in favour of the Shewans?

(3) Why did the B.C. court determine that the Shewans were poor role models who deserved to be punished for misconduct?

(4) If you were charged with deciding this case, which side would you favour?

(5) What is the significance of this landmark case for you as a teacher?

Complicating this issue is a 1983 case in Quebec in which a teacher was suspended for violating the principles of Catholicism by appearing naked at a nudist camp. This was discovered when a picture appeared in a small-town newspaper. A board of arbitration and, subsequently, the courts indicated that the Catholic school board had failed to prove that the employee's behaviour violated Catholic principles. It is possible that the school board would have been successful if it had provided evidence that nudity is contrary to Catholic religious doctrine (Piddocke, Magsino & Manley-Casimir, 1997).

How can one reconcile these two cases? *Shewan* is a landmark case because it has helped define the degree to which teachers' private lives are public. Critical to this being a case of misconduct was the decision by the Shewans to place their pictures in the public domain by submitting them to a magazine. This made it a case of lewdness rather than of lifestyle alone. (Similar public–private distinctions have emerged in freedom of speech cases concerning teachers.)

The second case, which focused on lifestyle alone, suggests that lifestyle choices that are lawful and private are not the concern of public schools, professional bodies, or the community.

It is worth noting how much things have changed since the examples listed at the beginning of this Teachers as Role Models section. Behaviours that would have resulted in dismissal and community outrage in the 1870s, or even the 1960s, were debated in the 1980s as raising interesting issues about teachers' privacy rights. Also, in both of the cases discussed above, there was never a danger that the teachers would be dismissed for their behaviour.

Teachers whose lifestyles may have been deemed inappropriate in the past, such as living in homosexual or non-marital heterosexual relationships, are now protected by the *Canadian Charter of Rights and Freedoms*. Indeed, as the case of *Trinity Western v. College of Teachers (British Columbia)* illustrates, teachers are expected to be respectful of these lifestyles.

Most lawful and private lifestyle choices are accepted, or at least tolerated, by school boards, professional bodies, and many members of the public. Nonetheless, teachers are advised to be sensitive to their legal and ethical duty to be role models. There is little doubt that the personal conduct of teachers could lead, fairly or unfairly, to a loss of respect by students and confidence by the community. This is why many teachers are discreet about their personal lives and, in some cases, choose not to live in the communities in which they work.

The exception to the increasing acceptance of teachers' lifestyle choices is the sexual exploitation of minors. As a Discipline Committee panel of the Ontario College of Teachers wrote:

> A member making and possessing child pornography and obtaining the sexual services of persons under the age of 18 years is not suitable to be in a position of trust and authority over children and should not be permitted to teach in Ontario or elsewhere. (*Professionally Speaking*, June 2007)

LIFESTYLES OF TEACHERS IN CATHOLIC SCHOOLS

Although teachers in private and public schools are held to the higher standard of conduct as role models, their lifestyle choices and teaching positions are protected by the *Canadian Charter of Rights and Freedoms* and provincial human rights legislation. Teachers in Catholic schools are held to a different standard.

In *Caldwell et al. v. Stuart et al.* (1985), the Supreme Court decided that Roman Catholic schools could use conformity with Catholic religious practices as a *bona fide* requirement for teachers in Catholic schools. This decision validating discriminatory practices in Roman Catholic schools was based on denominational rights enshrined in the *Constitution Act* (or *BNA Act*), *1867*. This was reaffirmed in *Casagrande v. Hinton Roman Catholic Separate School District* (1987) when the Alberta Court of Queen's Bench upheld the right of the school board to dismiss a teacher who had premarital sex, contrary to Catholic doctrine. In this case, the Court affirmed the school's expectation that Catholic teachers "are required to reveal the Christian message in their work as well as in all aspects of behavior." There are a number of cases in which teachers have been dismissed for pre-marital sexual intercourse, marrying outside the requirements of the Roman Catholic Church, and practising homosexuality.

In these early *Charter* cases, there was incontrovertible evidence to support the dismissals. A teacher dismissed for premarital sex was pregnant outside of wedlock. Two gay religion teachers in Catholic schools were dismissed after it was disclosed that they were joined together in a civil union ceremony (before same-sex marriage was legalized in 2003). A teacher was dismissed after it was discovered that she had not obtained an annulment and had remarried, outside the Roman Catholic Church.

It is safe to say that Catholic school boards in Ontario, particularly in suburban and urban areas, do not actively monitor the lifestyles of their teachers. Indeed, it would be fair to say that many administrators of Catholic boards are reluctant to pursue lifestyle cases. In general, a "don't ask, don't tell" policy prevails. While this may reflect cultural norms among contemporary Catholics, it may also be a response to concerns that the courts may now be less likely to defer to religious authority. For example, a gay teacher in a religious college was successful in having his dismissal overturned. The court ruled in *Vriend v. Alberta* (1998) that the "law does not draw any distinction between heterosexuals and other groups."

Teachers employed in Catholic boards are advised to adhere to accepted Catholic lifestyles or, at the very least, to be discreet about their practices.

Caution should especially be exercised in formalizing non-conforming relationships.

BELIEFS OF TEACHERS

Lifestyle choices are often intertwined with belief systems. And beliefs often inform practices. As a result, some employers may be reluctant to hire teachers with unconventional lifestyles or unorthodox beliefs, on the grounds that these teachers may implicitly promote their distinctive lifestyle or even explicitly teach their own personal beliefs in the classroom. This is often the basis for discrimination based on sexual orientation or religious beliefs.

A landmark case, *Trinity Western v. College of Teachers (British Columbia)*, brings together in an interesting manner the issues of sexual orientation and religious belief. The findings of the Supreme Court in this case are useful in delineating distinctions between teachers' private beliefs and public practice.

Trinity Western v. College of Teachers (British Columbia) (2001)

Trinity Western University (TWU), a private evangelical Christian institution, applied to have its teacher education program accredited by the British Columbia College of Teachers (BCCT). BCCT declined to accredit the program. The reason given was that the code of conduct for students and staff at TWU, which was grounded in evangelical Christian values, embodied discrimination against gays and lesbians.

TWU took BCCT to court, arguing that its freedom of religion was violated. The Supreme Court of Canada, which had the final word in this dispute, had to determine the balance between freedom of religion and the right to equality for gays and lesbians. As Brown & Zuker (2002) write, "In deciding in favour of the university, the Court found that the case could be decided in a way that was consistent with its interpretation of both these rights" (p. 308). At the heart of its decision was a distinction between off-duty beliefs and on-duty conduct.

TWU's admissions policy and code of conduct were found to be discriminatory. The court decision stated that "a homosexual student would not be tempted to apply for admission, and could sign the so-called student contract at a considerable personal cost."

The Court also recognized BCCT's duty to respect equality in Canadian society and to adhere to the public interest section of the *Teaching Profession Act*, which contains language prohibiting discrimination.

The Court also noted that TWU is a private religious institution and that as such its freedom of conscience and religion should be protected. As a result, unlike public schools and universities, it was entitled to discriminate on the basis of religion in its admissions policy and code of conduct.

The challenge for the Supreme Court was balancing these two fundamental rights. Underpinning its ruling was a commitment to pluralism. The Court quoted Justice Dickson's reasoning in an earlier Supreme Court decision: "A truly free society is one which can accommodate a wide variety of beliefs, diversity of tastes and pursuits, customs and codes of conduct." Given the rights of TWU under human rights legislation, the Court continued, "[w]hat the BCCT was required to do was determine whether the rights were in conflict in reality." In the absence of concrete evidence to the contrary, the Court concluded that TWU graduates would not have a detrimental effect on the learning environment in public schools. "Instead, the proper place to draw the line in cases like this ... is generally between belief and conduct." Thus, BCCT was wrong to make the assumption that discriminatory beliefs would lead to discriminatory conduct. BCCT should address only professional conduct that is discriminatory. Then it would be entirely appropriate for that teacher to be subject to disciplinary proceedings.

(1) Summarize the case.
(2) What is the Supreme Court's understanding of the equality rights of gays and lesbians?
(3) What is the Supreme Court's understanding of freedom of religion and conscience?
(4) How does the Supreme Court attempt to balance these competing rights?
(5) Do you agree with the decisions? Why or why not? Do you see any limitations or problems with the decision?

TEACHERS' FREEDOM OF SPEECH
ON EDUCATIONAL ISSUES

A major area of debate has been the balance between teachers' right to freedom of speech and their responsibilities as role models. A number of court cases have helped delineate a path between these two important principles. In this section, the focus is freedom of speech as it pertains to educational issues.

British Columbia Public School Employers' Association v. British Columbia Teachers' Federation (2005)

The British Columbia Teachers' Federation (BCTF), which was opposed to major education reforms proposed by the provincial government, created a report to parents outlining its opposition to larger class sizes and the loss of resources to teachers. Teachers distributed these documents at parent–teacher interviews. School districts opposed this strategy, which resulted in a labour grievance that eventually found its way to the British Columbia Court of Appeal.

The court recognized that the teachers' right to express their opinion on political issues could undermine public confidence in the education system and negatively affect parent–teacher meetings. Nonetheless, in a split decision, the majority of the justices found that the board had unreasonably curtailed the teachers' right to freedom of expression. The rights of teachers to free speech could exist alongside their obligation to conduct themselves professionally with students and parents.

---

(1) Summarize the case.

(2) What is the significance of this decision?

(3) Do you agree with the decision? Why or why not? Do you see any limitations or problems with it?

Before entering into such discussions, teachers need to recognize that there is a delicate balance to be maintained between their personal freedom of speech and their duties to students and school boards. The court decision discussed above affirms the right of teachers, individually and as federations, to engage in issues of importance to education. Teachers as professionals have the right to discuss school, board, and provincial policies with students, and to express disagreement. They should not, however, abuse their position of trust and power in the classroom. This particular case focused on events that took place during the course of parent–teacher interviews. The court may have taken a very different view of the matter if the teachers had used their position of authority in the classroom to hand out federation materials or promote their own political agenda.

Here are five questions to consider:

(1) Am I properly informed about the issue? (Teachers as professionals can be disciplined for irresponsible statements.)
(2) Am I risking being insubordinate? (Teachers have a duty to support the principal in the implementation of approved policies.)
(3) Am I risking being unprofessional in my conduct? (See standards of practice.)
(4) Am I risking being abusive? (See case below.)
(5) Have I checked with my federation? (Get the best advice possible before taking action.)

Case: Toronto (City) Board of Education v. O.S.S.T.F., District 15 (1997)

Bhadauria was upset with being turned down for promotion and wrote an abusive letter to the board containing perceived threats against the director and other senior officials.

After a psychiatric report confirmed that Bhadauria was of sound mind, the board passed a resolution terminating his contract. He filed a grievance with the board of arbitration, which ordered him reinstated. The Ontario Divisional Court disagreed and permitted the termination. The Ontario Court of Appeal sided with Bhadauria and his federation. In the end, the Supreme Court of Canada ruled that the termination was warranted. Subsequently, his licence to teach was revoked by the Ontario College of Teachers.

At the heart of the Supreme Court's decision was the teacher's duty to act as a role model. The arguments of the Court, which are featured at the beginning of this chapter, emphasize the duty of teachers under section 264(1)(c) of the *Education Act* to conduct themselves according to high moral principles.

---

(1) Summarize the case.
(2) What is the significance of this decision?
(3) Do you agree with the decisions? Why or why not? Do you see any limitations or problems with the decision?

Case: Cromer v. British Columbia Teachers' Federation (1986)

After attending a meeting at her son's school, Mrs. Cromer, a member of the B.C. Teachers' Federation, made negative comments in public about a teacher at the school for her teaching of human sexuality. As a result, Mrs. Cromer was charged with breaching the Code of Ethics of the British Columbia Teachers' Federation on the grounds that she had publicly criticized a colleague and fellow member.

The case was appealed to the courts, since Mrs. Cromer believed that she should not be disciplined for expressing her views as a concerned parent.

Justice Lambert, writing for the majority of justices on the British Columbia Court of Appeal, concluded that teachers have to exercise discretion when speaking about other teachers and administrators:

> I don't think people are free to choose which hat they will wear on what occasion. Mrs. Cromer does not always speak as a teacher, nor does she always speak as a parent. But she will always speak as Mrs. Cromer. The perception of her by her audience will depend on their knowledge of her training, her skills, her experience, and her occupation, among other things. The impact of what she says will depend on the content of what she says and the occasion on which she says it.

(1) Summarize the case.

(2) What is the significance of this decision?

(3) Do you agree with the decisions? Why or why not? Do you see any limitations or problems with the decision?

Taken together, these three cases confirm the right of teachers as professionals to speak about educational issues, so long as other teaching professionals are not criticized. As professionals and role models, they need to ensure that they are always appropriate in their conduct and speech. The words of the Supreme Court of Canada in *Ross v. New Brunswick District No. 15* are worth bearing in mind at all times:

> Teachers are seen by the community to be the medium for the educational message and, because of the community position they occupy, they are not able to "choose which hat they wear on what occasion"... teachers do not necessarily check their teaching hats at the school yard gate and may be perceived to be wearing their teaching hats off duty.

TEACHERS' FREEDOM OF SPEECH IN THE PUBLIC DOMAIN

In chapter 3, the *Morin* case was used to delineate the academic freedom of teachers in the classroom. So long as teachers work within the parameters of the curriculum guidelines, they have the academic freedom to adapt curriculum to meet the learning needs of their students. The *Keegstra* case, on the other hand, makes it clear that hate speech is never acceptable in the classroom.

What happens when teachers respect these limits in their professional practice yet express opinions in public that may be regarded as hateful? Should such teachers still be allowed to teach?

Case: Ross v. New Brunswick School District No. 15 (1996)

Malcolm Ross was a mild-mannered teacher at Magnetic Hill School while on duty, yet a notorious anti-Semite off-duty. In his published writing and television appearances, Ross remarked that Christianity was being undermined by an international Jewish conspiracy. The school board reprimanded Ross on more than one occasion, but he asserted his right to off-duty freedom of speech.

Ross was removed after the parent of a Jewish student brought forward a claim that the board's decision to allow Ross to teach constituted discrimination against her child by poisoning the educational environment. Because this case raised fundamental human rights questions, it ultimately wound its way to the Supreme Court of Canada. The Court, in upholding Ross's removal from the classroom, wrote:

> The school is an arena for the exchange of ideas and must, therefore, be premised upon principles of tolerance and impartiality so that all persons within the school environment feel equally free to participate … Teachers are inextricably linked to the integrity of the school system. Teachers occupy positions of trust and confidence, and exert considerable influence over their students as a result of their positions. The conduct of a teacher bears directly upon the community's perception of the ability of the teacher to fulfill such a position of trust and influence and upon the community's confidence in the public system as a whole.

Teachers could also face professional sanctions for publicly expressing views that may be offensive. In the case of *Kempling v. British Columbia College of Teachers* (2005), the British Columbia Court of Appeal upheld a decision made by the BCCT disciplining a public school teacher for an article and letters in a local newspaper that associated gays and lesbians with immorality, abnormality, perversion, and promiscuity. BCCT's disciplinary panel determined that the writings were discriminatory and that Mr. Kempling failed to accommodate core values of the education system. This off-duty conduct constituted professional misconduct, BCCT concluded, because it could contribute to a loss of public confidence in teachers and the public school system.

The Court of Appeal determined that BCCT had indeed infringed on Mr. Kempling's right to freedom of expression under the *Charter of Rights and Freedoms*. Despite this, the one-month suspension was upheld as reasonable and justified in a free and democratic society. This case serves as a warning to teachers to be respectful of all groups when expressing their views in the public arena.

On the whole, teachers are free to express their opinions in private and in public. There are many teachers who are actively involved in public issues and in the political process. These teachers, through their engagement in public discourse, could be viewed as positive models of citizenship for students. Kevin Kindred (2009), after studying relevant cases, concludes:

> teachers do have the right to freedom of expression within the school system. Such freedom definitely includes the right to take positions contrary to and critical of the employer ... (p. 152)

Even so, teachers need to be careful not to impose their views on students in class and to exercise a modicum of restraint in how they express themselves in public so students can enjoy an atmosphere of tolerance and respect (Oliviero & Manley-Casimir, 2009). Even if they are never at risk of a reprimand from their boards or the College of Teachers, teachers who exercise their freedom of speech in a manner inconsistent with being role models risk losing the respect of students, parents, and the community.

CHECKING YOUR UNDERSTANDING

- Teachers are expected to act as role models for students both in the classroom and in the community.

- Section 43 of the *Criminal Code* will protect a teacher who uses reasonable force to restrain or remove a child in appropriate circumstances. However, it is no longer considered reasonable for teachers to administer corporal punishment.

- As professionals, teachers must at all times respect the boundaries that exist between teachers and students.

- Failure to respect these boundaries or to meet the standards expected of them by the local community could lead to professional sanctions and board discipline or dismissal.

- "Sexual abuse" by a teacher of a student of any age is considered professional misconduct by the Ontario College of Teachers. "Sexual abuse" includes remarks of a sexual nature.

- "Sexual exploitation" by a teacher of a student who is sixteen or seventeen is a criminal offence, with a maximum penalty of ten years.

- "Sexual interference" or "invitation to sexual touching" by anyone with a person under the age of sixteen is a criminal offence, with a maximum penalty of ten years.

- Teachers have a legal and ongoing duty to report suspected child abuse directly to a children's aid society. For the purposes of the *Child and Family Services Act*, a child is defined as a person under the age of sixteen.

- Child abuse includes physical, sexual, and emotional abuse, as well as neglect.

- A teacher who reports another teacher for suspected sexual abuse of a student is not required to give the other teacher a copy of the report.

- The courts try to strike a delicate balance between teachers' human rights and the expectation that they act as role models.

- Lifestyle choices of teachers in public elementary and secondary schools are protected under the *Canadian Charter of Rights and Freedoms* and Ontario's *Human Rights Code*.

- Lifestyle choices of teachers in Roman Catholic separate schools could be a matter for discipline or dismissal, if the board is able to prove that the lifestyle is contrary to church doctrine.

- The courts have recognized the right of teachers to speak on political and educational issues, but teachers must avoid abusing their position of trust and power in the classroom.

- Despite the right to speak on political and educational issues, teachers could face professional sanctions for publicly expressing views generally considered hateful, offensive, or discriminatory.

APPLYING YOUR UNDERSTANDING

Sounding Off at the Diner

Raj and Al, recent B. Ed. graduates, were summer camp counsellors with the YMCA. While sipping sodas at the diner, Joe teased Raj about the dearth of South Asian players in baseball, and Raj yelled, "F____ off." Al responded with obscenities of his own and stormed out of the building.

Mrs. Wong, who was sitting in a booth with her eight-year-old daughter, was shocked at what she heard. Her daughter, who giggled as she witnessed this encounter between two of her counsellors, then told her mother that she heard Al swear as he fell on the baseball diamond and that Raj often said "oh shit" when he forgot something.

Mrs. Wong reported these incidents to Ms. Caputo, the manager of the summer camp. After a brief investigation, Ms. Caputo met with Raj and Al separately. They confirmed that they had sworn on these occasions, but minimized the significance of their off-duty use of obscenity.

Ms. Caputo reminded them that the Y's policy and procedures manual states that the "use of improper or inappropriate language in front of the children at any time" will result in dismissal. She then dismissed both Raj and Al for their behaviour.

Raj was very upset and decided to challenge his termination. He then met with Al, who agreed to join him in fighting the Y. Nothing like a common enemy to bring friends back together, Raj reflected.

(1) What was the basis of the dismissal of the two camp counsel-lors?

(2) What would be the basis of a challenge of their termination by Raj and Joe?

(3) How do you think the courts would rule on such a case?

(4) What do you think would happen if this incident had involved two classroom teachers?

(5) Do you think counsellors and teachers should be punished for off-duty use of obscenities?

Chapter 5

Avoiding Negligence: Acting as a Careful and Prudent Parent

After reading this chapter, you will understand:
- The importance of the educator's role of acting as a careful or prudent parent in order to ensure that schools are safe places for students to learn.
- The definition of negligence in civil law and the four elements necessary for a finding of negligence.
- The legal consequences when educators breach their duty of care, as laid out in education statutes.
- Legal concepts such as foreseeability, reasonableness, vicarious liability, voluntary assumption of risk, and contributory negligence (illustrated through legal cases).
- Ways in which educators can avoid negligence through professionalism and risk management.

A student trips on the extension cord for the overhead projector.

During a school field trip, a student is injured crossing the street.

A chemical squirts into the eye of a student during a science experiment.

Who is responsible? The student, teacher, principal, or school board?

Could the student successfully sue for damages in a civil court of law?

Educators must always be aware of potentially hazardous situations and think carefully when planning any activities that have an element of risk. By ensuring that adequate safety precautions are taken, they reduce the risk of harm for everyone and the likelihood of being sued.

WHAT IS NEGLIGENCE?

Negligence is defined as the failure to use reasonable care. Police can bring charges of criminal negligence when actions are considered to be grossly negligent. It is much more likely that negligence by an educator would lead to civil law proceedings. A teacher could be found guilty if his or her unintentional actions were judged to have contributed to an injury. Depending on the circumstances, both the teacher and the school board, who as the teacher's employer could be found vicariously liable, could be required to compensate the victim financially.

WHAT IS NEGLIGENCE IN CRIMINAL LAW?

In order for someone to be guilty of a crime, there must be evidence of both *actus reus* ("the guilty act") and *mens rea* ("the guilty mind"). Generally, a crime requires a deliberate intention to commit a wrongful act or knowledge that the act was against the law. Even though negligence is generally thought of as an unintentional act, the Crown can also establish *mens rea* by proving that the accused was criminally negligent. According to the *Criminal Code*, section 219(1), a person is criminally negligent who:

(a) in doing something, or

(b) in omitting to do anything that is his duty to do, shows wanton or reckless disregard for the lives or safety of other persons.

For example, when a five-year-old was run over while riding his bike unsupervised, his parents were charged with failing to provide the necessities of life to their son. Though they intended no harm, they were found guilty due to their wanton and reckless disregard for their son's safety. The judge was particularly upset that the parents had failed to heed previous warnings and sentenced the father to one year in jail and the mother to a conditional sentence of seven months.

Similarly, when a street race led to the deaths of two pedestrians, the two drivers were charged with criminal negligence.

Criminal negligence cases do not feature in education law, so it is highly unlikely that a teacher will ever be found criminally negligent. Civil cases against educators and school boards are very common, however.

WHAT IS NEGLIGENCE IN CIVIL LAW?

The failure to use reasonable care is often the basis for lawsuits in civil law. Negligence becomes the basis for lawsuits in civil law if the failure to act as a reasonably prudent person would do in such circumstance results in damage or loss to another person. This standard was established in 1856 in England (*Blyth v. Birmingham Water Works Co.*).

Negligence became recognized as a tort due to a landmark case in Scotland. In *Donoghue v. Stevenson* (1932), a brewer, Stevenson—the defendant—was found to owe a duty of care to Mrs. Donaghue—the plaintiff. His failure to notice a snail at the bottom of a bottle of ginger beer was a breach of that duty. This breach of duty was responsible for Mrs. Donoghue's subsequent illness. Stevenson was required to compensate her for the injury she sustained. The highest court identified the *neighbour principle*, which states, "You must take reasonable care to avoid acts or omissions which you can reasonably foresee would be likely to injure your neighbour."

The standard of care for teachers is even higher. Teachers must take reasonable care to avoid acts or omissions that could harm students, toward whom they have a duty to act as a careful or prudent parent would do.

ELEMENTS OF NEGLIGENCE

Four elements are necessary for a finding of negligence in a civil suit:

(1) The plaintiff is owed a duty of care by the defendant.
(2) The defendant breached that duty of care.
(3) Actual damage or loss was sustained.
(4) The breach of duty was the proximate cause of damage or loss by the defendant.

Cases of negligence fall under civil law, which operates under a set of principles collectively known as the law of *tort*. In tort law, redress for damages to the plaintiff takes the form of a financial award. Torts can be intentional (e.g., assault or sexual misconduct) or unintentional (e.g., negligence). The plaintiff's burden of proof is lower in a civil case than in a criminal case. The onus of proof is "a balance of probabilities" rather than "beyond a reasonable doubt."

DUTY OF CARE IN CIVIL LAW

Teachers and schools have a fiduciary relationship with students and the parents who entrust their children to the school. As a result of being *in loco parentis*, teachers and schools have an obligation to conduct themselves in a manner consistent with this trust. Generally the standard of a careful or prudent parent is used in assessing *fault* for an *act* or *omission*.

The duty of care of teachers and school boards is well established in law. The expectation that teachers in Canada act as prudent parents was established in *Williams v. Eady* (1893). In that case, a boy was severely burned in a flash fire caused by a boy lighting a bottle of phosphorous with a match. The teacher was deemed negligent for leaving the bottle of phosphorous in the conservatory where students could find it. While both sides in negligence cases tend to accept that there is a duty of care, they may dispute the nature of the duty given the specific facts of the case.

In Ontario, the duties of boards, principals, and teachers are set out in statute law. The *Education Act* and its associated regulations reflect the high standards set by society for educators.

Duties of School Boards

The school board assumes the overall responsibility for ensuring a safe and healthy learning environment for the schools in its jurisdiction. Section 170(1) of the *Education Act* delineates the following obligations for school boards:

Every board shall,
6. provide instruction and adequate accommodation during each school year for the pupils who have a right to attend a school under the jurisdiction of the board; ...

8. keep the school buildings and premises in proper repair and in a proper sanitary condition, provide suitable furniture and equipment and keep it in proper repair, and protect the property of the board;

9. make provision for insuring adequately the buildings and equipment of the board and for insuring the board and its employees and volunteers who are assigned duties by the principal against claims in respect of accidents incurred by pupils while under the jurisdiction or supervision of the board.

Duties of Principals

Principals are charged with the day-to-day responsibility of ensuring that each school is a safe and healthy learning environment. Section 265(1) of the *Education Act* lays out the following obligations for principals:

It is the duty of a principal of a school, in addition to the principal's duties as a teacher,

(a) to maintain proper order and discipline in the school; ...

(j) to give assiduous attention to the health and comfort of the pupils, to the cleanliness, temperature and ventilation of the school, to the care of all teaching materials and other school property, and to the condition and appearance of the school buildings and grounds; ...

(m) subject to an appeal to the board, to refuse to admit to the school or classroom a person whose presence in the school or classroom would in the principal's judgment be detrimental to the physical or mental well-being of the pupils.

This duty of the principal is further elaborated in *Regulation 298*, a regulation made under the *Education Act*.

11(1) The principal of a school, subject to the authority of the appropriate supervisory officer, is in charge of,

(a) the instruction and the discipline of pupils in the school;

(b) the organization and management of the school ...

11(3) In addition to the duties under the Act and those assigned by the board, the principal of a school shall, except where the principal has arranged otherwise under subsection 26 (3) ...

(a) supervise the instruction in the school and advise and assist any teacher in co-operation with the teacher in charge of an organizational unit or program;

(b) assign duties to vice-principals and to teachers in charge of organizational units or programs; ...

(e) provide for the supervision of pupils during the period of time during each school day when the school buildings and playgrounds are open to pupils;

(f) provide for the supervision of and the conducting of any school activity authorized by the board; ...

(k) provide for instruction of pupils in the care of the school premises;

(l) inspect the school premises at least weekly and report forthwith to the board,

(i) any repairs to the school that are required, in the opinion of the principal,

(ii) any lack of attention on the part of the building maintenance staff of the school ...

As the person charged with the responsibility for maintaining discipline and order in the school, the principal assumes wide-ranging authority and obligations. Recognizing the broad scope of the principal's duties, the act requires teachers to assist in keeping the school safe and orderly under the principal's direction.

Duties of Teachers

Teachers are charged with the duty of maintaining a safe and healthy learning environment within their classrooms. This responsibility also extends to their duties in other parts of the school.

Section 264(1) of the *Education Act* states:

It is the duty of a teacher and a temporary teacher: ...

(d) to assist in developing co-operation and co-ordination of effort among the members of the staff of the school

(e) to maintain, under the direction of the principal, proper order and discipline in the teacher's classroom and while on duty in the school and on the school ground.

Additionally, section 20 of *Regulation 298* outlines the duties of teachers in keeping with their obligation to cooperate with the principal in ensuring a positive learning environment:

20. In addition to the duties of the teacher under the Act and by the board, a teacher shall:

(a) be responsible for effective instruction, training and evaluation of the progress of pupils in the subjects assigned to the teacher and for the management of the class or classes, and report to the principal on the progress of pupils on request;

(b) carry out the supervisory duties and instructional program assigned to the teacher by the principal and supply such information related thereto as the principal may require; ...

(g) ensure that all reasonable safety procedures are carried out in courses and activities for which the teacher is responsible;

(h) co-operate with the principal and other teachers to establish and maintain consistent disciplinary practices in the school.

---

(1) What are the duties of the principal?
(2) What are the duties of the teacher in the classroom?
(3) What are the duties of the teacher outside the classroom?
(4) Did any of these duties surprise you? If so, why?

The *Education Act* and other legislation make it clear that teachers, principals, and boards all owe a duty of care to their students because of their special relationship of trust. Since parents are required to send their children to school, they are entitled to expect that reasonable precautions will be taken to ensure that they will be safeguarded from all foreseeable risks.

Case: Myers v. Peel County Board of Education (1981)

Myers, a fifteen-year-old boy, was practicing gymnastics in a room off the school gymnasium. The routine went smoothly until he attempted a straddle dismount, during which he fell awkwardly to the ground and broke his neck. There was no one to help break his fall, because the spotter had left that piece of equipment. Myers's parents sued the school board for negligence in a landmark case that reached the Supreme Court of Canada.

The court recognized that there was an element of risk in gymnastics that was known to the plaintiff. It also recognized that the plaintiff participated in the activity and executed the straddle dismount of his own free will. At age fifteen, Myers was old enough and in sufficient physical condition to engage in this activity. Therefore, it was not negligent to permit Myers to participate in gymnastics.

In its ruling, the court applied to the case the standard of care of the prudent parent. The court recognized the complexity of modern schools and the challenges of conducting activities with larger groups of students. It stated:

> Its application will vary from case to case and will depend upon the number of students being supervised at any given time, the nature of the exercise or activity in progress, the age and degree of skill and training the students may have received in connection with such activity, the nature and condition of the equipment in use at the time, the competency and capacity of the students involved, and a host of other matters which may be widely varied but which, in a given case, may affect the application of the prudent parent standard to the conduct of the school authority in the circumstances.

The court, nonetheless, accepted the contention of Myers, the plaintiff, that the school board had not exercised an appropriate duty of care. One reason was that the equipment was not adequate. The protective matting of two-and-a-half inches was deemed insufficient given that more protective matting could have been obtained. Another reason was that the activity was not properly supervised. Gymnastics was sufficiently dangerous that an adult supervisor should have been present in the room to minimize harm and ensure that safety procedures were observed. The court concluded that a prudent parent would have exercised this higher standard of care. Therefore, the school board's act or omission "materially contributed" to the cause of the accident.

Myers was held to be partly responsible for his injuries. The Court of Appeal held that

> there was contributory negligence ... in performing a difficult manoeu-vre, fraught with danger, without announcing his move and without the presence of a spotter in position to break his fall.

Nonetheless, the school board had to pay significant damages to Myers.

---

(1) What acts or omissions by the school board contributed to the accident?

(2) What acts or omissions by Myers contributed to the accident?

(3) Do you think that the Supreme Court ruling was fair? Why or why not?

(4) Think about this case in relation to a school situation in which you are likely to be involved (e.g., an art activity, science lab, or field trip). How might the lessons learned from this case inform your actions?

Modified Standard of Care

In the *Myers* case, the court applied the standard of care of a careful and prudent parent. Courts, however, modify the required standard of care depending on the circumstances of the case.

In *McKay v. Board of Govan School Unit 29 of Saskatchewan* (1968), a student was severely injured when attempting a dismount from the parallel bars. The physical education instructor had not demonstrated the dismount to students, and McKay had minimal experience with this exercise. The Court of Appeal determined that the careful parent standard did not apply to the facts of this case. Justice Woods wrote:

> A physical training instructor in directing or supervising an evolution or exercise is bound to exercise the skill and competence of an ordinarily competent instructor in the field. The standard of the careful parent does not fit a responsibility which demands special training and expertise.

The careful parent standard continues to be used, but the courts have adapted it to recognize the higher level of expertise expected of teachers as professionals.

This is most clearly expressed in the case of *Brown v. Essex (County) Roman Catholic Separate School Board* (1990). In this case, the plaintiff was using a sewing machine when the cloth bunched, causing the needle to stay in one spot. Because the teacher had not explained what to do if the cloth bunched, the student did not turn off her sewing machine. As a result, the needle broke into three pieces, one of which became imbedded in the student's eye. The court found that the sewing teacher "did not act as would a careful or prudent parent with her background and knowledge of sewing." The judge argued that "a *reasonably prudent sewing teacher* owed students the duty of care to have warned them of the particular dangers involved in sewing on the spot." This ruling elegantly acknowledges the careful and prudent parent standard while elevating the standard to acknowledge the additional expertise of a professional educator.

BREACH OF DUTY OF CARE

For a finding of negligence, the defendant must owe a duty of care. In addition, there must be evidence that this duty of care was breached due to an act or omission on the part of the defendant. In the *Myers* case, the court determined that poor equipment and a lack of adult supervision constituted breaches of the board's duty of care.

Case: Moddejonge v. Huron County Board of Education (1972)

Background
A tragic accident occurred during a field trip. The outdoor education instructor permitted a group of students to go swimming in a reservoir. The instructor had warned the students about the drop-off under the water, but the drop-off was irregular and poorly marked with buoys. A sudden breeze caused a student who could not swim to move beyond the drop-off. The student drowned, as did another student who attempted to rescue him.

Legal Question
The deaths were tragic, but did the outdoor education instructor breach his duty of care to the students? Had he warned them sufficiently? Was he responsible for the death of the boy who attempted a rescue?

Decision
The court ruled that a reasonably prudent parent would guard against these risks, which it regarded as foreseeable. Among the factors taken into account were:

- The instructor permitted students to go into water where there was a drop-off;
- He did not swim, and did not provide sufficient life-saving equipment;
- Once the wind came up, he did not take safety measures;
- The death of the rescuer was a foreseeable response to an emergency created by the instructor's negligence.

Legal Significance
Teachers are held to a very high standard of care. Teachers and school boards have to make an effort to foresee a wide range of consequences of their acts or omissions. Adopting risk-management strategies can limit the chances of injury and reduce the chances of a successful negligence suit. While the standards are high, they are not unreasonable, as the following excerpt from the Supreme Court of Canada ruling in *Stewart v. Pettie* (1995) makes clear:

One of the primary purposes of negligence law is to enforce reasonable standards of conduct so as to prevent the creation of reasonably foreseeable risks ... Tort law does not require the wisdom of Solomon. All it requires is that people act reasonably in the circumstances. The "reasonable person" of negligence law ... is not an extraordinary or unusual creature; he is not superhuman; he is not required to display the highest skill of which anyone is capable; he is not a genius who can perform uncommon feats, nor is he possessed of unusual powers of foresight. He is a person of normal intelligence who makes prudence a guide to his conduct. He does nothing that a prudent man would not do and does not omit to do anything a prudent person would do ... His conduct is the standard "adopted in the community by persons of ordinary intelligence and prudence."

Limits to Foreseeability

The standard of care does not require school boards or teachers to take precautions against accidents that are not reasonably foreseeable. As the court noted in *Ramsden v. Hamilton* (1942):

Human prudence would be taxed beyond reason, were it to endeavour to foresee every possibility of human ingenuity, or boyish mischievousness, in its search of opportunities to get into trouble, in even the remotest and most unlikely corners, nooks, or crannies.

Here are some unfortunate incidents that the court decided were not results of negligence:

- *Fraser v. Campbell River (Board of School Trustees of School District No. 72) (1987)*: A student jumped head-first into the snow in the schoolyard and injured himself. The teacher had conducted the class in a manner that was controlled and disciplined. The plaintiff's action was sudden and could not have been foreseen.

- *McCue v. Etobicoke (Board of Education) (1982)*: A high school student sustained an eye injury when another student flicked a paperclip before class began. It was not reasonable to expect the teacher to be present or to foresee this incident.
- *Crouch v. Essex County Council (1966)*: A student deliberately sprayed caustic soda into the eyes of another student. The teacher had warned of the dangers of caustic soda, maintained reasonable classroom management, and could not have foreseen such a deliberate act.

NEGLIGENCE OUTSIDE SCHOOL HOURS

It is clear that during the course of the regular school day teachers and schools have a duty of care to students. But what if an incident occurs during a special activity, or off campus, or outside school hours?

Note that students participating in authorized and approved school activities, such as field trips and intercollegiate sports events, remain under the care of the supervising teacher wherever they are and whatever time it may be. Students may need to be reminded that all the normal expectations of the school's code of conduct apply during activities like school dances or concerts. Overnight and extended trips can also present special problems, and supervising teachers should ensure that parents and students clearly understand that participants remain responsible to the principal for their behaviour just as if they were at school.

Schools need to be explicit in stating school opening and closing times so students and parents know not to presume that schools will provide supervision outside those times. Schools also need to be consistent in applying these rules; otherwise they may be viewed as negligent should an accident occur when the school was open unofficially.

It is crucial for teachers to avoid sending young students into danger. Consider a grade 1 student who is stranded at school due to a family emergency. It would be negligent to send her home at 4 p.m. so the teacher can get home. In-school detentions that cause students who are bused-in to miss their normal transportation home could also be deemed negligent.

What if a student is injured on the playground on the weekend? While the school has a duty of care to *students*, they are not students when playing on school property at night or on the weekend and the school is not responsible for their supervision. They are children, not students, during that time. The duty of the school board is simply to ensure that the condition of the grounds is not hazardous and that any equipment is properly maintained. If they do not do this, then the common law standard of occupier's liability is used against them rather than the standard of care of a prudent parent.

OCCUPIER'S LIABILITY

School boards, like all property owners, are responsible for ensuring that appropriate care is taken to prevent accidents to anyone using the property. This is why it is important for homeowners to ensure that their premises are safe (e.g., by keeping sidewalks clear of snow and ice). School boards own large amounts of property that are regularly used by students, staff, and members of the public. For this reason, board personnel, particularly principals and custodial staff, should pay attention to the condition of the premises at all times.

Section 3 of Ontario's *Occupier Liability Act* states that the occupier of the land and structures owes a duty to

> take such care as in all the circumstances of the case is reasonable to see that persons entering on the premises, and the property brought on the premises by those persons are reasonably safe while on the premises.

School boards must meet this standard in relation to regular users (e.g., staff and students during the school day), people who use the premises at other times (e.g., children using the playground after hours or adults cutting across the schoolyard), and even people using the property illegally (e.g., trespassers).

In *Kennedy v. Waterloo (County) Board of Education* (1999), the school board was sued after Kennedy crashed into a bollard while riding his motorcycle at a high speed. The plaintiff successfully sued the school board for failing to take reasonable care in not removing the bollards from that location. The school board was apportioned 75 percent of the costs, with the plaintiff being found contributorily negligent. Since school premises are regularly used by the public, appropriately or otherwise, school boards as occupiers must exercise a duty of care to anyone who might enter the grounds or buildings. As noted above, they are not considered to be *in loco parentis* for school-age children who use the premises outside school hours or activities.

Occupier's liability may also be an issue in cases of injury to students, especially when they are under the care of educators. In *Cox (Litigation Guardian of) v. Marchen* (2002), the student litigant injured her Achilles heel while leaving the building through an emergency exit door. Although the student knew that this locked door was not to be used, she and others regularly used it to go to the parking lot. The principal did not conduct regular inspections of the door, and it was not repaired until after the incident. The Ontario Superior Court found that although the student violated school rules, she had a reasonable expectation that the door would be safe. The court found the principal at fault based on both the standard of care in the *Education Act* and the standards contained in the *Occupier Liability Act*.

ACTUAL DAMAGE OR LOSS

While negligence is a failure to use reasonable care, not all negligent acts cause actual damage or loss. Courts will award a claim only to a plaintiff who can demonstrate that the breach of care has caused actual harm or loss. If Myers had not fallen from the gymnastic ring, for example, there would have been no loss, and legal action would not have succeeded.

Fortunately for everyone, most negligent acts do not lead to significant harm. Nonetheless, with over 110,000 teachers in Ontario, there are numerous negligence cases every year that do result in significant damage or loss.

CAUSATION

Once it is established that the defendant has breached the standard of care required of a teacher, the plaintiff must prove that the defendant's negligent act caused the harm sustained by the plaintiff.

In the case of *Myers v. Peel County Board of Education*, the courts carefully assessed the degree to which the school board's negligence contributed to Myers's injury. They applied the "but-for" test that courts often apply in negligence cases. If suitable protective mats had been used, would Myers have sustained fewer injuries? Would the presence of a teacher have altered Myers's behaviour or the actions of the spotter? In ruling in Myers's favour, the court decided that causation was likely. Similar questions led the court to conclude that Moddejonge's swimming death was caused by the outdoor education instructor's failure to foresee the consequences of his own acts and omissions.

VICARIOUS LIABILITY

A person or organization that did not directly cause the plaintiff's injury may be found liable in tort law. This is known as the principle of *vicarious* (substitute) *liability*. For example, if the person who caused a car accident did not own the vehicle, the owner could be held vicariously liable for lending it to someone not competent to drive safely. This is intended to ensure that owners exercise care in lending their vehicles. It also enables the plaintiff to obtain money from the insurance policy of the owner if the driver is not insured sufficiently.

In civil suits, the plaintiff tends to include as defendants anyone who could have played a role in the incident. Anthony Brown (2004), in *Legal Handbook for Educators*, writes:

> In many instances, the defendants in a tort action are the teacher involved, the principal (whether directly involved or not), and the school board. The plaintiff's lawyer will issue a statement of claim against everyone who is potentially liable because one cannot always predict how a judge or jury will find or apportion liability. (p. 110)

You may have noticed that the school board is one of the defendants named in all of the cases cited in this chapter. While the board as a corporate entity may have done nothing wrong, the board is often sued along with the teacher accused of negligence. The school board may have had clear guidelines in place, which a teacher, other employee, or volunteer disregarded. Nonetheless, the board may be found vicariously liable and required to pay the plaintiff. For example, in *Bain v. Calgary Board of Education* (1994), the teacher was found negligent in the serious injury of a student on a field trip.

While the board was not negligent in its actions, it was found vicariously liable and thus required to compensate the plaintiff. If the teacher had been the only party responsible in law, Bain would not have collected significant damages, given the defendant's meagre assets. The prospect of having to pay significant damages caused the board to pursue this case vigorously. The board could have sought indemnity from its employee, but this is rarely done because boards usually have much deeper pockets than their employees.

DEFENCES AGAINST NEGLIGENCE

The best defence against a negligence claim is that negligence did not exist or that the defendant did not owe the plaintiff any duty of care. The plaintiff, even if negligence is proved, may not be able to recover as much as expected if the court finds that the accident was unavoidable or that the plaintiff voluntarily assumed the risk or had also been negligent in the incident.

Unavoidable Accident

Injury or loss may result from a situation that is unavoidable, no matter what precautions a reasonable person might take.

- A school bus driver lost control of the vehicle because it was struck by lightning:
    - The unavoidability of the situation could be a full or partial defence against a negligence claim.
- A piece of ice fell from a passing plane and struck a student playing at recess:
    - The airline, not the school, would be liable for this unforeseeable event.
- A student suffers a brain aneurysm while at school:
    - The school would not be liable for a random and unavoidable event such as this.

Voluntary Assumption of Risk

For a *voluntary assumption of risk* defence to succeed, the defendant must prove that the plaintiff clearly knew of the risks of his or her action and made a choice to assume those risks. Negligence cases involving sports injuries often hinge on questions regarding the voluntary assumption of risk inherent in the particular sport.

Case: Thomas v. Hamilton (City) Board of Education (1994)

Thomas, an athletic grade 11 student, executed a routine tackle during a school football game. Unfortunately, as Thomas hit the ball carrier on the thigh with his head down, his helmet dislodged. Despite prompt medical attention, Thomas was rendered a quadriplegic by the incident.

Thomas sued, among others, the coach and the school board, arguing that their negligence caused his injuries. Much of the trial revolved around the question of voluntary assumption of risk. The plaintiff argued that he and his parents had not been warned of the risks inherent in football. It was further alleged that the coach had not trained Thomas in proper tackling technique and should have known that the plaintiff's "long, lean, swan neck" rendered him more susceptible to injury.

The defendants noted that Thomas, his parents, and his doctor had completed forms giving their informed consent. The court, in finding in favour of the defendant, stated that Thomas voluntarily assumed the risk, and that the coach and the school board had exercised appropriately the duty of care of a careful and prudent parent. Nor could they have reasonably anticipated the long-neck theory, which may or may not have been a factor.

The case eventually made its way to the Ontario Court of Appeal, which made the following statement about participation in dangerous sports:

> The appellant participated in his high school's junior football program of his own free will. He was aware of the risk of injury, even serious injury, that is inherent to participation in a contact sport such as football. However, he did not, through his consent to participate (and that of his mother), assume all risk of injury to the extent that school authorities were relieved of the duty of care that they owed to him.
>
> The appellant was not incapacitated, let alone obviously incapacitated ... He had his mother's consent, and his family doctor's certificate stating that he was fit to play football. He knew that football

was a contact sport which carried with it the risk of serious injury. He wore a "horse collar" because he was aware of the fact that his neck was exposed to injury. He said, as the trial judge noted in his reason for judgment, that even if he had specifically contemplated the risk of a catastrophic neck injury, he would probably have continued to play.

The appellant was appropriately and progressively coached. He was an excellent athlete who excelled in a number of sports, including football. His equipment was adequate. The injury he sustained occurred during a routine play and, although the consequences of his injury were, and continue to be devastating, the injury came within the ambit of those risks inherent in a contact sport such as football. He did not, of course, give a consent which would overcome negligent conduct on the part of the Board or his coaches. However, I agree with the trial judge that neither the Board nor the coaches were negligent and that his mother "consented to the normal risks of the game". I am not prepared to say that the trial judge was wrong in reaching that conclusion.

(1) Why were the coach and school board not found negligent for their actions or omissions in practice or during the game?
(2) Why did the plaintiff introduce the long-neck theory?
(3) Did the plaintiff and his family understand the risks they were assuming?
(4) What do you think of the statement by the Ontario Court of Appeal?
(5) As a result of this decision, Thomas received no money to assist him in his life as a quadriplegic. Was this fair?

While Thomas was ultimately unsuccessful, his case illustrates the scrutiny under which school boards and their employees are placed when it came to negligence cases.

First, it is incumbent on school boards to ensure that every reasonable safety measure is taken. In the *Myers* and *McKay* cases, faulty equipment, inadequate coaching, and the lack of proper supervision led to findings of negligence against the school boards. In *Thomas*, close scrutiny failed to reveal any negligent acts on the part of board employees.

Second, it is essential for teachers, schools, and school boards to obtain informed consent from students and their parents or guardians before students participate in activities such as extracurricular sports or trips off school property. In the *Thomas* case, the forms signed by the student, parents, and doctor left no doubt that they had been fully informed of the inherent risks before the student was permitted to play football. If the board had not obtained informed consent, this failure in itself could have constituted a form of negligence.

Bain v. Calgary Board of Education (1994), which is discussed below, illustrates that an act must be voluntary and that the assumption of risk must be explicit. Although nineteen-year-old Bain had gone on a voluntary, unsupervised hike on his own initiative, the court ruled that he had not given express or implied agreement to assume risk of injury; nor had he waived his right to claim damages due to a breach of care on the part of the instructor.

Teachers should exercise great care to ensure that informed consent forms are completed. This gives students and parents the opportunity to voluntarily assume the risks inherent in a particular activity. It is wise, in requesting and obtaining waiver forms, to include all potential risks, so students and parents cannot argue that they were unaware of them. Students should not be permitted to participate without written consent, because this could be grounds for a successful negligence suit. At times, teachers accept consent over the phone; this could be problematic because it leaves the school board open to a claim that the parent was not informed of all of the risks. On school outings, teachers should stick to the agreed itinerary and outline of activities and diligently follow school board policies and procedures. Finally, educators should remember that the purpose of informed consent is to address the potential hazards inherent in a particular high-risk activity. Informed consent does not absolve the supervising teacher from the duty to take all reasonable care to prevent foreseeable accidents. Waiver forms will not protect a teacher if it can be shown that an accident was caused by the teacher's negligence rather than by the natural risks inherent in the activity.

Contributory Negligence

At one time, under common law, a plaintiff found to be in any way at fault was denied the right to claim damages. Since then, common law has developed the notion of shared responsibility.

If both the plaintiff and the defendant are deemed to be negligent to some degree, damages are divided between them according to the principle of *contributory negligence*. Whereas normally the plaintiff must prove negligence against the defendant, in these cases the defendant assumes the burden of proof in asserting a defence of contributory negligence. The judge then apportions liability in accordance with Ontario's *Negligence Act*.

While teachers have a duty of care toward students, students also have a duty to conduct themselves responsibly and demonstrate reasonable care for their own safety. This is reflected in the duties of students in the *Education Act*. Section 23 of *Regulation 298* requires pupils to:

(b) exercise self-discipline;
(c) accept such discipline as would be exercised by a kind, firm and judicious parent;
(d) attend classes regularly and punctually;
(e) be courteous to fellow pupils and obedient and courteous to teachers;
(f) be clean in person and habits;
(g) show respect for school property.

As this section indicates, a pupil

is responsible for his or her conduct to the principal of the school that the pupil attends,
(a) on the school premises;
(b) on out-of-school activities that are part of the school program; and
(c) while travelling on a school bus that is owned by a board or on a bus or school bus that is under contract to a board.

The degree of care on either side will vary, depending on factors such as the age and mental ability of the students.

In *Myers v. Peel County Board of Education*, Myers was deemed to have contributed to his own gymnastic injuries, although the school board was still considered largely responsible. The same held true in *Brown v. Essex (County) Roman Catholic Separate School Board*, where the girl injured by the sewing needle was found partly responsible. On the other hand, in *Marshall (Litigation Guardian of) v. Annapolis (County) District School Board* (2009), a four-year-old kindergarten student hit by a school bus was considered too young to be held responsible for his injuries.

Case: Bain v. Calgary Board of Education (1994)

Bain, a nineteen-year-old grade 11 student at a vocational school for the learning disabled, was participating in a school-sponsored outdoor education activity. In the evening, a group of students asked permission to go on an evening hike rather than watch a movie as planned. The defendant teacher, after initially refusing, gave them permission and drove them to the start of the trail. The boys were poorly dressed and provisioned for the hike. Bain lost his grip at a rock face and fell off the cliff headfirst, sustaining serious permanent injuries. The school board countered Bain's claim for damages by arguing that he had voluntarily assumed risk (see above), was an adult, and contributed to his injuries by failing to take appropriate precautions.

The court ruled that the age of the student did not detract from the duty of care of the teacher, especially given the student's learning disability. In its decision, the court wrote:

> The forestry tour was an extension of the classroom, occurring during the school year, with the specific authorization of the school board and subject to its rules and regulations. The defendant teacher remained in control of the students to the same extent as if they were in the classroom, and he owed them the same or a higher duty of care ... The defendant teacher could have avoided the injury simply by following the agenda authorized by the school board and approved by the parents for that evening's activities. The risk of harm was foreseeable.

As a result, the teacher and school board were found 75 percent liable. Because Bain failed to "take proper steps for his own safety," he was held contributorily liable for 25 percent of the damages.

---

(1) What factors did the court need to factor into its decision to apportion responsibility between the plaintiff and the defendants?
(2) Do you agree with the court's decision?
(3) Although the board's rules and regulations were clear, it still had to pay damages. Why?

NEGLIGENCE AND THE ONTARIO COLLEGE OF TEACHERS

The Ontario College of Teachers is a regulatory body charged with monitoring the competence and professional conduct of its members. As illustrated in earlier chapters, professional misconduct is taken very seriously by the College. This includes disciplining teachers for "conduct unbecoming a member," whether in a professional setting or in a member's personal life. (See chapter 2.)

Although assessing negligence is a matter for courts and not regulatory authorities, negligence could lead to a complaint and professional sanctions against a member of the College for professional misconduct, in particular for "failing to maintain the standards of the profession" under the *Ontario College of Teachers Act, 1996*. Standards of the profession refers to The Standards of Practice for the Teaching Profession and The Ethical Standards for the Teaching Profession contained in the *Foundations of Professional Practice*. (See chapter 2.) These standards "articulate the goals and aspirations of a teaching profession dedicated to fostering student learning" (p. 4) and offer "guiding images that can foster a strong collective professional identity" (p. 17). Their "overarching purpose is to guide College members" (p. 27), not to prescribe specific practices. Indeed, it is very difficult to determine best practices that apply in all educational situations. As Daloz (1986) writes, if:

education is understood as the *development* of the whole person—rather than knowledge acquisition, for example—the central element of good teaching becomes the provision of *care*, rather than use of teaching skills or transmission of knowledge (p. xii).

In determining whether a failure to maintain the standards of the profession constitutes professional misconduct, the Investigation Committee is also required to consider whether the teacher has complied with the *Education Act* and its regulations. The committee, as with other forms of alleged misconduct, may then forward the complaint to the Discipline Committee or the Fitness to Practice Committee.

Elizabeth J. McIntyre and David I. Bloom (2002), in *An Educator's Guide to the Ontario College of Teachers*, note that "the standards of the profession are not specifically addressed in either the act or the professional misconduct regulation." Nonetheless, they argue, "while these standards do not have the force of the law, it is reasonable to expect that they will be considered and applied by the Committee by virtue of section 1, para. 5 of the professional misconduct regulation" (p. 74).

Investigations by the College, like those of other self-regulatory bodies in Canada, have often considered the opinion of fellow professionals in assessing professional misconduct (McIntyre & Bloom, 2002, p. 76). Likewise, the Investigation Committee of the College is also charged with determining whether an act or omission "would reasonably be regarded ... as disgraceful, dishonourable or unprofessional" by other members. In response to appeals, court judgments have made it clear that

> members of a profession who sit on disciplinary tribunals cannot rely on their own personal conception of what constitutes professional misconduct and that decisions must be based on evidence of professional standards regardless of how obvious they may appear to be. (p. 77)

In at least one case, *Ontario College of Teachers v. Teliatnik*, the committee did hear evidence regarding the standards of the profession. In a split decision, the majority wrote:

In addition to relying on the individual and collective experience of the majority in the education field, the majority did consider the profiles developed by Dr. Begley in determining whether Alexander Teliatnik is guilty of professional misconduct and is incompetent. The majority is of the opinion that Alexander Teliatnik undoubtedly met the minimum standards of performance. (O.C.T.D.D. (2001) No. 47, at para. 30)

A review of the investigations and hearings recorded in *Professionally Speaking*, the magazine of the Ontario College of Teachers, identified only a few cases that related to professional negligence. Some complaints that were considered by the Investigation Committee did not proceed further. On a number of occasions, the College recommended that these matters were more appropriately dealt with at the board level.

RISK MANAGEMENT

By being prudent and careful, teaching professionals can enhance student safety and avoid negligence claims. School boards, too, can be proactive in avoiding negligence. In fact, the high cost of litigation and successful claims for damages have led school boards to make every effort to act defensively in order to reduce the risk of harm and potential lawsuits. In the lingo of liability insurance, this is known as *risk management*. It has two benefits:

- Safety and training lead to fewer accidents.
- It is easier to defend a lawsuit when reasonable safety measures and appropriate training are in effect.

School boards and their employees can take many risk-management measures. These include:

- identifying potential dangers through "safety audits"
- current training of teachers and coaches
- staff training in first aid and CPR
- maintenance on a fixed schedule
- safety equipment in labs and gyms

- safe vehicles and transportation plans
- adequate supervision ratios in playgrounds and on field trips
- appropriate reporting and record keeping
- controlling communication after incidents occur.

The Ontario School Board Insurance Exchange (OSBIE), the self-funded non-profit insurer for 90 percent of the school boards in Ontario, offers a wide range of risk-management materials and services. (Go to www.osbie.on.ca for more information.)

As part of your duty of care to your student, take time to foresee risk and consider how you can make the learning environment safer for your students. Here are some practices to consider:

(1) Monitor your teaching area on a daily basis for potential hazards (e.g., damaged outlets, frayed cords, unsafe wall fixtures or loose ceiling tiles).

(2) Report any problem to the principal in writing on the same day, keeping a copy for your own records.

(3) Until the problem has been fixed, take whatever measures are necessary to keep the area safe for your students.

(4) If you come across a potential hazard in the school at large, report it to the principal.

(5) If you are supervising a field trip or other off-campus activity, make sure you follow board policy meticulously and know what to do in case of an accident or other emergency (always take a cell phone with you).

(6) If you are the teacher of a high-risk activity, such as technological studies, physical education, or science, be sure to follow all the appropriate safety protocols and procedures that apply in your subject area.

CHECKING YOUR UNDERSTANDING

- In tort law, negligence is the failure to use reasonable care. It can result from an act or an omission.

- Teachers are considered to be *in loco parentis* and therefore are expected to act in the role of a "careful or prudent parent" toward the students in their care.

- A modified standard of care means that in certain circumstances the standard of a careful or prudent parent is replaced by the standard of a careful or prudent expert teacher.

- The standard of care is influenced by the age of the students, the training they have received, the nature and condition of any equipment, and the number of students being supervised.

- Teachers are unlikely to be held liable for accidents that were not reasonably foreseeable.

- The four elements of negligence are: (1) the plaintiff is owed a duty of care by the defendant; (2) the defendant breached that duty of care; (3) actual damage or loss was sustained; and (4) the breach of duty was the proximate cause of the damage or loss.

- The burden of proof in a negligence case lies with the plaintiff.

- The duties of the school board include providing a safe and healthy learning environment.

- Principals must ensure a school environment in which order is well maintained and attention is paid to the health and comfort of students.

- Teachers, under the direction of the principal, are responsible for appropriate supervision of students, as well as for maintaining a safe learning environment.

- Teachers and schools are responsible for incidents that occur during school trips or during after-school activities.

- *Vicarious liability* means that school boards may be held legally liable for the actions of their teachers, even when the board did nothing wrong.

- As property owners, school boards are also responsible for ensuring that reasonable measures are taken to prevent accidents from happening to anyone entering their property.

- Two possible defences against negligence suits are unavoidable accident and voluntary assumption of risk.

- At times plaintiffs' own actions are regarded as contributing to their injury or loss.

- Negligence by a teacher could also lead to a complaint to the Ontario College of Teachers that the teacher failed to maintain the standards of the profession.

- School boards should promote risk-management strategies in order to reduce the risk of harm and, by extension, litigation.

APPLYING YOUR UNDERSTANDING

One Teacher's Excursion into the Garden of Negligence

Ms. Patel, a second-year teacher, was very excited about taking her grade 5 class on a field trip to the Royal Botanical Gardens (RBG). She had planned this activity as the culmination of her unit on the season of spring. The tulips and flowering trees would beautifully illustrate spring renewal while letting students enjoy the fresh air after a long winter of being cooped up in the classroom. As her twenty-six students jostled each other and spoke loudly while boarding the bus, it was evident that they shared her excitement.

Ms. Patel was relieved that she had not cancelled the trip due to the heavy rainfall overnight. She believed that everything would be fine as long as students stayed on the paths and followed the rules.

The two parent volunteers sat behind Ms. Patel, who herself sat beside Veronica. Veronica, who needed a wheelchair to get around, had been helped onto the bus by the driver.

As the bus pulled into the RBG driveway, Ms. Patel loudly reminded the rambunctious students that they needed to obey the guide and chaperones at all times. She also asked them to stay on the path and be extra careful because of the damp conditions.

After the guided orientation tour, students were free to roam through a couple of the gardens. A number of the boys ran around and played roughly. The chaperones tried to keep the students under control, but it was difficult to identify them because they were not wearing name tags. It was also difficult to distinguish them from students from other schools. One parent noticed later that she had lost an earring while breaking up a scuffle.

Meanwhile, Veronica's wheelchair, pushed by a student, slipped off the path, causing her to fall into the mud. Her feet remained soaked until her return home at the end of the day; she would remain in bed sick for two weeks as a result of the incident.

To make matters worse, the shop was demanding that the school reimburse it for a vase that a student had accidentally broken and some candy that it said had been shoplifted.

While Ms. Patel was disappointed that the field trip had not gone entirely as planned, she was proud of how she handled Faria's apparent anaphylactic (allergic) reaction. She had grabbed Paul's EpiPen and stabbed it into Faria's thigh. Faria was rushed to hospital where, according to a call from her parents, she was recovering well.

The next day, Mrs. Patel was shocked to learn that the principal had received complaints from many parents. Veronica and Faria's parents were particularly upset. They were threatening to involve lawyers.

(1) Should the field trip have been cancelled, given the conditions?

(2) Was there adequate supervision for the field trip?

(3) Should Veronica, Paul, and Faria have been permitted to go on the field trip? If so, under what conditions?

(4) Did the teacher use reasonable care? Were the four elements necessary for a finding of negligence evident in any specific situation?

(5) Could Veronica or Faria's families sue the school board?

(6) What is the responsibility of the school board to the gift shop?

(7) Could the parent sue for her lost earring?

(8) What is the effect of the "consent and waiver" forms signed by the parents?

(9) Is there a basis for a complaint to the Ontario College of Teachers?

(10) What is the principal's responsibility?

(11) If you were running this field trip, what procedures would you put in place to avoid these problems?

CHAPTER 6

ENSURING SAFE CLASSROOMS AND SCHOOLS

After reading this chapter, you will have a better understanding of the ways teachers, principals, and other members of the school community can ensure the safety of classrooms and schools. In particular, you will learn about:

- *The importance of actively developing a safe school culture, with a particular emphasis on the* Ontario Schools Code of Conduct.
- *The consequences of misconduct by students with regard to suspension, expulsion, and criminal charges.*
- *The implications of the principal's statutory duty to maintain order and discipline in the school.*

Jordan Manners, a fourteen-year-old student at C.W. Jeffreys Collegiate Institute, was shot dead, allegedly by another student, in June 2007.

While youth violence was not uncommon in this north Toronto neighbourhood, citizens were outraged that the sanctuary of the school had been so horribly violated.

Yet schools are not entirely safe places for students. Teachers, students, and intruders sometimes act in ways that put students at risk. One teacher at C.W. Jeffreys characterized the school as a "war zone" in which teachers and administrators were reluctant to discipline students for fear of hassles from parents, lawsuits, and human rights complaints.

Several weeks later, an independent investigation revealed that a fourteen-year-old girl had been sexually assaulted in a school washroom earlier in the school year. She was targeted, the investigation found, because the assailants believed that Muslim girls were less likely to report sex crimes due to cultural taboos and strict parents. This was one of several sexual assaults that had occurred at the school for which little or no action was taken to protect the victims or punish the assailants, according to the report of the School Community Safety Advisory Panel (2008), which investigated incidents at the school. The principal and other school administrators were suspended in June.

Was the school responsible for the murder of Jordan Manners?

Was the school responsible for the sexual assault?

Did the school have effective disciplinary processes?

Was the school a positive and safe place for students?

An independent panel led by lawyer Julian Falconer was appointed by the Toronto District School Board to consider how the above mentioned killing may have been prevented at C.W. Jeffreys. This report led to an increased awareness of school safety issues and to many administrative reforms. The recommendations in the report also led to the introduction of police officers into Toronto schools as "school resource officers."

SAFETY AND CULTURE OF SCHOOLS

Teachers work with young people on a daily basis yet often know little about what really matters to the students and what influences them. In *Freaks, Geeks and Cool Kids* (2004), sociologist Barry Milner, Jr., notes:

In large part, teachers and administrators tend to ignore subtle forms of cruelty when they can because they lack the knowledge and power they need to deal with them. More specifically, the way schools are organized means it is hard for them to know what is going on in the peer culture and that they have few effective sanctions to use against those who abuse others. (p. 186)

It is important for teachers and administrators to understand the underlying interactions of school life and, in particular, the nature and impact of peer dynamics. In his sociological study of student culture in schools, Milner examines how the elements of teenager, school, and consumerism interact.

> Our educational system plays a central role, not just in giving people technical skills, but also in molding their desires and ambitions. Life with one's peers, in and out of the classroom, powerfully shapes people's world views and personalities. (p. 169)

After studying 304 retrospective accounts by college and university students and observing students in schools, Milner was particularly struck by the profound importance of status differences in high school peer relations. Social standing in schools, he discovered, is a function of *coolness* derived largely from the display of consumer goods. Toward the top are athletic males and attractive females; toward the bottom are "geeks" and "nerds." Cliques and social marginalization are the natural result.

Teachers and administrators who have their finger on the pulse of student culture are better able to influence that culture and, by doing so, make schools safer places for students. While Milner's focus is on understanding school culture, he notes that one school in his study was very successful in breaking down these informal power structures. In this school, as one student wrote, "The goal of administration was to break up cliques throughout our four years in high school so that we would all become friends."

Ignoring the inevitable minor cruelties of students toward each other creates unsafe school cultures. Marginalization and bullying are often the result. Violent incidents, such as the sexual assault and murder at C.W. Jeffreys, are more likely to occur when teachers and administrators fail to understand and address student conduct in schools.

EDUCATION ACT AND THE
ONTARIO SCHOOLS CODE OF CONDUCT

Students have the right to learn in a safe place. The *Safe Schools Act* of 2000, which amended the *Education Act*, was an Ontario government response to public perceptions. These perceptions were fed by tragedies such as the Columbine massacre.

The Minister of Education stated in a news release (Ministry of Education, May 31, 2000):

> Many school boards have varying codes and rules for safety. But this legislation will ensure that there are clear, province-wide standards, especially for the most serious infractions, like bringing a weapon to school.

This set of amendments to the *Education Act*, in addition to setting forth mandatory consequences for serious unacceptable conduct in schools, empowered the Minister of Education to establish a code of conduct for all schools in Ontario. Note that the *Ontario Schools Code of Conduct* (2000) begins:

> A school is a place that promotes responsibility, respect, civility and academic excellence in a safe learning and teaching environment.
>
> All students, parents, teachers and staff have the right to be safe, and feel safe, in their school community. With this right comes the responsibility to be law-abiding citizens and to be accountable for actions that put at risk the safety of others or oneself.
>
> The Ontario Code of Conduct sets clear provincial standards of behaviour. It specifies the mandatory consequences for student actions that do not comply with these standards.
>
> The Provincial standards of behaviour apply not only to students, but also to all individuals involved in the publicly funded school system— parents or guardians, volunteers, teachers and other staff members— whether they are on school property, on school buses or at school-authorized events or activities.

The code calls on everyone involved in education to contribute to fostering safe school environments. Random acts of violence may not be preventable, but it is possible to create safer places in which all members of the school community can feel more secure.

Roles and Responsibilities

Principals have long been charged with the responsibility of ensuring that each school is a safe and healthy learning environment. Section 265(1) of the *Education Act* includes the following duties:

> It is the duty of a principal of a school, in addition to the principal's duties as a teacher,
>> (h) to maintain proper order and discipline in the school ...
>> (n) subject to an appeal to the board, to refuse to admit to the school or classroom a person whose presence in the school or classroom would in the principal's judgment be detrimental to the physical or mental well-being of the pupils.

In order to fulfill their responsibility, principals assume wide-ranging authority and obligations. Recognizing the broad scope of the principal's duties, the *Education Act* requires teachers to assist in maintaining order under the principal's direction. In particular, section 264(1)(e) calls on teachers "to maintain, under the direction of the principal, proper order and discipline in the teacher's classroom and while on duty in the school and on the school ground." In addition, *Regulation 298*, section 20(h), states that a teacher shall "cooperate with the principal and other teachers to establish and maintain consistent disciplinary practices in the school."

The duty of a teacher to maintain discipline and order outlined in section 264(1) of the *Education Act* speaks directly to the teacher's responsibility while teaching in the classroom or while on duty around the school. However, the duty to establish and maintain consistent disciplinary practices in the school outlined in section 20 of *Regulation 298* has a much broader scope. First, it suggests that teachers must follow school policies and procedures even when implementing discipline in their own classroom. For example, most schools have established protocols for dealing with students who are late to class. Second, it implies that a teacher should never ignore student misbehaviour, even if the students involved are not registered in the teacher's class, or if the teacher is not on duty at the time. This implied duty to respond to inappropriate student behaviour and report it where necessary to the principal has recently been made explicit through amendments to the *Education Act* and revised Ministry of Education guidelines.

The Ministry now requires board employees *who work directly with students*—including principals, teachers and non-teaching staff—to respond to any student behaviour that is likely to have a "negative impact on school climate," provided it is safe to do so. Such behaviour includes all inappropriate or disrespectful behaviour at any time while the student is at school or at a school-related activity. As the Ministry puts it, "the purpose of responding to incidents of inappropriate and disrespectful behaviour is to stop and correct it immediately so that the students involved can learn that it is unacceptable." Otherwise, as the Safe Schools Action Team (2008) notes, "Behaviour that is not addressed becomes accepted behaviour" (p. 9). In the case of serious incidents, *all board employees* who become aware that a student may have engaged in an activity for which suspension or expulsion must be considered are required to report the matter to the principal as soon as reasonably possible, but in any event no later than the end of the school day. Where immediate action is called for, the employee may make a verbal report, which must then be confirmed in writing, using the Safe Schools Incident Reporting Form. In addition to board employees, school bus drivers are required to report serious incidents to the principal in writing; and boards may also require other non-board employees who come into contact with students on a regular basis to report such incidents.

Section 23 of *Regulation 298* sets out a number of statutory requirements for *students* to help make the school a safe and orderly environment. In particular, students are expected to exercise self-discipline; accept such discipline as would be exercised by a kind, firm, and judicious parent; and be courteous to fellow pupils and obedient and courteous to teachers. In keeping with the January 30, 2004, Supreme Court ruling on section 43 of the *Criminal Code,* a clause has recently been added to section 23 of *Regulation 298* clarifying that the regulation does not authorize teachers to impose, or require students to accept, corporal punishment

The *Safe Schools Act* provided principals and school boards with strong disciplinary measures to support them in maintaining order and discipline. School boards were expected to develop codes of conduct consistent with the amendments to the *Education Act*. Principals, in consultation with school councils, could also develop a "local code of conduct" adapted to the specific needs of the school.

Ontario Schools Code of Conduct makes it clear that principals are expected to take a leadership role in guiding the school:

Principals, under the direction of their school board, take a leadership role in the daily operation of a school. They provide this leadership by:

- demonstrating care and commitment to academic excellence and a safe teaching and learning environment;
- holding everyone, under their authority, accountable for their behaviour and actions;
- communicating regularly and meaningfully with all members of their school community.

The code also requires teachers to support their principal in enforcing the school's code of conduct:

Teachers and school staff, under the leadership of their principals, maintain order in the school and are expected to hold everyone to the highest standard of respectful and responsible behaviour. As role models, staff uphold these high standards when they:

- help students work to their full potential and develop their self-worth;
- communicate regularly and meaningfully with parents;
- maintain consistent standards of behaviour for all students;
- demonstrate respect for all students, staff and parents;
- prepare students for the full responsibilities of citizenship.

In addition, parents and students are also assigned responsibilities under the code. Parents "have a responsibility to support the efforts of school staff in maintaining a safe and respectful learning environment for all students," while students are to be treated with respect and dignity. In return, they must demonstrate respect for themselves, for others and for the responsibilities of citizenship through acceptable behaviour. Respect and responsibility are demonstrated when a student:

- comes to school prepared, on time and ready to learn;
- shows respect for themselves, for others and for those in authority;
- refrains from bringing anything to school that may compromise the safety of others;
- follows the established rules and takes responsibility for his or her own actions.

The police and community members also play enhanced roles under the code. Community members are asked to "support and respect the rules of their local schools." Police are asked to "investigate incidents in accordance with the protocol developed with the local school board. These protocols are based on a provincial model developed by the Ministry of the Solicitor General and the Ministry of Education."

Standards of Behaviour
The *Ontario Schools Code of Conduct* establishes codes of behaviour to guide the behaviours of everyone involved in the education system:

Respect, civility and responsible citizenship
All school members must:
- respect and comply with all applicable federal, provincial and municipal laws;
- demonstrate honesty and integrity;
- respect differences in people, their ideas and opinions;
- treat one another with dignity and respect at all times, and especially when there is disagreement;
- respect and treat others fairly, regardless of their race, ancestry, place of origin, colour, ethnic origin, citizenship, religion, gender, sexual orientation, age or disability;

- respect the rights of others;
- show proper care and regard for school property and the property of others;
- take appropriate measures to help those in need;
- respect persons who are in a position of authority;
- respect the need of others to work in an environment of learning and teaching.

Physical Safety
Weapons
All school members must:

- not be in possession of any weapon, including but not limited to firearms;
- not use any object to threaten or intimidate another person;
- not cause injury to any person with an object.

Alcohol and Drugs
All school members must:

- not be in possession of, or under the influence of, or provide others with, alcohol or illegal drugs.

Physical Aggression
All school members must:

- not inflict or encourage others to inflict bodily harm on another person;
- seek staff assistance, if necessary, to resolve conflict peacefully.

These Standards of Behaviour were given teeth in the *Safe Schools Act*, which mandated the imposition of *mandatory consequences* for significant offences by students, such as swearing at a person in authority or possessing illegal drugs, or even more serious offences, such as possessing a weapon or committing sexual assault. The various grounds listed in the *Education Act* for which a student may be suspended or expelled are outlined below in the sections on suspensions (pp. 174–76) and expulsions (pp. 176–78).

On the one hand, media reports regarding events at C.W. Jeffreys Collegiate Institute suggest that the *Code of Conduct* may have been violated by educators and students alike. The suspension of senior administrators suggests that the school leadership struggled to maintain a safe learning environment. By failing to respond to the alleged sexual assault of a student, they failed to make students accountable for their behaviour and may have contributed to an unsafe culture in the school. It is entirely possible that ineffective enforcement of a code of conduct on an ongoing basis may have contributed to a culture of weapons and violence.

On the other hand, social and economic factors well beyond the control of the school administration should be taken into account. As the Final Report of the Task Force on Youth Violent Crime (2000), formed after the swarming death of a fifteen year-old student, found:

> ... the problem of violence amongst youth was not simply an issue of school violence. Youth violence had its roots in the community in general; schools only provided a gathering place where violence could occur. (p. 1)

Mandatory Consequences

A defining characteristic of the *Safe Schools Act* (2000) was its requirement that *mandatory consequences*, in the form of suspension or expulsion, be imposed for unacceptable student behaviours. The earlier version of the *Education Act*, section 306(1) stated that a principal "shall consider whether to suspend a pupil if he or she believes that the pupil has engaged in any of the following activities ..." The activities listed were very broad in definition and scope. The amended wording conveyed a much tougher law-and-order stance: "It is mandatory that a pupil be suspended ... if the pupil commits any of the following infractions ...," followed by a very specific and precise list of offences that leaves little room for the principal's discretion.

Many regarded mandatory consequences as too authoritarian. Barbara Coloroso (2003), an expert on school discipline, argues that harsh punishments and *zero tolerance* for violations of codes of conduct are not helpful. Instead, she proposes "authoritative (not authoritarian) adult-child interaction ... (backbone as opposed to brick-wall structure)" (p. 177).

The most contentious aspect of the *Safe Schools Act* was its zero tolerance policy. One among many criticisms was that the implementation of this policy was particularly harmful to racial minorities. These criticisms, which were given credence by an Ontario Human Rights Commission ruling, prompted the government to review the policy.

After consulting stakeholders, the Ontario government passed amendments to the safe schools legislation in June 2007, which came into force on February 2, 2008. In announcing the proposed legislation, the Minister of Education said:

> Our first priority is safer schools and discipline that works. Our proposed changes would strike a balance between the consequences for inappropriate behaviour and its causes, as well as provide programs so students can earn their way back into the classroom and complete their education. (News Release, April 17, 2007)

One amendment indicated that principals and vice-principals should receive training to help them better apply discipline in a non discriminatory manner. The government also announced that it would provide $31 million annually to support expelled students and students serving long-term suspensions. The previous government had failed to deliver on its promise to offer programs to help rehabilitate these troubled students.

Another important amendment enacted in June 2007 was the addition of bullying to the list of infractions for which a principal had to consider suspending a student.

Bullying. Bullying has been a problem since the inception of schools. Autobiographies and novels over the centuries have often featured vivid accounts of school bullies and their victims. Bullying is a natural, though not inevitable, outgrowth of school cultures in which some students are identified as cool and others as uncool. The victims of bullying are varied;

too often they are individuals perceived to be outsiders, belonging to groups that are marginalized by ethnicity, race, religion, or sexual orientation. The bullies, the bullied, and the bystander are all diminished by this cycle of violence and self-loathing that often begins in schools and is perpetuated in society.

Today, adults are no longer minimizing and trivializing bullying. High-profile cases of the problem, especially school shootings by victims of bullying, have contributed to calls for action by educators. Articles and books, such as Barbara Coloroso's *The Bully, the Bullied and the Bystander* (2003), have increased understanding of the complex dynamics underlying bullying in schools. In Ontario, the Safe Schools Action Team (2005) prepared a bullying prevention plan, *Shaping Safer Schools: Bullying Prevention Plan*. (See pp. 170–72.)

The Bully, the Bullied and the Bystander (2003)
by Barbara Coloroso

Colorosso examines the complex dynamics underlying bullying in schools. She identifies the bully, the bullied, and the bystander as three characters in a tragedy. She also explores ways in which families, school, and communities can break the cycle of violence and create circles of caring.

The Bully
"Bullying is a conscious, willful, and deliberate hostile activity, intended to harm, induce fear through the threat of further aggression, and create terror" (p. 13). This includes verbal bullying and name-calling (which accounts for 70 percent of reported bullying), physical bullying such as spitting, hitting, and property damage (under 33 percent), and relational bullying through ignoring, excluding, and shunning.

The Bullied

"No one deserves to be bullied" (p. 42). Almost anyone can be bullied when "a bully feels a need to put someone down in order to feel superior" (p. 43). Students who appear vulnerable or who may appear annoying to their peers may be attractive targets. The same is true of children with autism, who may have an unusual manner and poor social judgment.

The Bystander

Bystanders "are the supporting cast who aid and abet the bully through acts of omission and commission. They can stand idly by or look away, or they can actively encourage the bully, or they can join in and become one of a bunch of bullies. Whatever the choice, there is a price to pay" (p. 62).

Breaking the Cycle

"Breaking the cycle of violence involves more than merely identifying and stopping the bully. It requires that we examine why and how a child becomes a bully or a target of a bully (and sometimes both) as well as the role bystanders play in perpetuating the cycle." (p. xvi).

(1) Have you ever been a bully, been bullied, or been a bystander to bullying? How did it feel?
(2) How do you feel about it today?

**Shaping Safer Schools: A Bullying Prevention Action Plan
by Safe Schools Action Team (2005)
3.0 BULLYING PREVENTION PLANS
3.1 What Works**

In developing a comprehensive bullying prevention plan for
Ontario schools, we reviewed evidence about what has, and has
not, worked in various jurisdictions. This research was reinforced
throughout our consultations with stakeholders. Our conclusion
is that successful bullying prevention programs have the following components addressing, as appropriate, all members of the
school community—students, teachers, administrators, support
staff, parents, and other community partners:

• **Education** to develop a deeper awareness and understanding of
  bullying that helps foster prevention.

• **Assessment** to determine the extent and nature of bullying, perceptions around the issue, and effectiveness of prevention efforts.

• **Action** to provide identification and prevention strategies for the
  whole school community and targeted interventions for students
  that address:
      – school-wide education, embedded in the curriculum, for
      the entire school population;
      – routine interventions targeted for students involved in the
      early stages of bullying;
      – intensive intervention strategies for those involved in
      repeated bullying and victimization, with possible referral to
      community/social service resources.

• **Policy** to establish the framework within which bullying prevention in the school is defined, prioritized, implemented, and
  evaluated.

According to recent research on the effectiveness of bullying prevention programs, the most successful programs:

- define bullying;
- support students who are bullied, as well as students who bully;
- are characterized by strong leadership from the principal and teachers;
- take a comprehensive approach by including elements and roles for the whole school community;
- are appropriate for students at different levels (primary, junior, intermediate, and high school);
- address gender-based differences;
- embed bullying prevention within the curriculum;
- focus on developing healthy relationships skills and explaining the bullying dynamic;
- recognize bullying as a relationship problem that requires relationship-based solutions;
- involve parents;
- include a broader community involvement component;
- promote respect, tolerance, and empathy.

3.2 What Doesn't Work

We also took the time to study bullying prevention approaches that have not worked as well. The research indicates that the least successful bullying prevention programs:

- do not have different intervention strategies for students at different levels of risk (e.g. they may only provide programming targeted at the entire school population);
- are more likely to focus on students who bully, and do not support students who are bullied;
- are not based on improving the social and emotional

skills development of students, including those who bully, those who are bullied, and those who are bystanders;
- do not have a parental or community involvement component; and
- are less likely to have been evaluated.

(1) Drawing on experiences in schools, which of the strategies listed above do you think would be most useful in preventing bullying?
(2) As a classroom teacher, how can you help create a climate of mutual respect and understanding among students?

THE CONDUCT OF STUDENTS

Random acts of violence, such as the shootings at Columbine High School in Colorado and Dawson College in Montreal, have raised public awareness of the fact that children in schools are not entirely safe from terrible crimes. The sexual assault and murder at C.W. Jeffreys Collegiate Institute reinforced these perceptions and prompted calls for increased efforts to make schools safe from violence.

What is violence? Lawyer Eric Roher (1997), in *An Educator's Guide to Violence in Schools*, writes:

Many people believe that violence always involves some sort of physical contact or assault. In fact, conduct which does not involve physical contact with another person may be described as violent. For example, a black student who is subjected to racially motivated threats may be a victim of violence. Similarly, a gay or lesbian student who is teased, taunted or intimidated by homophobic classmates may be a victim of violence. Students who find themselves being bullied, harassed or subject to acts of extortion by older or larger students are also possible victims of violence.

None of these acts involves physical contact but they all result in the vic-
timization of a particular student. Violence, in a school context, has been
defined as "anything that jeopardizes the climate for an effective learning
and working environment". It can include abusive language, disruptive
or aggressive behaviour in the classroom, assaults, the carrying and use of
weapons, and emotional and verbal abuse. (p. 1)

It has long been understood that children and youth, while they do commit crimes, deserve to be treated differently from adult offenders. This was
recognized in our society with the *Juvenile Delinquents Act* of 1908. The *Young
Offenders Act* of 1984 added to the protection afforded young offenders but
was soon criticized for being soft on youth who commit serious crimes. In
2003, the *Youth Criminal Justice Act (YCJA)* became the new law governing
youth crime in Canada.

Children under the age of twelve are seen as not criminally responsible
for their actions, since they are deemed unable to appreciate fully the consequences of their actions. "Refractory behaviour by children," according to the
authors of *Children's Law Handbook* (Zuker, Hammond & Flynn, 2005), "is
typically addressed as a matter of child protection legislation and/or intervention by the school system" (p. 162).

Youths between the ages of twelve and eighteen are seen as bearing
some responsibility for their actions. The *YCJA* governs how the justice
system balances their vulnerability as youth with their responsibilities
as members of society. As a general rule, it encourages the resolution of
offences without the formal involvement of the youth justice system. In
particular, "extrajudicial measures" are encouraged so youth can be held
accountable for their misconduct without having to enter a courtroom. The
intention is to prevent crime by addressing young students' circumstances
and to rehabilitate these students before they become caught up in a cycle
of criminal behaviour.

This extrajudicial and rehabilitory concept is in tension with other aspects
of the act that seek to ensure that young people are subject to meaningful consequences, including serving adult sentences for serious crimes of violence.

What are the implications for schools? The preference for extrajudicial measures means that the police and the courts are increasingly likely to defer to the authority of principals in cases that take place in schools, especially when the offences are relatively minor or involve first-time offenders. *Ontario Schools Code of Conduct* serves as a guide to conduct, discipline, and punish offences in schools. The safe schools provisions in the *Education Act*, particularly the power to suspend or expel students, are critical tools for law and order in schools.

SAFE SCHOOLS PROVISIONS IN THE EDUCATION ACT

Suspension

In practical terms, the principal is the primary parent and disciplinarian in a school. The principal is expected to exercise careful judgment in ensuring that young people conduct themselves appropriately within a safe school environment.

While principals have less severe punishments at their disposal than the police do, they have lower evidentiary standards to meet in determining misbehaviour. Also, principals and teachers, as substitutes for parents, are more interested in remedying behaviour than meting out severe punishments.

While *Ontario Schools Code of Conduct* applies to all participants in public schooling, the consequences listed for violating the code apply only to students. Section 306(1) of the *Education Act* reads:

Activities leading to possible suspension

306. (1) A principal shall consider whether to suspend a pupil if he or she believes that the pupil has engaged in any of the following activities while at school, at a school-related activity or in other circumstances where engaging in the activity will have an impact on the school climate:

1. Uttering a threat to inflict serious bodily harm on another person.
2. Possessing alcohol or illegal drugs.
3. Being under the influence of alcohol.
4. Swearing at a teacher or at another person in a position of authority.

5. Committing an act of vandalism that causes extensive damage to school property at the pupil's school or to property located on the premises of the pupil's school.
6. Bullying.
7. Any other activity that is an activity for which a principal may suspend a pupil under a policy of the board.

The principal, when considering whether to suspend or recommend expulsion for a student, is also required to take into account any mitigating factors. These factors include:

- whether racial or other harassment was a factor
- whether progressive discipline has first been attempted
- the impact of suspension or expulsion on the student's continued education
- whether the suspension or expulsion may result in an aggravation of student's behaviour
- age of the student
- safety of other students
- in the case of a student with a disability, whether the behaviour was a manifestation of the disability and whether appropriate accommodation, based on the principle of individualization, had first been provided.

If the principal decides to suspend the student, the student is suspended from the school and from all school-related activities for a period of one to twenty school days. Students who are suspended for one to five days are expected to receive homework packages from the school. The board is required to provide an academic program for students who are suspended for six to ten days, while those who are suspended for eleven to twenty days must be offered an academic program and various supports to promote positive behaviour.

The principal is required to inform teachers of the suspension, and to make all reasonable efforts to inform a parent or guardian of the suspension within twenty-four hours. Written notice of the suspension is to be given "promptly" to the student and the parent (unless the student is over the age of eighteen and/or has withdrawn from parental control). The notice must include the reason for the suspension, the duration, information about any program for suspended students, and information concerning the right of appeal. The principal must also notify as soon as reasonably possible the parents of a student who has been harmed as a result of the activity leading to the suspension, unless the student is an adult or unless such notification would not be in the student's best interests. When so notifying parents, the principal must be careful to protect the privacy of the student who has been suspended.

Students, parents, or guardians may appeal a suspension within ten school days by giving written notice to the appropriate supervisory officer. The school board must then hear and determine the appeal within fifteen school days of receiving the written notice, unless both sides agree to a later deadline. Appeals must be heard by a panel of at least three school board trustees. In the meantime, the student remains suspended. The standard of proof at the hearing is a "balance of probabilities" rather than "beyond a reasonable doubt," and the school board's decision on an appeal of a suspension is final. The board may confirm the suspension, confirm the suspension but shorten its duration, or quash the suspension and expunge the record.

While most educators are pleased with the new suspension legislation, there are a number of concerns. First, the complexity of the mitigating factors could lead to confusion. Second, if there is a significant number of appeals, the appeals process and time lines could impose a tremendous burden on school administrators—especially on school board trustees. To avoid such an eventuality, boards may want to consider creative solutions such as peer mediation, detentions, community service, behavioural contracts, supervised withdrawals (time-outs) from class, and written agreements to expunge suspensions from student records at the end of the year if certain conditions are met.

Expulsion

Expulsion from school is a severe form of punishment meted out for very serious offences by students. Section 310(1) of the act reads:

SUSPENSION, INVESTIGATION AND POSSIBLE EXPULSION

Activities leading to suspension

310. (1) A principal shall suspend a pupil if he or she believes that the pupil has engaged in any of the following activities while at school, at a school-related activity or in other circumstances where engaging in the activity will have an impact on the school climate:

1. Possessing a weapon, including possessing a firearm.
2. Using a weapon to cause or to threaten bodily harm to another person.
3. Committing physical assault on another person that causes bodily harm requiring treatment by a medical practitioner.
4. Committing sexual assault.
5. Trafficking in weapons or in illegal drugs.
6. Committing robbery.
7. Giving alcohol to a minor.
8. Any other activity that, under a policy of a board, is an activity for which a principal must suspend a pupil and, therefore in accordance with this Part, conduct an investigation to determine whether to recommend to the board that the pupil be expelled.

The principal is to undertake a thorough investigation into the circumstances of the offence in order to determine whether to recommend to the board that the pupil be expelled. In the meantime, the student is placed in a program for suspended students and has no immediate right to appeal the suspension. The requirements for the principal to report to teachers and parents are the same as those described above under suspension protocols.

If the principal, on concluding the investigation, decides not to recommend expulsion, the original suspension is either confirmed, modified, or withdrawn. If the principal decides to recommend expulsion, then the principal must prepare a report for the school board summarizing his or her findings and recommending whether the student be expelled from his or her school only, or from all the schools of the board. In considering whether to recommend expulsion, the principal has to take into account any mitigating factors. The principal also must make a recommendation on the type of school or program that might benefit the student.

On receiving a principal's recommendation to expel a student, the school board holds an expulsion hearing with the principal, the student's parents (or the student, if an adult), and any other persons specified by board policy. After hearing submissions from all parties, the board may decide to expel the student either from the student's own school or from all the schools in the board. Students expelled from their own school are assigned to another school in the board; students expelled from all schools of the board are assigned to a program for expelled students operated by the board. There is no time limit for an expulsion from all the schools of a board, but a student is not entitled to be readmitted to a school until he or she has successfully completed a program for expelled students. The program consists of an academic and non-academic component. This helps ensure that expelled students have the opportunity to continue their education and develop "long-term positive attitudes and behaviours by identifying and addressing the underlying causes of the behaviour that led to the expulsion" (Policy/Program Memorandum 142: School Board Programs for Expelled Students, 2007).

If the school board decides not to expel the student, it may uphold, modify, or expunge the original suspension.

THE ROLE OF THE CRIMINAL JUSTICE SYSTEM

While the school system is better equipped to protect students from harm and to punish and reform student offenders, the police and the courts continue to play an important role in ensuring student safety.

The purpose of criminal law is to protect individuals and maintain order in society. Students, teachers and other people in schools are protected from violence and other offences by criminal law, and may themselves face criminal charges for violating the law of the land.

Violent Crimes

Violent crimes committed by students, particularly homicide or aggravated assault, are taken very seriously by the police and the courts. The *Youth*

Criminal Justice Act has increased the number of violent offences for which youth can be sentenced as adults.

The killing of another human being—directly or indirectly, intentionally or not—is a *homicide*, which may be deemed murder (first-degree or second-degree murder) or manslaughter.

Murder is the intentional killing of another individual. According to section 231(1) of the *Criminal Code* a charge or conviction of first-degree murder pertains to situations in which:

- the murder is planned and deliberate;
- one person hires another to commit murder;
- the victim is a law enforcement officer;
- the murder is caused while committing another serious offence, such as aggravated assault, sexual assault, or forcible confinement.

"Second-degree murder" refers to murders that do not fit the situations listed above. "Manslaughter" is defined as a killing resulting from a wrongful act, even if the killing was unintentional.

Criminal assault, the most common form of violent crime, refers to threatened or actual physical contact without consent. There are several levels of assault under the *Criminal Code*:

Level 1:   Threatening or pushing accompanied by (a) intentionally applying force; (b) attempting or threatening force by act or gesture; (c) accosting or impeding someone while openly wearing or carrying a weapon or imitation weapon.

Level 2:   Assault with a weapon or causing bodily harm, such that there are serious consequences for the victim's health or comfort.

Level 3:   Aggravated assault, which is defined as wounding, maiming, disfiguring, or endangering the life of the victim.

While relatively minor Level 1 assaults in the school may be handled using the powers of the principal under the *Education Act*, weapons offences and more serious allegations of assault will be referred to the police as well.

This does not mean that the principal will not take action against a student who has committed a serious criminal assault. The *Education Act* is clear that the principal is responsible for suspending such a student immediately, and possibly, after a thorough investigation, for recommending that the student be expelled.

Sexual assault, another very serious violent crime, ranges in severity from unwanted sexual touching to aggravated sexual assault. Teachers who witness these crimes must report them immediately to the principal and, possibly, the police.

Teachers and principals play important roles in preventing violence by creating positive learning environments and enforcing the school's code of conduct. Natural consequences and rehabilitation at the school level also serve a critical function in the justice system because the courts defer to the judgment of educators in minor cases.

Offences Against Property

Canadian society takes a dim view of crimes against property, such as theft, robbery, and vandalism.

Theft, which is the taking of property, permanently or temporarily, without the owner's permission, is the most common criminal offence. It is also very common in schools, though the items taken may be of relatively low value. Nonetheless, these are serious crimes that merit the school's, and possibly the police's, attention. For the most part, the police do not become involved in theft cases unless the items stolen are of high value. Robbery that includes violence or the threat of violence will nearly always involve the police.

Another common property crime in schools is vandalism: the intentional destruction of property. Examples of vandalism in schools include graffiti, damage to classroom fixtures, breaking windows, stopping up toilets, and setting potentially serious fires. Vandalism, which is very often a sign of larger discipline problems within the school, is a significant problem that is best handled internally, though the police may be called in to investigate serious cases. Again, extrajudicial measures by the principal are critical to reducing vandalism.

Alcohol and Drug Offences

The use of alcohol and illegal drugs is common among teenagers in Canada, even though alcohol is illegal before the age of nineteen and improper use of controlled drugs illegal at any age. While most students do not abuse alcohol or drugs regularly, many students do encounter problems related to their use. As a result, it is important for schools to monitor their use in school and at school events. It is also important for them to help students who exhibit dependency habits.

Generally, the police are not involved with alcohol or drug offences at school, except when they are hired to supervise school events such as dances. As with other crimes on school property, they defer to the judgment of the principal acting *in loco parentis*. Police and police sniffer dogs may be called into schools if the principal has reasonable grounds for suspecting a student of trafficking.

The youth criminal justice system's increasing reliance on extrajudicial measures is a double-edged sword for educators. On the one hand, it recognizes that educators acting *in loco parentis* are better able to understand, influence, and punish children and youth than distant officers of the court. On the other hand, along with the *Code of Conduct*, this reliance adds considerably to the responsibilities and disciplinary challenges that principals and teachers face.

THE PRINCIPAL'S DUTY TO MAINTAIN ORDER AND DISCIPLINE

The statutory duty of principals to maintain order and discipline under the *Education Act* has been an important theme throughout this chapter. Principals, working with staff members, have a key role to play in establishing a safe school culture. Principals are also responsible for determining appropriate disciplinary measures, and, where necessary, suspending a student or even recommending a student's expulsion.

After outlining the principal's responsibilities concerning visitors and trespassers, this section will examine how searches should be conducted in schools and the ways in which principals should carry out disciplinary investigations. While principals have great authority, their actions are subject to legal scrutiny.

VISITORS AND TRESPASSERS

- A non-custodial parent attempts to abduct his children from the school.
- A predator passes himself off as a student.

Although we think of schools as public places, members of the general public do not in fact have the right to enter or remain on school premises unless they are authorized to do so. Students, teachers, board employees, and parents are authorized to be on school premises on any day and at any time, within limits established by the local school board. The law also permits school trustees, local clergy, and the local member of Provincial Parliament to visit without reservation. Other people may be invited onto school premises for a particular purpose by the principal or vice-principal, or may be authorized to be on school premises by board policy. Even those people who are legally permitted to be on the property do not have access to all areas of the school. This means, for example, that parents who want to visit their child's classroom are expected to make arrangements through the principal. They do not have automatic right of entry to a particular classroom. It also means that teachers do not necessarily have free access to all areas of the school.

Volunteers and members of the community are valued partners in fostering the development of young people. Volunteers assist as tutors, helpers, and coaches. Concerns about the safety of schools have led many school boards to require that they and other regular visitors (such as student teachers) obtain criminal record checks. Other members of the public who have not been authorized by the school board or principal—for example, students from another school—do not have automatic right of access. Most schools have clear signs requiring such people to report to the main office. While physical access to secondary schools is still relatively easy, many elementary schools in Ontario lock their doors; visitors have to be "buzzed in" by the main office.

Access to schools is at the discretion of the principal, who has the right to exclude *anyone* whose presence is considered "detrimental to the safety or well-being" of others on the premises. This could include disruptive parents and members of the public. Others who may be carefully screened or denied entry are non-custodial parents because there have been cases of attempted abduction. Students serving suspensions or who have been expelled are also not permitted access.

SEARCH AND SEIZURE

R. v. A.M., which was featured in chapter 1, made it clear that constitutional protections against unreasonable warrantless searches apply to students in school. The police officers who used a sniffer dog to help them search St. Patrick's High School in Sarnia on November 7, 2002, neither obtained a warrant from a judge nor had a reasonable basis for suspecting that drugs were present in the school. This police action, therefore, was considered unreasonable under both criminal law and the *Education Act*, since the "entire school body" was "held in detention" for a "warrantless, random search."

The court added that a warrantless search by school authorities, rather than the police, would be appropriate if based on reasonable grounds and conducted in a reasonable manner. It is important to understand why school authorities are held to a lower legal standard than police officers.

Case: R. v. M. (M.R.) (1998)

Mr. Cadue, vice-principal of a Halifax junior high school, had been advised on more than one occasion that thirteen-year-old M.M.R. had been dealing drugs at the school. Cadue had reason to believe his student informants: they were acquaintances of M.M.R. and a previous tip they had given him had proven to be correct.

On the day of the dance, one of the informants told Cadue that M.M.R. was "carrying" at the dance. Cadue then called the police and requested that an officer be present. He then asked M.M.R. and his friend to come to the main office. He asked them if they were in possession of drugs, then advised them that he was going to search them.

The police officer watched as Cadue conducted a search of the students. A bulge in M.M.R.'s socks was revealed to be a cellophane bag. Cadue showed the bag to the officer, who identified it as containing marijuana. The officer then arrested M.M.R. and advised him of his rights.

---

(1) Did the vice-principal act appropriately?

(2) Did the police officer act appropriately?

(3) Was M.M.R.'s "right to be secure against unreasonable search and seizure" (*Canadian Charter of Rights and Freedoms*, section 8) violated?

School principals and teachers have a duty to ensure that schools are safe places for learning. Common law recognizes their duty of care while acting *in loco parentis*. The *Education Act* charges them with the duty to maintain order and discipline. They must be careful, however, not to violate the legal rights of students under the *Canadian Charter of Rights and Freedoms*.

R. v. M. (M.R.) (1998) raised interesting legal points and prompted the courts to weigh the rights and responsibilities of educators and students in balance. When and under what circumstances was a search by a school administrator or teacher considered unreasonable under the *Charter*?

An earlier case had already determined that a school administrator could conduct a personal search of a student. In *R. v. G. (J.M.)* (1986), the Supreme Court held that, while the student had a legitimate expectation of privacy, the school's duty to maintain a safe and orderly learning environment was more important. As a result, the principal's search and seizure of a marijuana joint found in the student's pant cuff was deemed to be appropriate. G.J.M. was found guilty of possession of a narcotic, a charge laid by a police officer who appeared on the scene after the search.

In *R. v. M. (M.R.)*, the police officer was present for the search. As a result, the youth court judge dismissed the evidence, arguing that the vice-principal was acting as an agent of the police through an "agreed strategy" between them. The appellate courts and, finally, the Supreme Court of Canada ruled the search reasonable and legal and ordered a new trial.

First, the courts determined that the decision of the vice-principal to conduct a search was reasonable, given the information with which he was provided. The Supreme Court identified, as reasonable grounds, information from a credible student source, from more than one student or teacher, from the administrator's own observations, and from any combination of the above.

Second, the Supreme Court determined that the decision to search was consistent with Cadue's duties under Nova Scotia's *Education Act* and was not arbitrary in nature. Education legislation in both Nova Scotia and Ontario authorizes the search of students under appropriate circumstances. The search was also conducted before a witness, the police officer. School authorities should conduct searches in the presence of another staff member or a police officer.

The Supreme Court seemed reluctant to usurp the role of educators in assessing the information provided to them, concluding: "Courts should recognize the preferred position of school authorities to determine if reasonable grounds existed for a search." Indeed, students were deemed to be aware that their rights in school were more limited. Justice Cory of the Court wrote:

> Students know that their teachers and other school authorities are responsible for providing a safe environment and maintaining order and discipline in the school. They must know that this may sometimes require searches of students and their personal effects and the seizure of prohibited items. It would not be reasonable for a student to expect to be free from such searches. A student's reasonable expectation of privacy in the school environment is therefore significantly diminished.

Third, the courts concluded that the police officer was not directly involved in the search. If the officer had been directly involved, and the higher legal standard for a search by an agent of the police had applied, the courts may have accepted the youth court judge's decision to dismiss the evidence.

Fourth, the courts found no evidence that there was an agreed strategy between the vice-principal and the officer.

Educators must act reasonably in exercising their greater scope in conducting searches. The case of *R. v. A.M.* made it clear that random searches in schools are not permitted. As legal scholar Greg Dickinson (2009) writes, it was not the intent of the Supreme Court "to allow a reasonably well-educated guess to constitute reasonable grounds" (p. 176). The Court went even further. It expressed concern that making it easy for principals and the police to conduct such searches would send negative messages to students about their fundamental rights as citizens.

School board/police protocols instruct school personnel when conducting searches to ask students to remove items from their personal property and clothing as opposed to removing the items from the students directly. These protocols also instruct school personnel not to conduct personal searches. It is up to the police to conduct personal searches, presumably with a warrant based on evidence of probable cause.

DISCIPLINARY INVESTIGATIONS IN SCHOOLS

The incidents described above focus on cases that ultimately led to criminal proceedings and sanctions. Most disciplinary incidents in schools, however, are handled by the principal under the *Education Act* and Ministry of Education guidelines. Principals have both the duty and the authority to investigate all cases of student misconduct, and, in the worst cases, to suspend or recommend for expulsion students who violate the school's code of conduct or education legislation.

Principals should conduct investigations in a timely manner and interview witnesses while events are fresh in their minds. When the police are involved, such as in weapons or drug cases, principals may wish to delay their own investigations to avoid hampering the police investigation. Principals should cooperate with the police and supply them with copies of all their investigation notes. If the police are involved, principals should attempt to contact parents as soon as possible. They should also keep in mind that police investigations are separate and distinct from school investigations.

Each witness should be kept in a separate room under supervision. Each witness and victim should be asked to provide written and signed statements independently. All interviews and other sources of information should be thoroughly documented and dated. Notes should be carefully maintained in a manner consistent with the privacy rights of those involved. Language should be clear, simple, and descriptive. Opinions, subjective comments, and judgments should be avoided; adjectives and adverbs should be used with caution because they may connote judgment.

In making decisions, principals should use a balance of probabilities to weigh the evidence and explain their reasoning clearly and succinctly based on the evidence.

They should bear in mind the importance of procedural fairness under the *Statutory Powers Procedures Act.* The actions of a principal may be reviewed for procedural fairness when suspensions and expulsions are appealed to the board or a tribunal, respectively. In addition, as the search and seizure cases above make clear, the criminal courts also assess the reasonableness of school authorities' actions.

Principals and teachers who act diligently and fairly in investigating misconduct in schools are more likely to have the results of their inquiries respected by all parties.

CONCLUSION

There is no simple formula for ensuring that schools are safe places for teaching and learning. *Ontario Schools Code of Conduct* has proven a useful guide to the roles and responsibilities of all members of the school community, even though the mandatory consequences it outlines have been deemed too severe. The increased emphasis on prevention, progressive discipline, and early intervention in the 2007 changes to the safe schools provisions in the *Education Act* reflects a growing understanding that school safety and student conduct are complex issues that are best addressed by educators who understand their students and schools. Educators who are aware of their ethical, legal, and professional duties are best able to balance the rights of individuals with the safety of the community.

CHECKING YOUR UNDERSTANDING

- *Ontario Schools Code of Conduct* sets clear provincial standards of behaviour for all people involved in the school system. It calls on everyone to contribute to fostering safe school environments.

- The principal has the overall statutory responsibility for ensuring that the school is a safe and healthy learning environment.

- Teachers are required by law to assist the principal in maintaining discipline and order in the school.

- Board employees who work directly with students must respond to any student behaviour that is likely to have a negative impact on the school climate.

- Students are also legally required to be self-disciplined, obey teachers, and accept such discipline as would be exercised by a "kind, firm and judicious parent." Such discipline does not include corporal punishment.

- The *Youth Criminal Justice Act* attempts to balance the vulnerability of young people with their responsibilities as members of society. It encourages the resolution of offences through "extrajudicial measures" without the formal involvement of the criminal justice system.

- The *Education Act* lists a number of specific activities for which the principal may suspend a student from school and from all school activities for a period of one to twenty days. Depending on the length of the suspension, the student may be assigned to a special program for suspended students.

- The *Education Act* also lists a number of specific activities for which the principal must immediately suspend a student and then carry out an investigation with a view to possibly recommending that the school board expel the student.

- All board employees and school bus drivers who become aware that a student may have engaged in an activity that could lead to suspension or expulsion are required to report the matter in writing to the principal as soon as possible.

- A board may expel a student from the student's own school or from all the board's schools. If from the student's own school, the student is assigned to another school in the board. If from all the board's schools, the student is assigned to a special program for expelled students that the student must successfully complete before being readmitted to a school.

- Parents (or the student if an adult) may appeal a suspension or expulsion to the school board or to a specially convened tribunal, respectively.

- Violent crimes committed by students will inevitably lead to police involvement as well as school-imposed sanctions. Less serious offences may simply be dealt with by the principal under the *Education Act*.

- Only certain people are legally authorized to be on the school premises. Other people may be invited by the principal. The principal has the authority to exclude anyone whose presence is detrimental to the safety and well-being of others. Even those permitted to be on the premises do not have access to all areas of the school.

- Students' expectation of privacy in schools is significantly diminished. School authorities may search a student's property and person if they have reasonable grounds to do so. A search should be non-intrusive and be conducted with a witness present.

APPLYING YOUR UNDERSTANDING

Conduct Unbecoming of Students or Teachers

A fourteen-year-old student, Sheldon, was in the school library playing computer games when a teacher, Mr. Hage, entered and told him to leave because he should not be playing computer games during school time. According to Mr. Hage, Sheldon got upset when Mr. Hage moved his chair to encourage him to leave. Mr. Hage said the student grabbed his hand and twisted it before stomping out of the room. Mr. Hage suffered a fracture of his hand.

Sheldon's story is somewhat different. He said that Mr. Hage yelled at him and another student, telling them to stop playing computer games. He claimed that the teacher pulled the chair out from under him, causing him to fall to the floor. Sheldon, bruised and seething, left the lab and marched into main office to speak to the principal.

---

(1) What are the main facts in the case?

(2) What are the main issues?

(3) What areas of education law are relevant to this case?

(4) What advice would you offer the principal in dealing with this case?

(5) What is the likely outcome for Sheldon? For Mr. Hage?

CHAPTER 7

THE RIGHTS AND RESPONSIBILITIES OF STUDENTS AND PARENTS

After reading this chapter, you will have a keener appreciation of the legal rights and duties of students and parents within the school system.

Teachers draw on their professional expertise to serve the needs of students, parents, and the wider community. The concept of service recognizes the importance of working together with students and parents in an atmosphere of mutual respect.

Educators owe a duty of care to their students. Acting *in loco parentis,* teachers have a legal responsibility to protect their students from harm, while at the same time recognizing and respecting their rights and freedoms under the Canadian Constitution. Although there is a dynamic tension between these two imperatives, effective educators treat all students with dignity and respect. They also recognize the importance of helping students prepare for their role as adult citizens of Canada.

E ffective educators understand and appreciate the critical role of parents in the lives of their children. Many engage parents as partners in student learning and are open to the perspectives parents have to offer. It is also increasingly recognized that engaging with parents of all backgrounds can have a significant impact on student learning. Epstein and Rodriguez Jansorn (2004) write:

Students who succeed in school are almost always supported by their families, while other students struggle without support from home. For a school to develop a partnership program involving all parents in ways that increase student success requires new ways of thinking about family and community involvement. All schools need a purposeful, planned partnership program creating a welcome environment and engaging families in activities that contribute to students' readiness for school, academic success, and positive attitudes and behaviors. (pp. 19–20)

This chapter discusses the legal rights and duties of students and parents. The rights of students include the right to attend school and the right to have their freedom of expression and freedom of conscience and religion respected. Both parents and students have the right to expect that a student's personal information will be kept safe from disclosure to others. Parents have a legal duty to ensure that their children are properly cared for and the right to make decisions about their children's schooling and medical care. They also have a duty to ensure that their children of school age attend school. Parents have the right to be involved in their child's schooling through the school council and through active engagement by teachers in student learning.

RIGHTS AND RESPONSIBILITIES OF STUDENTS

In 1959, the General Assembly of the United Nations proclaimed the *Declaration of the Rights of the Child*. This declaration, which was signed by Canada, recognizes that the child, "by reason of his physical and mental immaturity, needs special safeguards and care, including appropriate legal protection." Key to this document are the statements that "the child is entitled to receive education, which shall be free and compulsory" and that "the best interests of the child shall be the guiding principle of those responsible for his education and guidance. The prolamation says that this responsibility "lies in the first place with his parents."

Canadian common law and education legislation recognized the vulnerability of children, and the duty of teachers to care for them, long before this declaration.

Safe Schools

Students have a right to learn in a safe learning environment and are responsible for conducting themselves responsibly in their interactions with fellow students, teachers, and other members of the school community. Teachers, principals, and other school personnel have the duty to make the classrooms and schools safe for students.

School Attendance

Compulsory Attendance

The *Education Act* stipulates that all persons of "compulsory school age" must attend school unless they are legally excused from attending. They are required to begin grade 1 in the September of the year they turn six years old, and, with the passage of the *Education Amendment Act (Learning to Age 18), 2006*, must remain in attendance until they attain the age of eighteen.

It is important to note that section 21 of the *Education Act* sets out a number of legal reasons for non-attendance, one of which is that the student has completed all the requirements for an Ontario Secondary School Diploma (OSSD).

A person is excused from attendance at school if,

    (a) the person is receiving satisfactory instruction at home or elsewhere;

    (b) the person is unable to attend school by reason of sickness or other unavoidable cause;

    (c) transportation is not provided by a board for the person and there is no school that he or she has a right to attend situated,

        (i) within 1.6 kilometres from the person's residence measured by the nearest road if he or she has not attained the age of seven years on or before the first school day in September in the year in question, or

(ii) within 3.2 kilometres from the person's residence measured by the nearest road if he or she has attained the age of seven years but not the age of 10 years on or before the first school day in September in the year in question, or

(iii) within 4.8 kilometres from the person's residence measured by the nearest road if he or she has attained the age of 10 years on or before the first school day in September in the year in question;

(d) the person has obtained a secondary school graduation diploma or has completed a course that gives equivalent standing;

(e) the person is absent from school for the purpose of receiving instruction in music and the period of absence does not exceed one-half day in any week;

(f) the person is suspended, expelled or excluded from attendance at school under any Act or under the regulations;

(g) the person is absent on a day regarded as a holy day by the church or religious denomination to which he or she belongs; or

(h) the person is absent or excused as authorized under this Act and the regulations.

Parents are legally required to ensure that their children of compulsory school age attend school, and the school principal is responsible for monitoring attendance on a daily basis and reporting to the school board the names of students of compulsory school age who are not attending. A school attendance counsellor, appointed by the school board, could take action if parents or guardians neglect or refuse to cause their children to attend school. As a further measure to ensure attendance, the act makes it an offence for employers to hire a person of compulsory school age during school hours.

Parents may determine that it is in the best interest of their children to attend private schools or be educated at home, in accordance with section 21(2)(a) of the *Education Act* (see above). In such cases, they must take steps to legally excuse the children by notifying school board officials of their intentions. A failure to provide satisfactory instruction can be the basis of prosecution by the courts.

The *Education Act*, section 21(2)(a) makes provision for children "unable to attend school by reason of sickness or other unavoidable cause." In cases where a child needs to be educated at home for medical reasons, the principal may arrange for "home instruction." Home instruction is provided by a school board teacher under *Regulation 298*, section 11(11). This is not to be confused with "homeschooling." (See Homeschooling under Rights and Responsibilities of Parents below.) Other students could be excluded if they lack proper immunization documentation; they, too, could be eligible for home instruction.

Right to Attend

Since education in Canada is a matter of provincial jurisdiction, in Ontario the right to an education is enshrined in the *Education Act*, which gives all persons the right to attend school, without payment of fee, in the jurisdiction of the school board in which they qualify to be a "resident pupil." The qualifications to be a resident pupil may be broadly divided into elementary and secondary.

To qualify as a resident pupil for elementary school purposes, a person must meet three criteria: age, residence, and tax support. The person must be between the ages of six and twenty-one and live in the district, and the person's parent or guardian must also live in the district and be a tax supporter of the board.

Society sees value in having children begin school even earlier than age six. This has led to the requirement that all school boards offer optional kindergarten classes. Children may enter kindergarten in the year they become five years old. Some boards now offer junior kindergarten a year earlier. If a board does offer junior kindergarten, the right to attend begins effectively at the age of four.

Secondary school qualifications are much more complex and depend on the age of the person. Up to the age of sixteen, there are essentially only two criteria: the person and the person's parent or guardian must live in the district and must be a tax supporter of the board. Even the tax support requirement can be waived, because there is "open access" between coterminous public and separate school boards for secondary school students. A parent could, then, be a separate school supporter, but their child would still qualify as a resident pupil of the coterminous public school board. Notice that, unlike the elementary qualifications, there is no lower or upper age limit specified. However, there is wording elsewhere indicating that a student who has been promoted from elementary school must be admitted to secondary school, and that after seven years of secondary schooling the board could charge a fee. These two statements have the practical effect of setting lower and upper limits.

There are various other clauses applying to persons over the age of sixteen who may have withdrawn from parental control and to persons over the age of eighteen. The overall effect of this further legislation is to enable all persons to complete their education. Even the children of parents unlawfully in Canada are entitled to attend school. The child's right to an education is seen as having primacy over other concerns.

Society presumes that "parents should make all significant choices affecting children, and has afforded them a general liberty to do as they choose" (*B.(R.) v. Children's Aid Society of Metropolitan Toronto* (1995)). This means parents can elect from French- or English-language public or Catholic schools, depending on their inclinations and whether or not their children qualify for admission.

RIGHT TO LEARN

Students have the right to learn and the responsibility to conduct themselves appropriately in the learning environment.

This has particular implications for exceptional students. Canadian courts have ruled that school boards must make *reasonable accommodations* with special education needs. In a landmark case, *Eaton v. Brant County Board of Education* (1997), the Supreme Court stated that "it is the failure to make reasonable accommodations to meet a child's needs which results in discrimination against disabled persons." This ruling has had significant implications for students identified as exceptional. School boards were required to make every reasonable effort to adapt the integrated classroom to meet the special needs of exceptional children. Only if "aspects of the integrated setting which cannot reasonably be changed interfere with meeting the child's special needs'" will the principle of accommodation "require a special education placement" outside the regular classroom. This case made it clear that school boards have a *duty to accommodate* and that "certain adaptations to the classroom such as the provision of a special desk, physical assistance and extra supervision from educational assistants were reasonable." Previously, school boards could claim that these accommodations constituted *undue hardship.*

The Education Quality and Accountability Office (EQAO) is one instrument used by the Ministry of Education to monitor and improve education outcomes in Ontario. This independent body conducts standardized provincial tests, including literacy and numeracy tests that are taken by all grade 3 and 6 students and a grade 9 mathematics test and a grade 10 literacy test that must be taken by secondary school students. These tests are administered by board personnel. According to *Regulation 298,* section 20(j), teachers must "co-operate and assist in the administration of the test under the *Education Quality and Accountability Act, (1996)."* These tests are then publicly disseminated, with the results often publicized by local media.

Members of the public can easily access these data by going to school and school board websites. The results often prompt schools to create action plans to improve literacy and numeracy outcomes for their students. Lately the Ministry of Education has been helping schools with poor results by sending out teams of experts to help teachers improve their results. While EQAO has led to greater accountability and public discussion of literacy and numeracy, there are concerns that these tests are unnecessarily intrusive and often place undue stress on students, teachers, and schools in areas of low socio-economic status. This is particularly so with the grade 10 literacy test, successful completion of which is a requirement for a student to obtain a secondary school graduation diploma.

HUMAN RIGHTS

Citizens of Ontario, including students in schools, are guaranteed freedoms and rights. These are enshrined in the *Canadian Charter of Rights and Freedoms* and Ontario's *Human Rights Code.*

Students, by virtue of being under the supervision of teachers acting *in loco parentis,* have more limited rights than other people in society. Some of these limitations were explored in the previous chapter, which focused on issues of good conduct and safety in schools. Nonetheless, students' human rights should be respected in the school setting.

As discussed in chapter 1, the *Charter of Rights and Freedoms* protects fundamental freedoms such as freedom of expression and freedom of conscience and religion. It also includes a wide range of legal rights, including the right to fair legal processes and security from unreasonable search and seizure. (See chapter 6.)

Ontario's *Human Rights Code*, enacted in 1962, protects people from discrimination in: employment; accommodation; contracts; goods, services, and facilities; and membership in vocational associations and trade unions. There are now fifteen possible proscribed grounds of discrimination, including race, ethnicity, religion, sex, sexual orientation, disability, and family status. The preamble to the document describes the purpose of the code as follows:

> ... its aim [is] the creation of a climate of understanding and mutual respect for the dignity and worth of each person so that each person feels a part of the community and able to contribute fully to the development and well-being of the community and the Province ...

Persons who believe they have been discriminated against by any individual or organization in Ontario may bring a complaint to the Ontario Human Rights Commission, the overall function of which is to promote and advance human rights in the public interest. This includes reviewing statutes, regulations, and policies that may be inconsistent with the code (section 29,d) and conducting inquiries into "incidents of tension or conflict" involving human rights (section 29,e).

While most complaints are resolved through negotiation at the commission, applicants can apply to have their complaints heard by the Ontario Human Rights Tribunal. If discrimination is proven, the respondent will be required to make accommodations for the complainant, unless there is a *bona fide* reason for the discrimination or the accommodation would cause "undue hardship."

Right to Freedom of Expression

Advocate for Illegal Drugs or Free Speech?

Kieran King, a fifteen-year-old student at Wawota Parkland School in Saskatchewan, was sceptical about a classroom lesson on the dangers of marijuana. He researched the effects of alcohol and tobacco use and told classmates that he considered cannabis the least dangerous of the three. After being informed by a student, the school's principal, Susan Wilson, called Kieran's mother to express concern. She also indicated that she was going to call in the police.

Kieran believed his freedom of expression was being violated, and planned a school walkout by students in support of free speech. Members of the Saskatchewan Marijuana Party, which he had contacted, were scheduled to attend.

When Kieran and several other students attempted to leave the school, school officials barred the doors, ordered a lockdown, and brought in the RCMP to conduct a threat-assessment against Kieran. A school superintendent was also videotaped stating that Kieran had been accused of selling drugs in school. According to his mother, Kieran had never been investigated or charged with possession or trafficking. Kieran was suspended for trying to leave the school and missed his final exams in June 2007.

This event generated considerable publicity in 2007. While nobody doubted that the school administration had the interests of the student population in mind, it was generally agreed that the principal and the superintendent had overstepped their authority and violated this student's rights. Illegal drug use is a major problem, but King's intellectual stance was misinterpreted as dangerous speech and he was falsely vilified by the superintendent as a troublemaker and even a drug dealer. The administration, unduly alarmed about escalating drug problems, inflamed the situation and lost sight of the student's right to freedom of expression.

This freedom also became a public issue in the case of *Hall (Litigation Guardian of) v. Powers* (2002). Mark Hall, a gay student in the Durham Catholic District School Board, wanted to take his male partner to the school prom. The principal refused to allow this, citing Roman Catholic doctrine opposing homosexual acts. While the court granted the school board an injunction, preventing Hall from attending the prom until after court case was heard, the judge claimed that "the role of a school is to enlighten and guide students—not to control their private thoughts or behaviour. He also added that a prom "is not part of the religious education component of the Board's activity" and is "not educational in nature." While this case was not pursued by Hall once the prom was over, the words of Justice McKinnon suggest that both public and Catholic schools are expected to respect students' right to freedom of expression.

Right to Freedom of Conscience and Religion

Is Islam Compatible with Women's Soccer in Canada?

In February 2007, a girl was expelled from a soccer tournament in Quebec for wearing a hijab, a head covering worn by some Muslim women as a sign of modesty. Asmahan Mansour, age eleven, had played two games already when she was expelled by a Muslim referee in the third game and her team forfeited its remaining games in protest.

The soccer association claimed that this was not a religious matter but one of banning headgear that could be unsafe to her and other players on the field. There was a furor as public opinion in Quebec revealed underlying fears that society was making too many concessions to religious and cultural minorities. Even Premier Jean Charest defended the official decision as reasonable.

Islamic groups defended the hijab as religiously important and as perfectly safe when tucked into a shirt.

---

(1) What are the facts of the situation?
(2) What are the grounds for banning the hijab from soccer?
(3) What are the grounds for permitting the hijab in soccer?
(4) Who do you think is right? Why?

> (5) Are there any ways in which a "reasonable accommodation"
> can be reached between religious freedom and player
> safety?

This incident, which has not been pursued in court, has many similarities to the case of *Multani v. Commission Scolaire Marguerite-Bourgeoys*. (See chapter 1.) At issue in that case was whether or not Gurbaj Multani should be allowed to wear a kirpan in school. Ultimately, the Supreme Court ruled that Gurbaj was so entitled, as long as it was sewn into his clothing in order to address safety considerations.

The *Multani* case, following the precedent of the *Eaton* case, discussed above, makes it clear that school boards must make every reasonable effort to accommodate students and teachers who may wish to observe their religious beliefs through their manner of dress or in other ways. As Mackay (2009) writes, "Diversity properly accommodated in the schools produces a sense of inclusion and belonging that is conducive to a safe and welcoming environment" (p. 58).

The case of *Islamic Schools Federation of Ontario v. Ottawa Board of Education* (1997), in which the school board was successful in defending its policies, illustrates suitable measures to put in place in order to reasonably accommodate students from religious minorities. In arriving at its decision, the Ontario Divisional Court considered the following steps taken by the board: (1) students were able to observe holy days; (2) examinations and other major events were not scheduled on holy days; (3) a multi-faith calendar had been distributed to all schools; (4) a document outlining religious observances and needs of students had also been distributed to all schools; (5) a board multiculturalism advisory committee was in place; (6) an anti-racism and race relations policy existed; and (7) space was provided for noon prayer meetings.

Urban school boards have already had to grapple with the challenge of reasonably accommodating diverse student populations. Their policies will serve as useful templates for other school boards across the province as their classrooms become more diverse.

Teachers are advised to develop differentiated learning activities and assessment tools in order to reasonably accommodate minority students in their classes. Rather than expecting all students to be the same, teachers should consider alternative ways to meet teaching and learning objectives.

RIGHT TO PRIVACY OF STUDENTS AND PARENTS

Information is power. While teachers and principals may not consciously think of themselves as having such power, they are often the guardians of important and sensitive information about students and their families. Teachers, therefore, must always be aware of students' and parents' right to privacy. They should not disclose information that may be regarded as private and confidential.

Ontario school boards must adhere to a range of laws concerning the collection and use of student information, including the *Education Act* and the *Municipal Freedom of Information and Protection of Privacy Act* (*MFIPPA*). The former gives school boards the authority to collect personal information about students when they register. By registering their children, parents are consenting to the potential use of the information in the interest of their child. Access to this information comes with a duty of care to ensure that it is properly stored and judiciously disseminated. Under *MFIPPA*, data such as name, address, ethnic background, blood type, and fingerprints are all considered personal information and subject to privacy provisions. This legislation also applies to information on employment, criminal history, financial dealings, and health records. This means the school board must treat teacher records with the same care as student records.

While these laws and their implications for professional practice are outlined below, there are two guiding principles for dealing with personal information:

- Do not divulge personal information without explicit consent.
- When in doubt, check with the school principal before divulging information.

In "Student Privacy and You," published in *Professionally Speaking* (March 2008), Graham F. Scott draws on recommendations by the Information and

Privacy Commissioner of Ontario and the Access and Privacy Office of the Ontario government to recommend "seven virtues" of privacy protection:

(1) Collect only as much personal information as you need to do your job.

(2) Collect information directly from individuals, or for students under 18, directly from their parents or guardians—not from third parties.

(3) Explain why you need to collect the information and exactly how it will be used.

(4) Get consent from students, or for students under 18, from parents, for the collection, storage and use of personal information.

(5) Store personal information securely. Keep hard copies under lock and key, such as in a locked filing cabinet; keep electronic documents on a password-protected computer. A clean desk will help prevent sensitive information being misplaced or stolen.

(6) When in doubt, ask for advice from the school principal or the board staff member in charge of privacy. (Ontario law requires every board to have one such contact person.)

(7) When you no longer need the personal information to do your job, destroy it by shredding paper documents or securely erasing electronic ones.

ONTARIO STUDENT RECORD

The Ontario Student Record (OSR) is the single most common and sensitive document that is readily accessible to teachers and other school board employees. The OSR Folder includes:

- report cards
- Ontario student transcript
- office index card—which includes family contact information
- documentation file
- custody orders
- verification of changes of surname
- Identification, Placement, and Review Committee (IPRC) report

- Individual Education Plans (IEPs)
- Violent Incident Reports
- educational/psychological/health assessments.

Access to these confidential documents is restricted. They should be kept under lock and key in a secure office area, available only to those authorized by law. According to section 266 of the *Education Act*, the OSR is "privileged for the information and use of supervisory officers and the principal and teachers of the school for the improvement of instruction of the pupil." Teachers and principals often review OSRs to develop an understanding of a student's progress over time. Educational assessments are particularly useful for teachers working with students who have identified exceptionalities. Although section 266 of the act makes it clear that student records are for the use of all the teachers in the school, many schools have established protocols to help maintain confidentiality and ensure appropriate use of the files.

These documents are also available for review to students of any age, as well as to the parents and guardians of minors (under the age of eighteen). Both custodial and non-custodial parents have a legal right to "access" the OSR, but this right may be thought of as a read-only privilege. The principal of the school determines the contents of each student's OSR, in accordance with the provision of the *Education Act*, subject to the authority of the appropriate supervisory officer. Section 266 of the act sets out an appeal process for parents who disagree with the principal's decision. Parents also have the right to meet with teachers to discuss their child's progress and attend Identification, Placement and Review Committee meetings. If they request copies of the file, the school may charge five dollars plus photocopying fees. The local medical officer of health has limited access to a student's OSR. An adjudicator appointed by the Ministry of Education may also review an OSR if there is a dispute regarding its contents.

Disclosure may also be permitted if information is requested through a court order under the criminal code, in a civil suit, or under the *Child and Family Services Act*. In such cases, the principal is advised by the Ministry of Education to consult school board legal counsel before turning over any records.

AVOIDING INAPPROPRIATE DISCLOSURES

Teachers are often very accommodating and eager to help. These virtues can sometimes land them in trouble when it comes to the disclosure of confidential information. Following are a few examples that may serve as cautions.

Scenario 1

Two teachers talk about a student while in a coffee shop. One casually mentions that the student has an educational exceptionality, and the other wonders if this may have contributed to his failing grade. A relative of the student overhears the conversation and complains to the school principal.

Lesson: Do not casually disclose/share confidential information about students, especially in public places.

Scenario 2

John is socially awkward and many students are annoyed by his rude and insensitive conduct on the playground. In order to help John, a teacher explains to the other students that John has mild autism, which makes it difficult for him to read social situations. She urges them to be more forgiving and accommodating. John's mother later telephones the teacher to object to this unauthorized disclosure of personal information.

Lesson: Never disclose or divulge confidential information about a student to other students or parents without the prior written consent of the individual student's parents or adult student, as the case may be.

Scenario 3

A teacher is contacted by someone purporting to be a lawyer representing one of a child's parents. The lawyer asks about the student's IPRC and grades. The teacher states that she is busy and offers to call back once she has collected information. The principal then cautions her not to divulge this information without the written permission of the parent or a court order. Later, she calls the lawyer's office number (which verifies his legitimacy) and is careful not to knowingly reveal information from the OSR.

Lesson: It is wise to verify the identity of a person requesting confidential information and to check with the principal to ensure that you are protecting the student's privacy rights. The same principles apply when dealing with Family and Child Services or local medical officials.

Scenario 4

A principal is routinely visited by the liaison officer of the local police division. The two regularly swap information about students (and staff) involved with the law. When requested, the principal shares a copy of the school yearbook for police investigation purposes. She believes she is being a good citizen by assisting the police.

Lesson: Conversations with the police involving the exchange of information should be conducted with care to ensure that private information is not offered without appropriate authorization. Technically, the names and photos of students in a yearbook constitute personal information.

CONSEQUENCES OF BREACHING PRIVACY

While wilfully disclosing personal information can result in a fine of up to $5,000 under *MFIPPA*, this is rare because most privacy breaches are inadvertent or accidental. Parents could also sue the school board in civil court but this is unlikely given the cost of litigation and the need to prove harm. Breaches of privacy could also involve a complaint being filed with the College of Teachers, possibly leading to a finding of misconduct. While the penalty may be little more than a reprimand, it is a needless blemish on a teacher's career.

The penalties are relatively minor, yet these laws and the scenarios above serve as cautionary tales to ensure that teachers make every effort to be sensitive to the privacy rights of students and their parents.

RIGHTS AND RESPONSIBILITIES OF PARENTS

"The joys of parents are secret; and so are their griefs and fears," wrote the sixteenth-century philosopher Francis Bacon (1597; 1965, p. 15).

The word *parent* has multiple layers of meaning. Obviously it is understood to refer to maternity and paternity. More generally, it is a legal term referring to parents by birth or adoption. Finally, the term may include the legal guardians, stepparents, or someone standing in the place of the parent. In this chapter, unless otherwise specified, the word is broadly defined to include parents and guardians as identified in law.

As society changes, our understanding of parents and families evolves. Teachers working in increasingly multicultural schools need to come to terms with very different conceptions of family and good parenting. They also need to recognize that changes to the legal definition of marriage and adoption laws mean that more children will grow up in non-traditional family units.

Teachers should always bear in mind that parents are the most important people in the lives of their children. Rich childhood experiences can contribute significantly to happiness and success in school and beyond. As Michael Howe (1990) writes in *The Origins of Exceptional Abilities*:

> Effective mothering in early childhood will usually give a child a good start in life. In most cases that will have beneficial long-term consequences, partly through a kind of snowballing effect. Other things being equal, a child who, as a result of the mother's effectiveness as a teacher, gains useful abilities that facilitate the acquisition of further useful skills will thereby have a definite advantage over less-favoured children. (p. 115)

Parents, like teachers, have a small number of rights and a large number of responsibilities. Instead of fundamental rights, they have conditional rights: rights connected with their obligation to provide for the rights and best interests of their children. The *Criminal Code* states that parents have a duty to give their children the "necessaries of life" until age sixteen. These include food, clothing, shelter, medical care, and education. Failure to supply these is punishable by up to two years in prison. The code also makes it illegal for a parent to abandon a child or expose a child under ten to danger. Ontario's *Child and Family Services Act* empowers the state to remove children from abusive parents. These legal responsibilities often pale in comparison with the moral and practical responsibilities that weigh heavily on parents.

Outside the home, schools are the most important institutions in most children's lives. The time they spend in school is critical to their intellectual and social development. Parents, as caregivers, have every right to take an interest in the education their children are receiving during this time. While teachers as professionals are empowered to make educational decisions for the students in their classrooms, they are also accountable to parents. Parents' requests and demands on the school system, which sometimes may seem unreasonable to teachers, stem from their secret joys, griefs, and fears.

Teachers and schools can be most effective in the education of children when they keep in close communication with the home and work together in an atmosphere of mutual respect and understanding.

EDUCATIONAL RIGHTS AND RESPONSIBILITIES

As noted earlier, a child has a fundamental right to be educated, and parents have a legal responsibility to ensure that a child of mandatory school age attends school. Failure to do so can result in prosecution.

It was also noted that parents have the right to make decisions regarding where and how their children are educated. This includes choosing publicly funded education from English-language or French-language boards and between public and Catholic education. The *Education Act* also excuses a person from attendance at school if "the person is receiving satisfactory instruction at home or elsewhere" (section 21(2)(a)). This permits parents to enrol their children in private school or to opt for homeschooling.

Homeschooling

According to section 21(2) of the *Education Act*, parents may choose to have their children educated at home instead of at school so long as they are receiving "satisfactory instruction" (which is not defined). Over the years, the number of children who are schooled at home has risen to more than 20,000.

Homeschoolers are highly diverse. They include families that duplicate school at home, complete with textbooks, assignments, and report cards. They also include families that have a conception of learning involving children and adults living and learning together in a holistic manner. Some Christian homeschoolers select the homeschooling option because they are not comfortable with the values underlying publicly funded schooling in Ontario. Others, such as parents of students with special education needs, may believe that the school system cannot meet their children's unique learning needs. Students may be homeschooled for their entire education, or they may mix that form of schooling with periods of time in public or private schools.

Homeschooling involves a significant commitment by families. Parents must invest considerable time ensuring that their children learn. Many families make significant financial sacrifices to allow a parent to stay at home with the children. Many of these families enter into relationships with other homeschoolers in their communities. The Internet has also made it easier for parents to access quality educational resources at home, including lesson plans and assessment instruments.

The Ministry of Education, in Policy/Program Memorandum #131 (June 2002), requires parents who are homeschooling their children to provide their school board annually with a letter of intent. This letter is to include names, ages, and gender of the school-age children and an indication that the parents understand their responsibility to provide for the education of their children as indicated in section (21)2 of the *Education Act*. The memorandum also directs school boards to excuse children of compulsory school age from attendance at school once the board has received this notification from the family. School boards are no longer required to investigate the adequacy of homeschool instruction, unless they are given reason to do so. Indeed, "the board should accept the written notification of the parents each year as evidence that the parents are providing satisfactory instruction at home" and provide educational resources to support homeschooled children. These changes reflect the success of the homeschool movement in articulating its case to policy-makers and in presenting clear evidence that homeschooling does not diminish educational outcomes.

IMMUNIZATION OF STUDENTS

Schools, as public places in which large numbers of children congregate, are particularly susceptible to outbreaks of disease. The *Immunization of School Pupils Act* was enacted to ensure that students are immunized against designated diseases. Parents are now required to have their children immunized in order to be admitted to school. One school board created a local controversy when it notified delinquent parents that their children would not be allowed to attend school if they had not completed an immunization form or a form exempting their child for medical reasons or for reasons of religious or conscientious belief.

The local medical officer of health may order a school to suspend students who have not been immunized to avoid an outbreak or in the event of an outbreak. Principals are also required to refuse admission to persons whom they believe are infected with or have been exposed to communicable diseases.

HEALTH AND MEDICAL INFORMATION IN SCHOOLS

Parents are responsible for the health and well-being of their children. They bear the responsibility to inform the school of any medical or health information that the school may need in order to respond to medical emergencies, allergic reactions, or other health situations that may arise. They then have the right to assume that the school acting *in loco parentis* will take reasonable steps to use this information to ensure the safety of their children. Indeed, one of the duties of the school principal, according to section 265(j) of the *Education Act*, is to "give assiduous attention to the health and comfort of the pupils." In order to assist the school, parents are required to provide updated medical and health information on their children. Teachers, as appropriate, are then informed of health risks and how to prevent or respond to situations that may arise.

Medication in Schools

In the past, principals and teachers have sometimes been reluctant to administer medication to students, and have sought to have the parents themselves administer the medication at home or at school. Students have the right to take medication in school, and parents in our day and age cannot reasonably be expected to be available during the school day. As a result, schools now have a duty to administer medication when necessary. This duty is balanced with parental obligations.

The *"Medication" Procedure (PR 536 SCH)* of the Toronto District School Board (TDSB) illustrates the obligations of schools and parents in ensuring children's right to good health. It states that designated staff members are authorized to administer essential medication, but only when it is:

- prescribed by a physician
- essential to the student's attendance at school
- required to be taken during school hours
- unable to be self-administered
- not reasonably able to be administered by the parents at school.

The TDSB also stipulates parental obligations. A parent and a physician are required to complete *Form 536A, The Administration of Prescribed Medication* before medication can be administered. This form requires the following:

- a set of clear instructions
- one week of medication, clearly labelled
- encouragement of the student to wear medical alert bracelet/ pendant
- dissemination of information by principal to staff/volunteers
- Waiver of Liability (which does not cover negligence).

Sabrina's Law, 2005

Sabrina Shannon, a thirteen-year-old from Pembroke with a dairy allergy, died at school in 2003 after eating French fries containing traces of cheese. Two years later, a private member's bill passed in the Ontario legislature requiring all Ontario school boards to have protection plans in place by January 2006.

Sabrina's Law states that school boards shall establish and maintain policies to deal with the health needs of students with anaphylactic allergies. These policies are designed to reduce risk of exposure to causative agents by disseminating information on life-threatening allergies, and providing regular training for all employees and others in direct contact with students on a regular basis.

Principals are required to develop an individual plan for each pupil with an anaphylactic allergy. These plans should include:

- sharing detailed information with all employees
- asking all parents/pupils about allergies at registration
- keeping a current file of treatment information, instructions from physician/nurse, and emergency list.

CONSENT FOR HEALTH CARE

If an individual has the capacity to provide consent under the *Health Care Consent Act*, teachers and principals need to receive consent before beginning treatment. This consent is for the *administration* of medication and in no way implies that the school board employee is responsible for the treatment itself (e.g., determining the appropriateness of the medication or the dosage).

The law offers no specific age of consent, but common law suggests the following general guidelines. If the student is over sixteen, s/he is capable of giving informed consent. If the student is under twelve years of age, s/he cannot give informed consent. Educators are advised, when dealing with the intermediate range, ages twelve to sixteen, to obtain consent from both parents and students.

With regard to emergency situations, Sabrina's Law authorizes school employees to administer epinephrine or other prescribed medication without preauthorization. They are also immune from civil court action for damages if they acted in good faith, unless they are found guilty of gross negligence.

DEFAMATION AND PARENTAL HARASSMENT

Concerns about the educational process can often lead to strong emotions in students, teachers, and parents. While the vast majority of people discuss issues and concerns thoughtfully and respectfully, some cross the line and behave unacceptably.

Defamation, in the educational context, refers to intentional, false statements about a student, teacher, or parent, damaging to his or her reputation. While defamation can involve any of these parties, it is parents who are most likely to be charged with defamation. The courts recognize that parents have a qualified privilege to file complaints against educators, but court rulings in cases such as *McKerron v. Marshall* (1999) demonstrate that there is little sympathy for malicious public statements.

Teachers and administrators have sometimes been accused of defamation for the comments they make on student report cards or teacher performance appraisals. Brown and Zuker (2002) write in *Education Law* that judgments made by school personnel "are not defamation, assuming that they are statements of fact or *bona fide* professional observations" (p. 122). There is a growing recognition of parental harassment among educators, who are increasingly taking stands against disruptive parents. In a national poll on school violence, the Canadian Teachers Federation found that 59 percent of principals across the country in 2001 had witnessed at least one parent verbally abuse a teacher that year; 23 percent reported seeing a parent physically assault or intimidate a teacher. It is possible that criticism of teachers in the media has made parents more aggressive and teachers more defensive.

One way to address these issues is to develop effective lines of communication with parents. Teachers who provide parents with regular newsletters and telephone calls are more likely to enjoy positive relations with parents. Regardless of the level of communication, intimidation and harassment are never acceptable behaviours.

Educators who think they are being harassed should document all incidents and consult the principal for direction, which may include consulting board guidelines for responding to harassment. Options in serious cases may also include contacting the police to investigate possible criminal harassment charges, and pursuing civil action such as defamation suits or restraining orders. In most cases, the principal's power to exclude the parent from the school premises is sufficient to address the issue.

School boards are beginning to develop parent harassment protocols in order to prevent, and, when necessary, respond to harassment. These protocols are included in parent handbooks. Lawyer R.G. Keel (2001) writes:

> Boards should consider any case of harassment to be the responsibility of the board and not the individual employee. Otherwise, the failure to act can create morale issues or could result in friction with a union or association representing the employee. (p. 64)

Tips for Effective Parent–Teacher Collaboration

Presume Good Intentions
- Parents and teachers want what is best for the child but may differ in how to achieve it.
- Each brings knowledge (e.g., observations on behaviour and past actions) and expertise that are crucial to enhancing learning.
- Overworked teachers should be sensitive to the stresses facing parents today.
- Exhausted parents need to respect the challenges of teaching diverse students in today's classrooms.
- Each child is special and deserves consideration of his/her unique learning needs.
- Parents and teachers who presume good intentions and work as allies are effective in helping the child grow.

Strategies for Teachers Working in Collaboration with Parents
1. Avoid Conflict by Acting/Appearing Professional
   - Provide detailed information.
   - Record multiple assessments and observations.
   - Save samples of student work.
   - Present materials in a polished manner.
   - Celebrate the student, even as you raise areas for improvement.
   - Offer some strategies that other parents have found useful.
   - Be careful not to explicitly or implicitly criticize their parenting.

2. Set the Stage for Success
   - Arrange ample time to talk.
   - Greet parents warmly, and acknowledge their commitment, knowledge, and expertise.
   - Commit to working together to help their child learn.

- Share information about the student's performance in school, past and present.
- Ask for information about the child at home and in other contexts.
- Ask about family experiences that may help you better understand the child.

3. Develop and Implement an Education Plan
   - Teacher and parents together prioritize needs.
   - Teacher develops a plan of action for student learning at school.
   - Parents develop strategies to support the education plan.
   - Ongoing communication—e.g., e-mailing list of upcoming assignments, occasional notes or telephone calls—about good and bad news.
   - Review progress and adapt expectations accordingly.
   - Recognize that learning involves change, and that trial and error is part of the process.
   - Support one another in the challenges you are facing together.
   - As you address the educational challenges, always think of the student as a worthwhile person to be nurtured.

SCHOOL COUNCILS

There is a growing trend toward greater parental involvement in education. Since 2000, school boards in Ontario have been required to establish school councils for each school in their jurisdiction (*Education Act*, section 170). These councils must meet at least four times a year, and meetings are open to the public. According to *Regulation 612/00*, their purpose is, through the active participation of parents, to improve pupil achievement and to enhance the accountability of the education system to parents. The primary means by which school councils achieve their purpose is making recommendations to the principal and school board on educational matters. The operative word here is *recommendations*, because the school council is not a decision-making body with authority over the principal or school board. Nevertheless, the principal or school board is required to advise the council of the action taken in response to a recommendation.

Regulation 612/00 outlines a number of areas where the school board and principal must consult the council. School councils may *make recommendations* to the principal on such matters as:

- school year calendars
- codes of student behaviour
- curriculum priorities
- programs and strategies to improve school performance on provincial and school boards tests
- safe arrival programs (elementary schools)
- communications to parents and communications to the community
- community use of the school, and community programs and services provided at the school through school-community partnerships
- school board policies that will affect the school
- selection of principals.

However, it would not be appropriate for the council to discuss individual teachers or students.

Parents must form a majority of the school council members. The principal is a member, though s/he is not eligible to vote. Other members include: a teacher (elected by peers); another employee of school (elected by secretaries, custodians, educational assistants, etc.); a student representative (selected by student council in secondary schools); at least one community member appointed by school council; and, where appropriate, a representative appointed by the home and school association. There are guidelines in place concerning the announcement and reporting of school council activities.

Many school councils are not very active and do not attract many parents or teachers to their meetings. This is unfortunate, for two reasons. First, such councils can be co-opted by disgruntled parents with specific agendas or grievances. Second, they have the potential to bring teachers and parents together to support one another's work. Although the school council, as noted above, has no authority over the principal, a wise principal will try to work with the council as much as possible. In many schools, the school council is active in raising supplementary funds for school activities. Also, school council meetings can serve as a place for principals to vet potentially controversial issues with parents. For example, a new sex education unit or anti-bullying initiative may be presented to parents for feedback.

Some visionary principals strive to attract large gatherings by promoting these meetings and inviting interesting guest speakers. These principals understand that the school council can be an enormous force for good in a school. The members of the council are often the school's strongest supporters and can help the school develop as a learning community that promotes excellence for all students.

Regulation 612/00 also permits school councils to engage in fund-raising activities, provided that the activities are conducted in accordance with board policy and the purpose of the fundraising is also authorized by the board. Although fund-raising is not one of the stated purposes of school councils, many councils do spend considerable time and energy on various fund-raising projects throughout the year, providing supplementary resources for the school.

ONTARIO COLLEGE OF TEACHERS

If students or parents think that their rights have been violated by a teacher, they can file a written complaint with the Ontario College of Teachers. The mandate of the College is to investigate complaints against members in order to ensure that the students, parents, and the general public have confidence in the education system. If a teacher's or principal's behaviour toward students or parents is deemed to constitute professional misconduct, the member may be disciplined by the College.

Teachers can be investigated for incompetence based on a complaint by a member of the public. For example, after a dispute resolution, one teacher who "lacked the skills for effective delivery and evaluation of the required curriculum and for effective classroom management" took a course of instruction and accepted additional conditions after a complaint from a member of the public (*Professionally Speaking*, September 2005).

Another teacher, who "used inappropriate language and shared unacceptable personal information," was cautioned for lacking appropriate boundaries in his interactions with students (*Professionally Speaking*, March 2007).

The importance of respecting the Educational Quality and Accountability Office's procedures for ensuring accountability was highlighted in a case involving a school superintendent. ARB was reprimanded and suspended for "failing to adequately supervise persons under his professional supervision" when he "remained silent where teachers under his supervision advised scribes to disobey protocols established by EQAO in the administration of the OSSLT [Ontario Secondary School Literacy Test]. The panel found that ARB's silence constituted tacit agreement that EQAO protocols should be disregarded" (*Professionally Speaking*, March 2007).

CHECKING YOUR UNDERSTANDING

- Both the right to an education and the obligation to attend school are enshrined in Ontario's *Education Act*.

- All persons between the age of six and eighteen must attend school, unless legally excused. Legal excuses include homeschooling, attendance at a private school, illness or other unavoidable cause, and achievement of a secondary school diploma.

- All persons have the right to attend school, without payment of fee, in the jurisdiction of the school board in which they qualify to be a resident pupil.

- Schools are required to make every reasonable accommodation to meet the educational needs of individual students.

- Schools must try to balance the rights of the individual with the safety of everyone.

- Every student has an Ontario Student Record, including report cards, documentation file, office index card, and transcript (in secondary schools).

- The OSR is for the use of supervisory officers and the principal and teachers of the school "for the improvement of instruction" of the student.

- "Students of any age and parents of students who are minors are entitled to examine the OSR," according to section 266(3) of the *Education Act*.

- The contents of the OSR are confidential and must not be disclosed to a third party without the written consent of either the parents of a student who is a minor or the student who is an adult.

- Parents who homeschool their children have to provide the school board with an annual letter of intent. The school board is not required to monitor homeschooling unless there is reason to do so.

- Students who are not immunized against certain diseases may be excluded from school.

- Schools are expected to administer necessary medication to students within board guidelines.

- Sabrina's Law requires all school boards to have policies and procedures in place to deal with anaphylactic allergies. School personnel may administer prescribed medication without prior authorization in emergencies.

- Parents and teachers are most effective when they work together as partners in the education of children. Teachers who are subject to defamation or harassment by parents should consult their principal and federation representative.

- Every school in Ontario is required to have a school council, consisting of a majority of parents. The council's role is to make recommendations to the principal/board in an effort to improve the effectiveness of the school. The principal/board must advise the council of action taken in response to a recommendation.

• Although the council may make recommendations on any matter, it would not be appropriate for the council to discuss individual teachers or students.

• When the rights of parents and students are not being met, a complaint could be lodged with the Ontario College of Teachers.

APPLYING YOUR UNDERSTANDING

Accommodating Religious Diversity

June Callwood Public School is a diverse school in a suburb of a large city. Immigration in recent years has caused a dramatic increase in the number of students from Sikh households. The school has made efforts to accommodate students of different religious backgrounds by informing staff of Sikh customs and holidays, not scheduling major assignments on Sikh holidays, providing a prayer room for Muslim students, and permitting days off for religious observance. At the school council meeting, a group of parents demanded that the school and school board schedule Sikh holy days into the school year calendar. They said they intended to pursue their right to religious accommodation in the courts if their demands were not met.

(1) What are the human rights issues? How might Ontario's *Human Rights Code* and the *Canadian Charter of Rights and Freedoms* apply in this case?

(2) Has the school made reasonable accommodations? Explain.

(3) Do you think the parents would be successful if they pursued this case before the courts? Explain.

CHAPTER 8

SPECIAL EDUCATION LAW: MEETING THE NEEDS OF STUDENTS WITH EXCEPTIONALITIES

After reading this chapter, you will be familiar with the legislative frame-work for special education in Ontario, including the processes involved in identification, placement, and review. Decisions by the courts and the Ontario College of Teachers will be used to illustrate the rights of students with exceptionalities and the responsibilities of the educators who serve them.

Eli has struggled in school from the beginning. His grade 2 teacher wonders if he has a learning disability, but Eli's parents do not want him tested. What can be done?

Mr. Arar sits at his desk exhausted at the end of another day of teaching a challenging class that includes four students with identified exceptionalities, three students learning English as a Second Language, and several other students who are having difficulty academically. The principal drops by to inform him that a parent has formally complained that Mr. Arar is not following the detailed strategies listed in her daughter's Individual Education Plan. What can be done?

The school team would like to place Toni in a regular grade 5 class. Her parents believe that her needs will be served better in a self-contained special education classroom. What is best for Adele? Who decides?

The right to an education is a fundamental tenet of liberal democracy. This right is enshrined in the *Declaration of the Rights of the Child* (United Nations, 1959) and implicit in Canada's *Charter of Rights and Freedoms* of 1982. In Ontario it is made explicit in the *Education Act*, where every person who qualifies has the right to attend a school free of charge (section 32(1)). The educational needs of students who are "exceptional," however, were often neglected prior to the 1980s. Even today, in an era when special education programs and placements exist across Ontario, the education of students with exceptionalities remains an issue of contention in schools and in the courts.

Two pieces of legislation have played a critical role in ensuring that special education is provided to meet the needs of exceptional learners in Ontario: the *Canadian Charter of Rights and Freedoms* and the *Education Amendment Act*, generally known as Bill 82.

The *Charter* guarantees every Canadian "the right to life, liberty, and security of the person" (section 7). This right has been interpreted by courts to include the right to an education (*R. v. Kind* (1984)). The court ruling on *Andrews v. Law Society of British Columbia* (1989) further clarified *Charter* rights by stating that the "accommodation of difference ... is the true essence of equality." This decision has led to provisions such as wheelchair ramps in buildings and permission for alternative testing for persons with learning exceptionalities. Canadian courts now expect that school districts will make reasonable efforts to accommodate students with identified special needs. Section 15 of the *Charter*, which guarantees equality before the law, has been used by parents to challenge schools boards in cases involving a student's right to reasonable accommodations.

Bill 82 (*Education Amendment Act*) amended the *Education Act* in 1980 to include provisions for special education in Ontario schools. Whereas school boards previously had the option of providing special education services, the principle of universality underlying Bill 82 means that all public school boards are now obliged to offer programs and services to all students with identified exceptionalities. Due process and the right to review identification and placements were also enshrined in the legislation. The process for identifying and placing students with exceptionalities today has changed little from what was outlined in this landmark piece of legislation, which reflected a shift from ignorance—ignoring, marginalizing, and institutionalizing exceptional learners—to an awareness that all learners benefit from being full participants in diverse learning environments.

While "special education has become a normal, integral, and functional part of the system" (Bennett & Dworet, 2008, pp. 18–19), the identification, placement, and review processes can involve parents, teachers, and principals in considerable debate, paperwork and, at times, litigation. It is important that all educators have a broad understanding of the rights of learners with exceptionalities, special education law in Ontario, and the administrative processes involved.

SERVING THE NEEDS OF STUDENTS WITH EXCEPTIONALITIES: PAST AND PRESENT

Until recent times, people with special needs were generally ignored. The Greek philosopher Aristotle believed that people who were deaf were incapable of reason. In medieval times, intellectual or behavioural disabilities were often regarded as signs of demonic possession. Carnival freak shows in the nineteenth century often exhibited physically disabled people such as John Merrick (the Elephant Man). By the early twentieth century, institutions were established to meet the needs of some people with disabilities. In particular, segregated settings provided services for children with physical exceptionalities: for example, sign language for those with hearing impairments, Braille for those with visual impairments, and wheelchairs for those who could not walk. On the other hand, people with intellectual or behavioural exceptionalities were often harshly treated in asylums and reformatories. As Bennett & Dworet (2008) write:

> Under a principle of concern for the public good, and a seemingly well-intentioned concern for the less able, supporters of eugenics were successful in effecting a policy that not only segregated people with special needs, but in practical terms, isolated them. (p. 8)

In the 1960s and 1970s, advocacy by parents and educators dissatisfied with unsatisfactory educational opportunities for students with exceptionalities led to increased awareness. These efforts culminated in the *Individuals with Disabilities Education Act* (1977) in the United States and Bill 82 in Ontario (1980).

Programming, placements, and curriculum for students with exceptionalities have changed considerably since the 1970s. Instead of focusing on "presumed underlying cognitive processes that caused disabilities ... teachers shifted toward providing remedial academic instruction at each student's level of functioning" (Gersten, Baker, Pugach, Scanlon & Chard, 2001). Many excellent special education programs have been developed to meet the needs of special education students generally as well as the specific needs of students with particular exceptionalities.

There is also a general understanding that persons with disabilities have fundamental rights. This is reflected in Canada's decision to ratify the *United Nations Convention on the Rights of Persons with Disabilities* in 2010. By becoming a signatory to this agreement, the federal government committed Canada to:

- change laws that discriminate against individuals with disabilities
- eliminate barriers to accessibility in schools, hospitals, parks, and new housing
- ensure that people with disabilities are treated equally in the justice system
- accommodate students with disabilities in elementary and secondary schools in their community
- foster respect for the rights and dignity of people with disabilities.

This treaty could lead to an increased commitment to special education in Canada and to a greater role for the courts in affirming and promoting education rights for learners with exceptionalities.

Currently, in Ontario and around the world, there is a movement to inclusionary schooling as the primary means of addressing exceptional learning needs. Segregation in special classrooms is increasingly viewed as a violation of human rights, because it denies access to the larger learning environment (McPhail & Freeman, 2005). Bunch & Valeo (2004) call on classroom teachers to take responsibility for all learners in the class. Attention has shifted to "the creation of forms of teaching that can reach out to all learners within a class and ... the establishment of school conditions that will encourage such conditions" (Ainscow, 2008, p. 244). In 2007 there were 191,902 students identified as exceptional in Ontario's publicly funded school system who were receiving special education services, and another 98,823 not formally identified but still receiving services (Ministry of Education, as cited in Bennett & Dworet, 2008). Both ethical and economical concerns therefore suggest the need for greater inclusivity.

Inclusion has become the norm in Ontario since the Supreme Court ruled in the case of *Eaton v. Brant County Board of Education* (1997). While advocates for learners with exceptionalities were disappointed that the court rejected the parents' insistence that their child be placed in a regular classroom rather than a special class, they were pleased by the court's affirmation that consideration must first be given to placement in regular classroom with appropriate special education supports. In response to the public debate concerning this issue, the Ontario Ministry of Education strengthened its resolve to favour inclusion, as is evident from the *Special Education Transformation* report (Bennett & Wynne, 2006). This report clearly states that, in cases in which special education classes are the only option, these "placements would be duration-specific, intervention-focused, and subject to regular reviews" (Bennett & Wynne, 2006, p. 8).

For inclusion to be successful, regular classroom teachers will need extensive professional development. Their thinking and teaching methods need to be shifted so they can support the 15 percent of students who require some form of special education services. There is evidence to suggest that initial teacher education and ongoing professional development go a long way in engendering in teachers and principals the attitudes and skills needed to effectively address the learning of all students (e.g., Praisner, 2002).

THE EDUCATION ACT ON SPECIAL EDUCATION

Special education provisions were incorporated into the *Education Act* when the *Education Amendment Act* of 1980 (Bill 82) received royal assent. While the broad provisions of Bill 82 remain, the last thirty years have seen many amendments to the legislation. The key provisions regarding special education in the current *Education Act* are identified below. Section 170(1)(7) states that it is the responsibility of school boards to "provide or enter into an agreement with another board to provide in accordance with the regulations special education programs and special education services for its exceptional pupils." Section 1(1) states: "Special education program ... means, in respect of an exceptional pupil, an educational program that is based on and modified by the results of continuous assessment and evaluation and that includes a plan containing specific objectives and an outline of educational services that meets the needs of the exceptional pupil." An "exceptional pupil" is defined in section 1(1) as "a pupil whose behavioural, communicational, intellectual, physical or multiple exceptionalities are such that he or she is considered to need placement in a special education program." The responsibility of the Minister of Education, according to section 8, subsection 3, is to "ensure that all exceptional children in Ontario have available to them, in accordance with this Act and the regulations, appropriate special education programs and special education services without payment of fees by parents or guardians." This section also indicates that the minister shall "provide for the parents or guardians to appeal the appropriateness of the special education placement" and that, to this end, the minister shall:

(a) require school boards to implement procedures for early and ongoing identification of the learning abilities and needs of pupils, and shall prescribe standards in accordance with which such procedures be implemented; and

(b) in respect of special education programs and services, define exceptionalities of pupils, and prescribe classes, groups or categories of exceptional pupils, and require boards to employ such definitions or use such prescriptions as established under this clause.

The *Education Act* also provides for the establishment of an Ontario Special Education Tribunal to provide final and binding arbitration in disagreements between a parent and school board concerning the identification or placement of an exceptional pupil.

Special Education Regulations in Ontario

The provisions in the *Education Act* are supplemented by a number of regulations made under the authority of the act. These include:

- *Regulation 181/98: Identification and Placement of Exceptional Pupils*, which governs: the identification and placement of exceptional pupils; IPRC reviews; appeal procedures; and the role of parent(s)/guardian(s) in these processes.

- *Regulation 306: Special Education Programs and Services (SEP)*, which defines the requirement for each school board to maintain a special education plan for the delivery of special education programs and services under the authority of the Minister of Education.

- *Regulation 464/97: Special Education Advisory Committees*, which outlines the role, requirements, and scope of Special Education Advisory Committees (SEACs) at the school board level. A SEAC, which is comprised of representatives of parent advocate groups and school board trustees, is charged with the responsibility of making recommendations "in respect of any matter affecting the establishment, development and delivery of special education programs and services for exceptional students of the board" (*Regulation 464/97*, section 11(1)). This group also plays a significant role in the review of SEP and the budget for special education services.

Other legislation relevant to special education is included in *Regulation*

298: Operation of Schools-General and *Regulation 296: Ontario Schools for the Blind and Deaf.*

Special Education Policy Documents

While the overarching legal requirements governing special education are outlined in the *Education Act* and its accompanying regulations, teachers are guided in their professional practice by many policy and planning documents issued by the Ministry of Education.

For example, *Individual Education Plans: Standards for Development, Program Planning and Implementation* (2000) outlines in considerable detail the standards teachers and principals need to apply in developing, implementing, and monitoring Individual Education Plans (IEPs).

Special Education: A Guide for Educators (2001) is a good general guide to the topic. In addition, many of the elementary and secondary program and curriculum policy documents also include guidance for teachers working with students with exceptionalities.

Education for All: The Report of the Expert Panel on Literacy and Numeracy Instruction for Students with Special Education Needs, Kindergarten to Grade 6 (2005) offers recommended practices "based on research, that would allow Ontario's teachers to improve and reinforce instruction of reading, writing, oral communication, and mathematics to students from Kindergarten to Grade 6 who have special education needs" (p. 1). *Learning for All*, scheduled for publication in 2010, builds on the principles in *Education for All* and applies them to elementary and secondary education.

These and other educational resources from the Ontario Ministry of Education can be found at http://www.edu.gov.on.ca/.

THE IDENTIFICATION, PLACEMENT, AND REVIEW PROCESS

While the regular school curriculum and program meets the needs of most students, some students require modifications—or even significant accommodations—to the program in order to have the opportunity to learn.

The process typically begins when a teacher or parent identifies a student whose learning needs merit discussion. The first intervention may involve the teacher and resource teacher adjusting the instructional practice or the program to meet specific needs. Alternatively, or subsequently, the student may be referred to the "in-school team"—which generally consists of the principal (who leads the team), a special education resource teacher, one or two classroom teachers and possibly, other personnel—who may be called on to recommend other interventions and develop an Individual Education Plan for the student.

The "response to interventions" is then assessed by the team. If the team determines that problems still persist despite the steps taken so far, it may recommend that the principal initiate the formal referral process for identification and placement.

The principal of the school may then decide to refer the student, with written notification to the parents, to an Identification, Placement, and Review Committee (IPRC). An IRPC consists of at least three members, one of whom must be a principal or superintendent of the board.

Note that although the process outlined above is typical of many schools, the legal responsibility for referring a student to an IPRC rests with the principal, who could initiate the referral process at any time. The principal must also refer a student to an IPRC at the written request of the parents.

Parents of the student (and students who are sixteen years of age or older) are entitled to be present and participate in all IPRC discussions about the student. They are also entitled to be present when the committee's decisions are made, although they are not entitled to be part of the final decision making. Experts such as educational psychologists may be called on to administer a battery of educational tests and provide an overall assessment of the student's level of exceptionality. Once students are identified as exceptional, they are placed in a classroom setting appropriate to their needs and an

Individual Education Plan is developed. The regulation governing the identification and placement of exceptional pupils directs the IPRC to consider the integration of exceptional pupils into regular classes before considering a placement in a special education class, provided that this meets the pupil's needs and is consistent with parental preferences. There are also processes for reviewing the student's situation each year and parents have opportunities to appeal school board decisions if they believe their children's needs are not being served.

The schema below, which was developed by Sheila Bennett and Don Dworet for *Special Education in Ontario Schools* (2008), outlines the main features of *Ontario Regulation 181/98*.

Figure 9-1

IDENTIFICATION AND PLACEMENT OF EXCEPTIONAL PUPILS

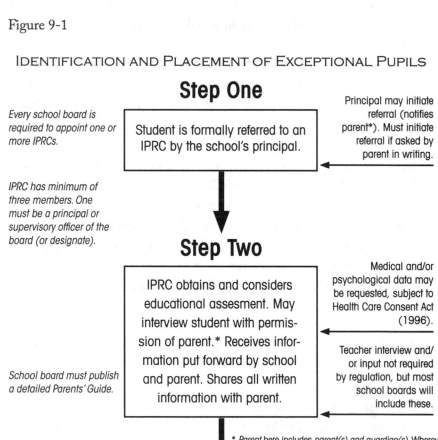

Step One

Every school board is required to appoint one or more IPRCs.

Student is formally referred to an IPRC by the school's principal.

Principal may initiate referral (notifies parent*). Must initiate referral if asked by parent in writing.

IPRC has minimum of three members. One must be a principal or supervisory officer of the board (or designate).

Step Two

IPRC obtains and considers educational assesment. May interview student with permission of parent.* Receives information put forward by school and parent. Shares all written information with parent.

Medical and/or psychological data may be requested, subject to Health Care Consent Act (1996).

Teacher interview and/ or input not required by regulation, but most school boards will include these.

School board must publish a detailed Parents' Guide.

* *Parent* here includes *parent(s) and guardian(s).* Wherever *parent* appears, note that students 16 years and older may be part of the process along with parent.

Step Three

IPRC must consider all information and proposals for special education programs and services.

Parent may present proposals in addition to those from school board.

Parent entitled to have a representative of choice present.

Parent and representative may participate in all discussions except decision making.

Written decision of IPRC goes to parent, referring principal, and school board.

Parent may request IPRC meet again to reconsider.

Step Four

IPRC decides student is not exceptional.

or

IPRC identifies student as exceptional, and decides on a placement. May make recommendations (but not decisions) regarding programs and services.

Process ends, unless parent appeals, or requests follow-up meeting.

Decision statement must list placement, category(s) and definition(s) of exceptionality, and student's strengths/needs.

Placement to be regular class if it meets needs, and if parent wishes. IPRC must give reasons if special class is chosen.

Within 30 school days principal of school where student is placed must see to development of IEP and for 14 year olds and older, a Transition Plan.

Rights and requirements as in Step One to Five.

Step Five

Student is placed according to IPRC decision. IEP is developed and implementation begun.

If parent signs consent or if consent is not signed, but parent does not appeal.

Step Five stayed if parent appeals.

Identification and Placement
How the IPRC works
A recommendation in the fall of 2006 from the then Deputy Minister outlined what for some school boards across Canada would be a shift in practice with regard to IPRC. The memorandum suggested that school boards re-examine their procedures around IPRC and consider dispensing with a formal IPRC process in those cases where the board and parent were in agreement that the student's placement be in the regular classroom.

Review

Student's situation to be reviewed at least once every school year by an IPRC. Parent may request review after three months.

Reviews confirm existing situation, or may make changes. Principal to review and update IEP.

In Cases of Appeal
Step One (A)

Parent may appeal identification as exceptional, or placement, or both.

Parent and/or representative entitled to participate in all discussions except decision making.

School board convenes a three member Appeal Board to review the IPRC material and decisions.

One member chosen by board; one by parent; the two select a third as chair (in case of disagreement, chair is chosen by MoE).

Step Two (A)

Written recommendation to parent, principal, school board and chair of IPRC.

Appeal Board agrees with IPRC and recommends its decisions be implemented,
or
disagrees with IPRC and makes recommendation to school board about identification or placement or both.

May interview anyone whom Appeal Board chair feels has information to contribute.

Written reasons must accompany written statement of recommendation.

Step Three (A)

School board considers recommendation and decides what action to take.

School board is not limited to recommendation of Appeal Board.

Written decision of school board goes to all parties.

Step Four (A)

School board decision is implemented.

If parent signs consent
or
if consent not signed but parent does not appeal.

Step Four (A) stayed if parent appeals.

Final appeal stage is to Special Education Tribunal.

Identifying Students with Exceptionalities

In the *Education Act*, section 1(1), under the definition of "exceptional pupil," five broad categories of exceptionality are recognized: (1) behavioural; (2) communicational; (3) intellectual; (4) physical; and (5) multiple. The categories and definitions of exceptionalities are outlined in *Standards for School Boards' Special Education Plans* (Ontario Ministry of Education, 2000, pp. 32–34) as follows:

Behaviour

A learning disorder characterized by specific behaviour problems over such a period of time, and to such a marked degree, and of such a nature, as to adversely affect educational performance, and that may be accompanied by one or more of the following:

  a) an inability to build or to maintain interpersonal relationships;

  b) excessive fears or anxieties;

  c) a tendency to compulsive reaction;

  d) an inability to learn that cannot be traced to intellectual, sensory, or other health factors, or any combination thereof.

Communication

Autism

A severe learning disorder that is characterized by:

  a) disturbances in:

   – rate of educational development;

   – ability to relate to the environment;

   – mobility;

   – perception, speech, and language;

  b) lack of the representational symbolic behaviour that precedes language.

Deaf and Hard-of-Hearing

An impairment characterized by deficits in language and speech development because of a diminished or non-existent auditory response to sound.

Language Impairment

A learning disorder characterized by impairment in comprehension and/or the use of verbal communication or the written or other symbol system of communication, which may be associated with neurological, psychological, physical, or sensory factors, and which may:

a) involve one or more of the form, content, and function of language in communication; and

b) include one or more of the following:

- language delay;
- dysfluency;
- voice and articulation development, which may or may not be organically or functionally based.

Speech Impairment

A disorder in language formulation that may be associated with neurological, psychological, physical, or sensory factors; that involves perceptual motor aspects of transmitting oral messages; and that may be characterized by impairment in articulation, rhythm, and stress.

Learning Disability

A learning disorder evident in both academic and social situations that involves one or more of the processes necessary for the proper use of spoken language or the symbols of communication, and that is characterized by a condition that:

a) is not primarily the result of:

- impairment of vision;
- impairment of hearing;
- physical disability;
- developmental disability;
- primary emotional disturbance;
- cultural difference; and

b) results in a significant discrepancy between academic achievement and assessed intellectual ability, with deficits in one or more of the following:

- receptive language (listening, reading);

- language processing (thinking, conceptualizing, integrating);
- expressive language (talking, spelling, writing);
- mathematical computations;

c) may be associated with one or more conditions diagnosed as:
  - a perceptual handicap;
  - a brain injury;
  - minimal brain dysfunction;
  - dyslexia;
  - developmental aphasia.

Intellectual

Giftedness

An unusually advanced degree of general intellectual ability that requires differentiated learning experiences of a depth and breadth beyond those normally provided in the regular school program to satisfy the level of educational potential indicated.

Mild Intellectual Disability

A learning disorder characterized by:
  a) an ability to profit educationally within a regular class with the aid of considerable curriculum modification and supportive service;
  b) an inability to profit educationally within a regular class because of slow intellectual development;
  c) a potential for academic learning, independent social adjustment, and economic self-support.

Developmental Disability

A severe learning disorder characterized by:
  a) an inability to profit from a special education program for students with mild intellectual disabilities because of slow intellectual development;
  b) an ability to profit from a special education program that is designed to accommodate slow intellectual development;
  c) a limited potential for academic learning, independent social adjustment, and economic self-support.

Physical

Physical Disability

A condition of such severe physical limitation or deficiency as to require special assistance in learning situations to provide the opportunity for educational achievement equivalent to that of pupils without exceptionalities who are of the same age or developmental level.

Blind and Low Vision

A condition of partial or total impairment of sight or vision that even with correction affects educational performance adversely.

Multiple

Multiple Exceptionalities

A combination of learning or other disorders, impairments, or physical disabilities, that is of such nature as to require, for educational achievement, the services of one or more teachers holding qualifications in special education and the provision of support services appropriate for such disorders, impairments, or disabilities.

Special Education in Ontario Schools, sixth edition (2008)
by Sheila Bennett and Don Dworet with Ken Weber

This book, written for new and practicing teachers, provides an overview of special education in Ontario, including government policies, administrative procedures, and classroom practices.

It also includes chapters on particular exceptionalities. These chapters, accompanied by short case studies, begin by identifying misconceptions, defining the exceptionality, and listing characteristics. They include information about how these students are served in Ontario schools. Each chapter concludes with a list of strategies for teachers.

The Placement of Students with Exceptionalities

Once a student has been identified as exceptional through a written decision of the IPRC, the next step is to identify an appropriate placement in the school system. If a student's needs cannot be met in the regular classroom, a range of placement options is available. These include:

- *A regular class with indirect support* where the student is placed in a regular class for the entire day and the teacher receives specialized consultative services.
- *A regular class with resource assistance* where the student is placed in a regular class for most or all of the day and receives specialized instruction, individually or in a small group, within the regular classroom from a qualified special education teacher.
- *A regular class with withdrawal assistance* where the student is placed in a regular class and receives instruction outside the classroom, for less than 50 percent of the school day, from a qualified special education teacher.
- *A special education class with partial integration* where the student is placed by the IPRC in a special education class in which the student–teacher ratio conforms to *Regulation 298*, section 31, for at least 50 percent of the school day, but is integrated with a regular class for at least one instructional period daily.
- *A full-time special education class* where the student–teacher ratio conforms to *Regulation 298*, section 31, for the entire school day.

Another option is for the IPRC to refer a student to a provincial committee for consideration of eligibility for admission to one of the provincial schools for blind, deaf, or deaf-blind students, or to one of the Provincial Demonstration Schools for students with severe learning disabilities.

Although a parental preference for a regular classroom setting must be taken into account, the committee may decide that a special education setting is more appropriate to the student's needs. A parent who agrees with the identification and placement made by the IPRC is required to consent in writing to the statement of decision. A parent who does not agree may request a meeting with the committee to discuss revising the decision. If these discussions do not result in an amended statement of decision, the parent has the right to appeal the decision to a special education appeal board convened at the local level. A parent who is still dissatisfied with the decision of the appeal board may appeal to a provincially appointed Special Education Tribunal. Its decision is final and binding.

As the decision in *Eaton v. Brant County Board of Education* affirmed, while parents have the right to express a preference for regular rather than special classes, it is nevertheless up to the IPRC, appeal board, or, ultimately, provincial tribunal to determine what is in the best educational interests of the child. The role and legal rights of parents will be explored in more detail later in this chapter.

Individual Education Plan

Good educators, recognizing that the starting points for lesson planning are the students not the textbook or curriculum document, adapt their teaching to the learning needs and preferences of their students (Ontario Ministry of Education, 2007). One way of meeting these needs and preferences is to develop individual student learning profiles. Such profiles, which are beneficial to any students who need extra attention, are legally required for students who have been formally identified as exceptional and are receiving accommodations or modifications to their programs.

An Individual Education Plan (IEP) is a written plan that describes the special education program and/or services to be provided for a particular student. According to *Individual Education Plans* (2000), an IEP

> identifies learning expectations that are modified from or alternative to the expectations given in the curriculum policy document for the appropriate grade and subject or course, and/or any accommodations and special education services needed to assist the student in achieving his or her learning expectations. (p. 3)

Accommodations are the teaching strategies, supports, and/or services that provide students with access to the curriculum and enable them to demonstrate learning. Modifications are changes made to the grade-level curriculum expectations for a subject or course to meet the needs of the student.

As noted above in the discussion of the IPRC process, IEPs are often created for students with special education needs, even if they have not been formally identified. However, *Regulation 181/98* requires educators, once a student has been formally identified as exceptional and placed in a suitable classroom environment, to develop an IEP. Standards for developing such plans are outlined in *Individual Education Plans* (2000) by the Ontario Ministry of Education. As with the identification and placement, parents have thirty days to appeal the contents of the IEP.

While the IEP outlines all the necessary accommodations and modifications, teachers are expected to use their professional judgment in how they incorporate these provisions into their daily lesson planning. Many lesson plan templates include space for teachers to identify curriculum and instruction modifications for exceptional learners.

One of the main benefits of an IEP is that it helps teachers and parents monitor and discuss a student's progress and, as appropriate, periodically update the record to reflect student progress over time. Continuous assessment and evaluation of student achievement culminates in an annual review of goals and learning expectations. While regular and special education teachers are primarily responsible for the implementation of the IEP, the principal and the school board are responsible for ensuring that IEP requirements are met.

Review of Identification and Placement
A review of the identification and placement must be performed at least annually, unless the parent dispenses with the review in writing to the principal. The principal of the school may refer a student to an IPRC for review at any time. Note that a parental request for review may be made only *after* the placement has been in effect for three months. From then on, such a request may be made only once in every three-month period. The guidelines for the review process are set out in *Regulation 181/98: Identification and Placement of Exceptional Pupils,* section 21. Most of the time, the focus will be the refinement of the IEP to better meet the needs of the child or to revise expectations and strategies in

response to changing developmental and learning needs. Of particular concern may be the student's transition from elementary to secondary school or transition out of schooling. The review process may also be an opportunity for educators or parents to challenge the identification or placement, except in the cases of students who are identified as gifted.

Funding for Special Education

Special education is primarily provided at the local level. The Ontario Ministry of Education allocates funding to each school board using a formula that is based on student enrolment and the unique needs of students in each board. Most of the funding comes in the form of a Foundation Grant providing a basic level of funding for each student. This is supplemented by a Special Education Grant (SEG), which provides additional funding for students who need special programs, services, and equipment; this funding is enveloped so it can be used only for the students who have been funded through this grant.

Most of the SEG comes in the form of a Special Education Per-Pupil Amount (SEPPA) allocated to boards on the basis of total enrolment. SEPPA recognizes the cost of providing additional assistance to the majority of students with special education needs. This is supplemented by the High Needs Amount and Special Equipment Amount to address the additional costs of supporting students who require supports well beyond that required by most students with exceptionalities.

RESOLVING IDENTIFICATION OR PLACEMENT ISSUES

The identification, placement, and review process works well for most of Ontario's 290,000 students who receive special education programs and services. Through consultation and discussion, parents, administrators, teachers, and support professionals are generally able to agree on the needs of the student and on the programs and services that will best meet those needs.

Appealing an IPRC Decision

There are times when parents and the school board cannot agree on special education programs and services. Parents who are not satisfied have several options under special education legislation. The first step is to request a follow-up meeting with the IRPC. If the two sides are still not in agreement, the parent has thirty days to appeal the decision in writing to the school board's Special Education Appeal Board. The final administrative body to which a parent may appeal is the *Ontario Special Education Tribunal* (*Education Act*, section 57). This body, which has statutory powers of decision making, is required to hold a hearing if asked to do so, and both parties have the right to be represented by lawyers, call witnesses, and cross-examine witnesses. The decision of this body is final and binding on both parties, though either side can request that its decision be reviewed by a court.

The courts have played a useful role in clarifying sensitive special education issues. The *Eaton* case provides clarification concerning a school board's right to determine that a special education placement may be preferable to an integrated placement. An appeal could be made to the Divisional Court, where a three-judge panel would hear arguments from lawyers for both sides. The first category of judicial review concerns procedural fairness. The appellant would need to prove that the Special Education Tribunal failed to meet the standards of procedural fairness outlined in the *Statutory Powers Procedures Act* or rules of procedural fairness in common law. A challenge could also be made concerning the tribunal's decision. The courts "exercise a considerable degree of deference to administrative tribunals when reviewing the substance of their decisions" (Bowlby, Peters & Mackinnon, 2001, p. 160).

This was evident in the Supreme Court's ruling in favour of the school board in the *Eaton* case. The Court acknowledged that special education is a necessary adaptation for students with exceptionalities. It also gave legal recognition to the benefits of social integration. While the Court placed a high burden on school boards to justify limiting access to programs and services, it made clear that the right of access is not an absolute right. While reasonable accommodations should be made, they are subject to "reasonable limits," such as not imposing "undue hardships" on the system. This ruling was reinforced by the Supreme Court's decision in *Auton v. British Columbia (Attorney General)* (2004). The Court declined to order the government to fund Applied Behaviour Analysis (ABA) for children with autism, arguing that it was a non-core medical service.

The Court's deference to education authorities is also evident in a land-mark Ontario case involving students with autism spectrum disorders. The rights of autistic children has been an area of recent litigation as the diagno-sis of autism has dramatically increased and as effective yet expensive treat-ments have emerged. Can parents compel school boards to provide and pay for highly expensive ABA?

Wynberg v. Ontario (2006)

The government of Ontario began providing funding for a form of Applied Behaviour Analysis, an intensive early intervention program, for children up to five years old with autism spectrum disorders. This one-to-one therapy, generally recommended for very young children, typically ranged from twenty to forty hours a week for one to two years. Because of high demand, and a lack of qualified service provid-ers, many children were unable to access this service before the age cut-off. The parents in this case sought to require the government or school boards to extend similar assistance to school age children with autism.

In the initial trial, the judge agreed with the parents that exclusion from the program and the failure of schools to provide ABA constituted discrimination on the basis of age and disability, thus violating equality guarantees in the *Charter of Rights and Freedoms*.

The Ontario Court of Appeal subsequently overturned the decision of the trial judge on the grounds that equality rights had not been infringed. The court ruled that the program had been targeted at the two-to-five age group since its inception and that this was generally viewed to be most effective with children in that age group.

Furthermore, the appeals court concluded that the Ministry of Education was not obliged to provide a particular program of special education. It has the option of offering other appropriate programs or services to that group. The judges found that "the existing jurisprudence does not permit us to interpret section 7 of the *Charter* as imposing a constitutional obligation on the appellant to ensure that every school-age autistic child has access to specific educational services." Schools had the option of offering other appropriate programs or services to that group, including ones that were not as costly as ABA.

> (1) Why did the Ontario Court of Appeal overturn the decision of
>   the trial judge?
> (2) Do you agree with this decision? Consider the implications for
>   parents and educators.

Legal scholar Wayne Mackay (2009) argues that while the equality provisions in section 15 of the *Charter* have not led to significant changes in
special education legislation,

> the greater impact of s. 15 on special education has been to provide a
> vehicle through which parents can challenge school board and govern
> ment decisions on the programs and services to be provided to excep-
> tional students. (p. 83)

Mediation

As the legal process is slow, cumbersome, and costly, the Ministry of
Education has been actively promoting mediation as an alternative means
of resolving special education issues. The *Special Education Transformation*
report (Bennett & Wynne, 2006) promotes this mediation as preferable to
appeal boards and tribunals. Also, given that the courts have consistently
respected the judgment of school boards, parents are more likely to have an
impact in this forum.

Mediation is a voluntary and consensual dispute resolution process. The
mediator, an experienced and neutral third party, works with the two parties to resolve the issues under dispute. Both parties typically agree that the
matters discussed in mediation are protected from disclosure in court should
mediation not be successful.

As Bowlby, Peters & Mackinnon (2001) observe:

> Mediation is also an extremely flexible method of dispute resolution.
> Mediation provides parties the opportunity to be creative in finding a

resolution to their dispute. The parameters of the resolution are not limited by the possible outcomes of litigation but only by the imagination of the parties. (p. 98)

Once an agreement is reached, a mediation agreement is drawn up and signed by the mediator, the school board, and the parents.

Shared Solutions: A Guide to Preventing and Resolving Conflicts Regarding Programs and Services for Students with Special Education Needs (Ontario Ministry of Education, 2007)

The best way to prevent, minimize and/or resolve conflicts concerning special education is for educators and parents to treat each other with respect and work together through transparent decision-making processes. This document by the Ontario Ministry of Education offers strategies that can help prevent and resolve problem.

For example, it indicates that a "culture of collaboration" can help parents and educators work constructively together to address concerns related to programs and services before they become sources of conflict. To create such a culture, boards and schools need to promote a positive school climate and establish effective lines of communication among parents, students, and educators (p. 19).

The document has the following to say about a shared perspective between parents and educators:

> Disagreements may arise and strong emotions may surface when people discuss complex issues such as programs and services for students with special education needs. Knowing how to prevent conflicts from escalating and/or resolve them cooperatively helps maintain a climate where all students thrive. Where the parties already have a good relationship,

options and seeking creative, student-focused solutions to problems.

While both educators and parents are seeking solutions to address complex problems, it is important for all parties to balance strong advocacy of their own views with a commitment to inquiry—a willingness to ask and respond to questions to clarify all parties' understanding of the issues and positions under discussion. Inquiry and exploration enable participants to discover or disclose their own and others' reasoning and assumptions and enhance each party's awareness and appreciation of other points of view. The use of an inquiry approach allows participants to avoid over-commitment to unrealistic positions, to build on one another's insights, and to work together to arrive at a shared solution (pp. 20–21).

This document is available at: http://www.edu.gov.on.ca/eng/general/elemsec/speced/shared.pdf.

Special Education and the College of Teachers

According to the Ontario College of Teachers' standards of conduct, teachers have a professional responsibility to attend to the learning needs of their students. Specific responsibilities related to special education include:

- following board policies and procedures for special education
- working with parents and special education staff to develop and review IEPs for students with exceptionalities
- implementing the IEP in the classroom
- communicating progress to parents.

Teachers who work with exceptional learners have a particular obligation to be sensitive to the heightened vulnerability of their students and to their specific learning needs. In the OCT case quoted below, it is likely that the vulnerability of the exceptional student was a factor in the decision to revoke the teacher's professional certification.

Case #1 (March 2006)
Decision: Certificates Revoked

A panel of the Discipline Committee held a public hearing October 17, 2005, into allegations of professional misconduct against EA, otherwise known as SA. EA was certified to teach in 1985 and was employed as a learning resource teacher by the Hamilton-Wentworth District School Board. The member did not attend the hearing nor was she represented by counsel.

EA faced eight allegations of professional misconduct related to inappropriate conduct with male students.

In the absence of the member, the chair of the panel entered a plea of not guilty on EA's behalf.

The panel heard that during the 2000–01 school year, EA was a learning resource centre teacher at a high school. Her role was to support students identified with exceptionalities through the Identification, Placement, and Review Committee.

A former student at the school where EA taught testified that he met her outside the school on a number of occasions including at his home and at hers. The student said that on one occasion, when EA had invited him to her home to learn more about Judaism and Sabbath customs, the member kissed him. Although he stopped her and became upset, she asked him to go to bed with her. The student then left.

The student said that, following the incident, he was uncomfortable in EA's presence in the learning resource centre and called in sick if he thought he couldn't avoid meeting her. The student testified that EA made many calls to him, which he tried to avoid by checking the call display whenever he could.

EA also came to his home to deliver personal gifts on a number of occasions, some of them accompanied by cards or notes signed "Love S."

The student told the panel that he felt that his failure to complete his secondary education was a direct result of his interactions with EA and the anxiety they produced in him.

College counsel presented evidence of a number of e-mails from EA to the student, most of them signed with the member's first name, in which she disclosed personal information about herself, her relationship with her family, employer and friends. EA also continued to communicate with the student after saying she would not.

A superintendent of the Hamilton-Wentworth District School Board told the panel that attempts to interview EA about the allegations resulted in one session with the member and her counsel, who ended the meeting. EA's employment was terminated in January 2004.

The panel found that EA was guilty of professional misconduct in that she violated the boundaries that should exist in the teacher-student relationship and engaged in sexual abuse in kissing the student and inviting him to make love to her.

The panel ordered that EA's Certificates of Qualification and Registration be revoked.

In its written reasons, the panel said that EA had the power to influence the conduct and actions of students and had exercised that power against the best interests of the student. Since EA did not attend to present a defence, the panel felt it could not determine if she would engage in similar misconduct if placed in a position of trust and authority over other students.

---

1. What evidence is there that the teacher's conduct was unprofessional?
2. Why might this conduct be particularly harmful to a learner with an exceptionality?
3. Do you think that the penalty imposed by the Discipline Committee was appropriate?

The College also requires teachers to treat students with exceptionalities equitably. While the OCT case summary quoted below does not reveal the teacher's motivation for not including the student with special needs on the field trip, it is possible that the teacher wanted to avoid extra work or responsibility.

Case #2 (September 2007)
Decision: Caution by the Investigation Committee

Following notification by an employer, the Registrar initiated a complaint against a member of the College. The Registrar alleged that the member lied to the parent of a student with special needs regarding the existence of a class trip.

As a result of the incident, the board placed a letter of reprimand on the member's file.

On May 25, 2007, the Investigation Committee ratified an MOA between the member and the College, in which the member:

- admitted the above-described conduct
- agreed to be cautioned, in writing, by the Investigation Committee
- agreed to complete a course of instruction, pre-approved by the Registrar, regarding appropriate and effective communication
- agreed to provide the Registrar with a written report, prepared by the course practitioner, indicating her successful completion of the course.

Teachers should also be vigilant in complying with the standardized testing procedures of the Education Quality and Accountability Office (EQAO) when providing supports for students taking provincial tests. A teacher (KP) was reprimanded, suspended for six months, and required to complete a course on professional ethics. The summary of the decision in *Professionally Speaking* (September 2007) states:

> In reaching its decision, the panel considered the fact that, but for the circumstances related to the charges, many in her professional community consider KP to be a dedicated, capable and caring teacher.

The panel wrote:

> The protocols of EQAO were clearly defined in detailed written instructions to schools and provided to the member. The member deliberately chose to disregard the protocols, particularly with respect to scaling of individual students' tests, time allowances and responding inappropriately to students' queries during the test. By these actions, the member failed to maintain the standards of the profession.

With regard to suspension of her certificates, the panel considered KP's demotion and transfer by her board, consequent loss of salary, and damage to her reputation. The panel wrote:

> The reprimand, the six-month suspension and the course on ethics are appropriate in these circumstances. These sanctions act as specific deterrents to ensure that the member understands the consequences of her behaviour and will not engage in similar behaviour.

CONCLUSION

Teachers, whether in a regular or special education classroom, have a duty to ensure that they attend to the identified learning needs of students with exceptionalities in their classes. While they do not necessarily need a detailed knowledge of all special education policies and procedures, they should have a heightened awareness of these students' statutory right to an education that is consistent with their Individual Education Plans. Teachers who attend to the special learning needs of these students can have a very positive impact on their success in school and life.

CHECKING YOUR UNDERSTANDING

- Bill 82 (*Education Amendment Act*) amended the *Education Act* to include provisions for special education in Ontario schools.

- The *Canadian Charter of Rights and Freedoms* has been interpreted by the courts to mean that school boards should make reasonable efforts to accommodate students with identified special needs.

- The *Education Act* requires school boards to provide special education programs and services, including early and ongoing procedures for identifying students with special needs and abilities.

- The school board is also required to establish a Special Education Advisory Committee (SEAC), which may make recommendations about any aspect of the board's special education program and services.

- The *Education Act* identifies five broad categories of exceptionality: (1) behavioural; (2) communicational; (3) intellectual; (4) physical; and (5) multiple.

- The principal of the school may, with written notice to the parents, refer a student to an Identification, Placement, and Review Committee established by the board, one of whose members must be a superintendent or principal of the board.

- The principal must refer a student to an IPRC at the written request of the parents.

- Although the parents (and students over sixteen) may participate in the IPRC deliberations, they are not part of the final decision making.

- The IPRC is required to consider the integration of exceptional pupils into regular classes before considering a placement in a special education class.

- A review of the identification and placement must be performed at least annually, unless the parent gives written notice to the principal dispensing with the review.

- Parents who are dissatisfied with the IPRC's decision may ask to have it revisited. If still dissatisfied, they may appeal to a local appeal board and, ultimately, a provincial tribunal the decision of which is final.

- Because the appeal process is lengthy and expensive, the Ministry of Education encourages mediation as an alternative means of resolving special education issues.

APPLYING YOUR UNDERSTANDING

Special Gifts, Special Classrooms

Raheem Singh is identified as intellectually gifted in an IPRC meeting. The committee develops a series of enrichment recommendations for his teacher to implement.

Raheem's parents are sceptical that his gifts, particularly his prodigious mathematical abilities, can be nurtured in a regular classroom setting. They have observed Raheem becoming increasingly bored, distracted, and socially isolated at school. Also, they have observed that his academic motivation has declined significantly and worry that he will not be able to reach his potential unless he leaves the mainstream classroom. They are convinced that the best placement for their son is a classroom with other gifted learners.

The school board does not have any "congregated" gifted classrooms and, instead, relies on classroom teachers to differentiate the program in order to serve high ability students.

The Singhs refuse to sign the report of the Identification, Placement, and Review Committee.

(1) What are the next steps in the process?
(2) What can the IPRC do to allay the concerns of Raheem's parents?
(3) What options are available to the Singhs?
(4) What are some possible outcomes of this case?

CHAPTER 9

TEACHERS IN THE WORKPLACE

After reading this chapter, you will have a greater understanding of employment law issues, the teacher appraisal process, and several operational issues that affect the daily lives of teachers.

Can I be fired if I refuse to carry out an order by the principal?

How many times will I be evaluated each year? Who will carry out the evaluation?

I am qualified to teach in the Primary/Junior divisions but my principal wants me to teach a grade 7 class. Can she do this?

A student in my grade 6 class refuses to stand for *O Canada*. He says it is against his religion. What should I do?

How often can I be asked to carry out playground duty each week?

A senior student keeps signing himself out of my class, saying he is an adult. Is he allowed to do this?

This book has laid great emphasis on teaching as a professional activity grounded in a legislative framework and an ethic of caring. It is important to remember that teachers are also employees of school boards. As such, they have the same duties and responsibilities to their employer as any other person employed in a workplace setting.

THE TEACHER AS AN EMPLOYEE OF THE SCHOOL BOARD

Teachers' professional lives are governed by many laws. As you have seen in earlier chapters, the professional rights, responsibilities, and duties of teachers are outlined in common law, school acts, and similar legislation governing publicly funded schools, and in codes of professional conduct.

The *Education Act* empowers school boards to hire and fire teachers. It also establishes a framework for collective agreements between school boards and teacher federations. These collective agreements, which have become increasingly complex, govern issues ranging from salaries to hours of instruction to procedures for dealing with grievances by school boards or employees.

PERSONAL CRIMINAL HISTORY

Under *Regulation 521/01*, school boards are required to collect a "personal criminal history" of everyone who is either an employee of the board or a service provider at one or more school sites. As employees, teachers are required to submit a criminal background check before they begin employment with the board and an offence declaration before September 1 during each subsequent year of employment.

LINES OF AUTHORITY

Although a teacher may be interviewed and hired by the school principal or a specially convened hiring committee, legally the local school board is the teacher's employer and the individual contract of employment is between the school board and the teacher.

The school board has the overall responsibility at the local level for running the school system, but individual trustees have no executive authority. School boards have authority only insofar as they act as a corporation to formulate and approve board policy. Under the *Education Act*, the director of education appointed by the school board acts as chief executive and chief education officer with ultimate administrative and executive authority, working within the frameworks of board policy and provincial legislation.

The superintendents appointed by the board to assist the director in carrying out the various administrative functions are generally assigned responsibility for a family of schools within the board. Each family may consist of one or two high schools along with their elementary feeder schools. These area superintendents may often be seen in schools, meeting with the principal or individual teachers, and representing the senior administration at ceremonial occasions, such as graduation and awards assemblies.

Classroom teachers are under the direct authority of the school principal. Under the *Education Act*, the board is required to appoint a principal for each school in its jurisdiction, and, as has already been noted, the principal has overall authority for the organization and administration of the school, subject to the authority of the appropriate superintendent. As mentioned earlier in this book, principals may properly be considered, from a professional point of view, as the principal teacher of their school, because principals are also bound by many of the same legal duties as teachers. However, in labour relations terms, the principal, as the board's agent, is the manager of the school and therefore the immediate supervisor of teachers in the school. Principals often experience tension between their role as principal teacher and as manager. This tension was inevitably heightened by the removal of principals and vice-principals from the Ontario Teachers' Federation in 1997. Since they are no longer fellow federation members, principals and vice-principals are often viewed as administrators with little in common with the daily concerns and practice of the classroom teacher. Wise principals tread a very careful line between these two roles. They understand the difference between management and leadership, and the truth of the adage that one can only lead with the consent of the led.

The role of vice-principal is not defined precisely in the *Education Act*. A board is not required to appoint a vice-principal for a school, although most secondary schools and large elementary schools have at least one or two full or part-time vice-principals. The vice-principal is required to perform duties as assigned by the principal of the school and, in the absence of the principal, be in charge of the school and perform the duties of the principal. In hierarchical terms, the vice-principal may be thought of the second in command, who shares the authority of the principal in the daily operation of the school.

Getting Along with Your Principal
- Be committed to your classroom and your students.
- Be modest and appreciative.
- Know school procedures, as outlined in handbooks and memos.
- If you're not sure, don't be afraid to ask, but "bundle" your questions.
- Keep a file or binder of memos from the office.
- Obey the rules.
- Share with your principal the interesting things you are doing in the classroom.

Teachers in Charge of Organizational Units

The *Education Act* does not clearly define the place of department heads in the chain of command in a secondary school or of division leaders in an elementary school. Boards are not required to appoint people to these roles, although most secondary schools and some large elementary schools do have personnel in various positions of responsibility. The number of such positions and the nature of the units for which they are responsible are usually matters negotiated between the board and the local federation affiliate. For example, while many boards have maintained traditional subject discipline departments in secondary schools, some have chosen to amalgamate these departments into larger groupings, each overseen by an area chair. Section 14(3) of *Regulation 298* sets out the terms of reference for such teachers:

> A board may appoint for each organizational unit of an elementary or secondary school a teacher to direct and supervise, subject to the authority of the principal of the school, such organizational unit.

While the words *in charge of* and *direct and supervise* indicate the leadership role of the department head or division leader, the lack of any explicit statutory powers or duties makes it difficult to determine the precise nature of their authority. For example, these heads or leaders play no direct role in the performance appraisal of teachers but may be asked to assist a teacher who is perceived by the principal as needing improvement. Board policy could, of course, elaborate the expectations for positions of responsibility, provided that the expectations remain within the terms of reference of the *Education Act*. Even though the place in the chain of command of teachers in positions of responsibility is not well defined, classroom teachers do have a legal duty to cooperate with them, as well as with consultants and coordinators. This duty is established in *Regulation 298*, section 20(c):

> Where the board has appointed teachers under section 14 or 17, [a teacher shall] co-operate fully with such teachers and with the principal in all matters related to the instruction of pupils.

At the very least, teachers in the organizational unit should be willing to attend department/team meetings convened by the teacher in charge, collaborate in developing third-generation curriculum documents at the school level, and cooperate fully in ensuring consistency across sections of the same course in secondary schools and among classes at the same grade level in elementary schools.

TEACHING ASSIGNMENTS

Because it is the duty of a teacher "to teach diligently and faithfully the classes or subjects assigned to the teacher by the principal" (*Education Act*, section 264(1)(a)), a teacher has a legal duty to teach the classes or subjects assigned by the principal.

While teachers may express preferences, it is ultimately the principal, as the person in charge of the organization and management of the school, who has the authority to assign classes and duties to teachers. In secondary schools, department heads, in consultation with members of their department, may be given the responsibility for drafting a proposed allocation of classes and courses, but these are just recommendations to the principal, who makes the final determination.

The legal authority of the principal to assign classes is limited by further wording in *Regulation 298*, which limits the nature of the classes that teachers can be assigned. Section 19 essentially states that teachers can be assigned or appointed to teach *only* those classes or subjects that they are qualified to teach according to their certificate of qualification issued by the Ontario College of Teachers. The principal, therefore, cannot insist that a teacher teach a class for which the teacher does not hold appropriate qualifications, if the teacher is unwilling to do so.

There are two subsections elsewhere in section 19 that provide some flexibility in the match between qualifications and classes assigned, provided that both the teacher and principal are in agreement. To understand these subsections, it is important to understand the distinction made in the legislation between "general studies" and "technological education." For convenience, general studies may be thought of as any subject or course that is not listed in the technological education guidelines.

The first subsection providing some flexibility states that a teacher whose certificate indicates qualifications in the primary division, junior division, intermediate division in general studies, or senior division in general studies may, by mutual agreement of the teacher and the principal (and with the approval of the appropriate supervisory officer), be assigned or appointed to teach in a division or a subject in general studies for which no qualification is recorded. For example, a teacher in an elementary school who is qualified in the primary/junior divisions could, by mutual agreement, teach in grade 7 or 8. A secondary school teacher qualified to teach geography and physical education in the intermediate/senior divisions could teach mathematics, if the teacher is willing to do so and is deemed to have an appropriate background.

There are some important limitations to this flexibility. For example, a teacher without the necessary qualifications cannot be placed in charge of a school library program, guidance program, or special education program. In some subject areas, teachers without the relevant qualifications cannot teach more than the equivalent of two credit courses a year. These areas are art, business studies, guidance, family studies, instrumental and vocal music, and physical education. And there are other subjects that can be assigned only to teachers who have the appropriate qualifications. These include French as a second language, English as a second language, design and technology, technological education, and special education.

The second subsection providing some flexibility in the regulation applies to teachers qualified in technological education. Such teachers may teach a subject in technological education for which no qualification is recorded on their certificate of qualification, by mutual agreement of the teacher and the principal (and with the approval of the appropriate supervisory officer). However, technological education teachers cannot teach senior division courses in technological education unless they have grade 11 and 12 qualifications in the area.

There are other provisos and exceptions in section 19 of *Regulation 298*, but the above summary gives a general outline of the way in which the principal's right to assign teachers to classes and subjects is limited by legislation. *Regulation 298* says nothing about the number of classes or courses that the principal may assign; this matter is for school boards and federations to negotiate.

THE ROLE OF THE FEDERATION IN THE WORKPLACE

Although the Ontario Teachers' Federation plays no formal part in the hierarchical structure of the district school board, the local affiliates do provide the classroom teacher with advice and support, including legal support where necessary.

Each of the four affiliates—Elementary Teachers' Federation (ETFO), Ontario Secondary Teachers' Federation (OSSTF), Ontario English Catholic Teachers' Association (OECTA), and l'Association des enseignantes et des enseignants franco-ontariens (AEFO)— is recognized as a trade union under the *Ontario Relations Labour Act* and bargains collectively for its members.

The local branch of the affiliate in each jurisdiction negotiates a separate collective agreement with the individual school board. The collective agreement includes a salary grid for teachers based on years of experience and category placement. OSSTF has its own internal system for providing Certification Rating Statements to its members for category placement purposes. The other three affiliates require their members to apply to the Qualifications Evaluation Council of Ontario (QECO) for a Statement of

Evaluation. Teachers are rated on the basis of their academic background and trade records.

Several other job-related items in addition to salary scale are typically negotiated at the bargaining table by the local affiliate. These include: insured benefits, such as coverage for prescription drugs and dental services; sick leave entitlement and retirement gratuity; working conditions, which typically cover such matters as preparation time, supervision time, and the number of hours a teacher can be required to teach in a day; provisions regarding seniority, transfer, and lay-offs; and a "just cause" clause, without which employers would be able to discipline teachers or terminate their employment far more easily.

Most contracts also include a detailed grievance procedure, which sets out the protocols to be followed if an individual teacher, the local affiliate as a whole, or even the school board believes that the terms of the contract have been violated. From the classroom teacher's perspective, the grievance procedure means that the local affiliate will support and assist a teacher who it believes has been given an inappropriate assignment or required to carry out an order contrary to the intention of the collective agreement. Typically, grievance procedures include an informal stage during which the immediate supervisor is given an opportunity to resolve the matter within a limited time period, and a formal stage that may include mediation and ultimately lead to arbitration. Since most grievance procedures have a strict set of time lines, a classroom teacher who thinks that he or she has been unjustly treated by the principal or vice-principal should immediately consult the federation representative at the school level. The representative will be able to advise the teacher how best to proceed and will help the teacher through the process.

Collective Agreements

Each district of the Federation affiliate individually negotiates a collective agreement with the local school board. There is no reason, then, why the wording in different contracts concerning the number of classes and duties that can be assigned to teachers should be the same. In practice, the four affiliates (AEFO, ETFO, OECTA, and OSSTF) each tend to work closely with their various local branches to achieve some measure of consistency across the province.

Elementary School Collective Agreements. In elementary schools, where most teachers are assigned a single group of students for the whole day, collective agreements tend to focus on the following variables: the length of the instructional program each day; the maximum amount of supervision time a teacher can be assigned in any given cycle of days; and the minimum amount of preparation time a teacher must be assigned in any given cycle of days. For example, the collective agreement between Grand Erie District School Board and its Elementary Teachers' Federation affiliate for the period 2004–2008 included the following contract wording:

> The instructional day shall be 300 instructional minutes commencing with the start of opening exercises or the start of instruction, whichever comes first and ending with the students' dismissal from school for the day exclusive of lunch and recess break(s) ...
>
> The Board shall ensure that no teacher is required to perform in excess of 100 minutes of supervision time in a five day instructional cycle. In addition, the Board shall make every reasonable effort to reduce the amount of supervision time each teacher is required to perform to a maximum of 80 minutes in a five day instructional cycle ...
>
> Exclusive of morning and afternoon recesses and lunch periods, each teacher on a full-time assignment shall be assigned, in blocks of not less than forty (40) minutes, at least two hundred (200) minutes free from supervisory, teaching or other duties within each period of five instructional day cycle.

Secondary School Collective Agreements. In secondary schools, collective agreements tend to focus on the number of teaching periods in a day that a teacher may be assigned and the maximum amount of supervision time. In schools on a semester system, full-time teachers are typically expected to teach three out of four classes each semester and may be assigned a certain amount of supervision, usually expressed in half periods per cycle. Some contracts also spell out designated preparation time. If there is no wording about preparation time, unscheduled time on the teacher's timetable is considered to be preparation time. For example, the collective agreement between Toronto

District School Board and OSSTF District 12 for the period 2004–2008 included the following wording concerning preparation time, teaching time, and supervision time:

> Every full-time Teacher's timetable shall include an amount of assigned preparation time which, over the course of a school year is equal to the time equivalent of one credit course as time tabled in that Teacher's school in that school year ...
>
> All full-time Teachers will be assigned core professional responsibility for six teaching periods or equivalent out of eight ...
>
> A teacher who is assigned core professional responsibility for six teaching periods shall not, as a requirement, be assigned in a semester teaching duties of more than 3.0 teaching periods or equivalent except by written mutual consent ...
>
> A Teacher may be assigned by the principal for coverage, or supervision from time to time of one half period per week on average over the school year to a maximum of 27 such half period assignments. A Teacher may be scheduled for an assignment during a preparation period or during time free from teaching duties.

Electing Federation Officers

Teachers' federations play a crucial role in the professional lives of their members. It is therefore important for teachers to understand their role in the negotiation of salaries, benefits, working conditions, and arbitration procedures.

It is also important for teachers to take seriously their democratic rights and responsibilities as federation members. As members, they will be called on to elect school representatives and district leaders, give a strike mandate to teams negotiating collective agreements, and vote to accept or reject contracts.

DISCIPLINE AND DISMISSAL OF TEACHERS

The discipline of teachers by school boards is governed by education legislation, school board policies, and collective agreements. Disciplinary action can range from minor reproof (such as an oral reprimand) to severe actions (such as suspension without pay or dismissal).

There are three broad grounds for discipline or dismissal: professional misconduct, insubordination, and incompetence.

In all cases, the principal and other school officials must ensure substantive due process (fundamental fairness) and procedural due process (adherence to formal process). This includes giving teachers notice of specific charges and sufficient time to defend themselves and, where appropriate, improve. Discipline should also adhere to the principle of progressive discipline: for example, the first or second failure to arrive at school fifteen minutes before classes begin may result in an oral warning only; the third or fourth time in a formal written reprimand. At this stage, the superintendent may meet with the teacher to emphasize the seriousness of the situation and warn of possible suspension. If the teacher continues to ignore the principal's direction, the teacher may be suspended for a period of time. Given that most teachers are dedicated professionals, with a strong sense of their professional obligations and legal responsibilities, it is most unlikely that a teacher would ever reach this stage of the disciplinary process.

Note that it is not always necessary or appropriate for the principal to use the progressive discipline steps sequentially. Some instances of misconduct are so egregious that they may call for an immediate formal written reprimand or suspension.

A copy of the record of an oral warning or a written reprimand will normally be placed in a teacher's personnel file. Depending on board policy, these files will be kept either in the teacher's school or at the board office, or duplicates may be kept in both places. Under the *Municipal Freedom of Information and Protection of Privacy Act*, teachers have the right to look at the information contained in their file and ask for something to be corrected. If the principal or board declines to make the requested change, the teacher can request that a statement of disagreement be attached to the information.

Teachers should consult their union representatives in order to ensure that their interests and rights are protected.

Professional Misconduct

Teachers are required to adhere to their duties as outlined in the *Education Act* and other educational legislation. For example, a teacher who uses obscene language, views pornography on a school computer, or is found in possession of controlled substances could be disciplined for his or her actions. More serious misconduct, such as sexual conduct with students or possession of child pornography, could lead to dismissal and criminal charges. Professional misconduct could also lead to professional sanction by the Ontario College of Teachers.

Insubordination

Insubordination may be thought of as the refusal to carry out an order given by someone with the proper authority to give that order. In the school workplace, the person with proper authority is clearly the principal or vice-principal. A classroom teacher, then, must carry out a direction given by the principal or vice-principal.

Failure to comply with such a direction constitutes insubordination in most circumstances. If a principal disciplines a teacher for insubordination, the discipline will be upheld if it is proven that the conduct violated an order, the order was reasonable or valid, the violation was willful, and the discipline is proportionate to the offence.

Given the complexities of collective agreements, education statutes, and common law, teachers are advised to obey the principal, especially if the request is timely in nature. They should do so even if they think the task at hand is not something the teacher would normally be asked to perform, or contravenes the teacher's understanding of the terms of the local contract made between the branch of the federation affiliate and the district school board. They can then consult their teachers' federation representatives at a later time and if appropriate file a grievance against their principals.

There are three circumstances in which it is legitimate to refuse to carry out an order given by the principal or vice-principal. First, if the teacher genuinely believes that doing so would endanger his or her own health and safety. Second, if the teacher is being asked to perform an illegal act. Third, if carrying out the order would expose the teacher to potential liability.

The range of tasks assigned to teachers on a daily basis does not tend to include any that fit these criteria, because principals are experienced educators, chosen largely for their integrity and professionalism.

At all costs, avoid insubordination or even the impression of insubordination, because these could lead to complex disciplinary procedures and even dismissal.

Incompetence

Incompetence is generally defined as inadequate work performance. In education, this usually involves inadequate teaching or supervision, failure to maintain classroom discipline, and willful neglect of duty. The Teacher Performance Appraisal process must be followed before a teacher with a permanent contract can be dismissed for incompetence. New teachers go through a similar performance appraisal process before they are offered permanent contracts; failure to meet the competency standards could lead to non-renewal of a contract. Both teacher performance processes involve many stages and provide teachers with multiple opportunities to improve their practice.

TEACHER PERFORMANCE APPRAISAL

All workers, including professionals such as teachers, benefit from meaningful performance appraisals. The challenge is to develop a system of appraisal that is rigorous and fair and provides teachers with plenty of opportunities to grow professionally.

Teacher performance appraisals have been a politically sensitive issue in Ontario since the late 1990s. The teachers' federations resisted the efforts of the Progressive Conservative government during that time to reform the education system. Among the reforms resisted was one that established a mandatory teacher appraisal process.

The subsequent Liberal government has continued the previous government's provincial teacher appraisal system but has worked to develop processes that are acceptable to teachers, principals, and members of the public. This includes the development of the New Teacher Induction Program (NTIP), which is a requirement for all teachers who are new to Ontario's publicly funded schools system and who are hired as permanent teachers, either full-time or part-time. Under certain circumstances, new teachers who are hired on long-term occasional contracts are also required to participate in some elements of the program. In addition, the Teacher Performance Appraisal (TPA) system, mandatory for experienced teachers, was modified in 2007 to build on the NTIP performance appraisal process. This growth-focused appraisal process is designed for teachers as they move through the various stages of their careers.

NEW TEACHER INDUCTION PROGRAM (NTIP)

New teachers often find it difficult to make the transition from pre-service teacher education programs to the everyday reality of classroom teaching. The journey from survival in the first years to successful classroom practice to the development of instructional expertise is not an easy path for many (Berliner, 1994).

It is increasingly recognized that teachers in their first years of practice benefit from systemic support. In the United States, which has been facing high attrition rates among education graduates (Guarino, Santibanez & Daley, 2006), a great deal of effort has been put into the development of teacher induction programs and the training of mentors for new teachers.

The Ministry of Education in Ontario describes the purpose of the NTIP in the following way:

> The New Teacher Induction Program (NTIP) has been designed to support the growth and professional development of new teachers. It is the second step in a continuum of professional development for teachers to support effective teaching, learning, and assessment practices, building on and complementing the first step: pre-service education programs. It provides another full year of professional support so that new teachers can develop the requisite skills and knowledge that will enable them to achieve success as experienced teachers in Ontario. (Retrieved in September 2007 from http://www.edu.gov.on.ca/eng/teacher/induction.html.)

For the purposes of the program, new teachers are defined as all new teachers certified by the Ontario College of Teachers who have been hired into permanent positions or, in certain circumstances, have been hired on long-term occasional contracts.

Beginning in 2006–2007, publicly funded school boards were required to systematically address the diverse learning needs of large numbers of new teachers. This institutional undertaking offers opportunities to maximize the potential of a large pool of highly qualified new teachers. Several school boards have already developed interesting and effective projects in response to this challenge.

All school board programs consist of three interrelated elements:

- orientation for all new teachers to the school and the school board
- mentoring for new teachers by experienced teachers
- professional development and training appropriate for new teachers.

School boards are encouraged to develop relationships among these components and situate the induction of new teachers into the larger continuum of building excellence in the profession.

The role of the principal is critical to the effective induction of new teachers. This role includes ensuring that the induction components are responsive to the needs of the new teacher. Principals can make a difference by providing effective school orientations, identifying effective mentors, and providing guidance in the selection of professional development sessions.

The principal is also the appraiser who determines whether a new teacher has been successfully inducted into the profession. Successful completion of the program is evidenced by two satisfactory performance appraisals conducted by the principal (or vice-principal). The Ontario College of Teachers then places a notation on the Certificate of Qualification of the teacher who has successfully completed the program.

Participation in the Program

All new teachers, regardless of experience, must receive an orientation. Teachers who have never taught before in permanent positions must participate in all three elements of the program. Teachers who have taught before but who were certified elsewhere in Canada or internationally are required to participate in the elements of the program that complement their particular teaching experience and help orient them to the Ontario curriculum and educational context. The principal is responsible for working with the new teacher and the teacher's mentor to determine the precise content and delivery mode of each element of the program.

Beginning teachers who are hired on a long-term occasional contract of at least ninety-seven days for the same teacher must also be included in the induction elements of the NTIP. Other non-permanent first-year teachers, such as those hired on short-term occasional contracts, are not required to participate in the NTIP, but school boards may offer them the opportunity to do so. Neither of these two groups of teachers is eligible for the notation of successful completion on their certificate, but if they subsequently enter into a permanent contract, their previous participation may be taken into account by the principal when determining which elements of the program they still need to complete.

Performance Appraisal Process

According to the Ministry of Education's *New Teacher Induction Program: Manual for Performance Appraisal of New Teachers*, the performance appraisal process is part of a growth-oriented effort to promote excellence in teaching and learning:

In conjunction with the orientation, mentoring, professional development and training elements of the New Teacher Induction Program, the performance appraisal process for new teachers has been designed to support and promote the continued growth and development of new teachers. In the larger context of school improvement, the performance appraisal system provides principals and teachers with processes and procedures that can bring about improvements in teacher and student learning. The appraisal can also foster the collaboration and relationship building that are essential to creating and sustaining a professional learning community in schools. It is especially important to see the appraisal process as a supportive and effective way of helping new teachers develop into confident and proficient Ontario teachers. (p. 9)

There are five components of the performance appraisal framework for new teachers:

- **Competency statements** based on the Ontario College of Teachers' Standards of Practice for the Teaching Profession. The sixteen competency statements were developed with all teachers, new and experienced, in mind. For this reason, the appraisal process for new teachers is based on a subset of *eight* competency statements that focus on the immediate needs of teachers new to Ontario's classrooms. (See Figure 9-1.)
- **Appraisal meetings.** The principal must arrange a pre-observation meeting with the teacher in preparation for the classroom observation, and a post-observation meeting. These processes are outlined in detail in the manual.
- **A summative report** that formally documents the appraisal process. The form is a standardized Ministry of Education document.
- **A rating scale and rubric** to assess overall performance and provide feedback about strengths and weaknesses. The scale for new teachers is *Satisfactory* or *Development Needed*. The scale in subsequent appraisals for a teacher who receives a *Development Needed* is *Satisfactory* or *Unsatisfactory*. The manual also outlines an extensive process for providing additional support to new teachers who struggle to meet the satisfactory level needed to be successfully inducted into the teaching profession.

Boards may establish additional requirements for the performance appraisal process of new teachers, such as additional competencies or procedures to be followed, provided they do not conflict with the requirements set out in the *Education Act*.

In the process of determining a new teacher's performance in relation

Figure 9-1

THE SIXTEEN COMPETENCY STATEMENTS WITH EIGHT COMPETENCIES HIGHLIGHTED FOR NEW TEACHERS

DOMAIN	COMPETENCY
Commitment to Pupils* and Pupil Learning	• Teachers demonstrate commitment to the well-being and development of all pupils. • Teachers are dedicated in their efforts to teach and support pupil learning and achievement. • Teachers treat all pupils equitably and with respect. • Teachers provide an environment for learning that encourages pupils to be problem solvers, decision makers, lifelong learners, and contributing members of a changing society.
Professional Knowledge	• Teachers know their subject matter, the Ontario curriculum, and education-related legislation. • Teachers know a variety of effective teaching and assesment practices. • Teachers know a variety of effective classroom management strategies. • Teachers know how pupils learn and factors that influence pupil learning and achievement.
Professional Practice	• Teachers use their professional knowledge and understanding of pupils, curriculum, legislation, teaching practices, and classroom management strategies to promote the learning and achievement of their pupils. • Teachers communicate effectively with pupils, parents, and colleagues. • Teachers conduct ongoing assessment of pupils' progress, evaluate their achievement, and report results to the pupil and parents regularly. • Teachers adapt and refine their teaching practices through continuous learning and reflection, using a variety of sources and resources. • Teachers use appropriate technology in their teaching practices and related professional responsibilities.
Leadership in Learning Communities	• Teachers collaborate with other teachers and school colleagues to create and sustain learning communities in their classrooms and in their schools. • Teachers work with professionals, parents, and members of the community to enhance pupil learning, pupil achievement, and school programs.
Ongoing Professional Learning	• Teachers engage in ongoing professional learning and apply it to improve their teaching practices.

Note: Principal must provide a comment for each of the eight highlighted competencies as a minimum requirement in the Summative Report Form for New Teachers.

*In the *Education Act*, students are referred to as "pupils."   Ontario Ministry of Education to the eight competencies and any additional board-established criteria (see Figure 9-1), a principal must take into account not only the classroom observation but also the teacher's participation in the New Teacher Induction Program and any other relevant data.

As Figure 9-2 illustrates (see p. 271), the program provides new teachers with multiple opportunities to develop their skills in order to meet the standards expected of a satisfactory teacher.

The *New Teacher Induction Program: Manual for Performance Appraisal of New Teachers* states:

> The appraisal process for new teachers is designed to strengthen schools as learning communities in which new teachers are provided with plentiful opportunities to engage in professional exchange and collective inquiry that lead to continuous growth and development. It provides a framework to encourage improvement efforts aimed at ensuring student success. Essential in this process is the engagement of new teachers in professional dialogue that deepens their understanding of what it means to be a teacher as described in the *Ontario College of Teachers' Standards of Practice for the Teaching Profession.* (p. 6)

If this initiative is successful, the benefits could be great for new teachers, their students, and the quality of education in Ontario.

PERFORMANCE APPRAISAL SYSTEM FOR EXPERIENCED TEACHERS

Experienced teachers in Ontario are also required to be part of a teacher performance appraisal process. In response to concerns about the original Teacher Performance Appraisal process, the Ministry of Education consulted with the Education Partnership Table of educational stakeholders, including teacher federations, for advice on how to improve the system. A revised process was implemented in September 2007 that is more streamlined and teacher-friendly than the previous appraisal process.

The Ministry of Education describes the system in the following way.

Figure 9-2

PERFORMANCE APPRAISAL OF NEW TEACHERS FLOW CHART
NTIP YEAR ONE (two appraisals are required in the first 12 months after the teacher begins teaching)

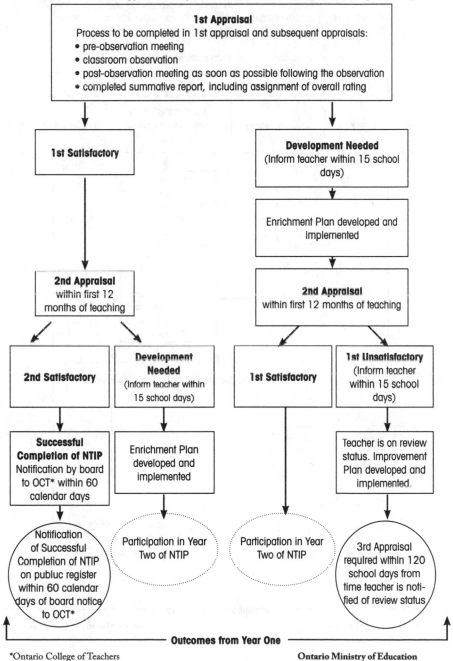

1st Appraisal
Process to be completed in 1st appraisal and subsequent appraisals:
• pre-observation meeting
• classroom observation
• post-observation meeting as soon as possible following the observation
• completed summative report, including assignment of overall rating

1st Satisfactory

Development Needed
(Inform teacher within 15 school days)

Enrichment Plan developed and implemented

2nd Appraisal
within first 12 months of teaching

2nd Appraisal
within first 12 months of teaching

2nd Satisfactory

Development Needed
(Inform teacher within 15 school days)

1st Satisfactory

1st Unsatisfactory
(Inform teacher within 15 school days)

Successful Completion of NTIP
Notification by board to OCT* within 60 calendar days

Enrichment Plan developed and implemented

Teacher is on review status. Improvement Plan developed and implemented.

Notification of Successful Completion of NTIP on publuc register within 60 calendar days of board notice to OCT*

Participation in Year Two of NTIP

Participation in Year Two of NTIP

3rd Appraisal required within 120 school days from time teacher is notified of review status

Outcomes from Year One

*Ontario College of Teachers   **Ontario Ministry of Education**

NTIP YEAR TWO–IF REQUIRED (must be completed within the teacher's first 24 months of teaching)

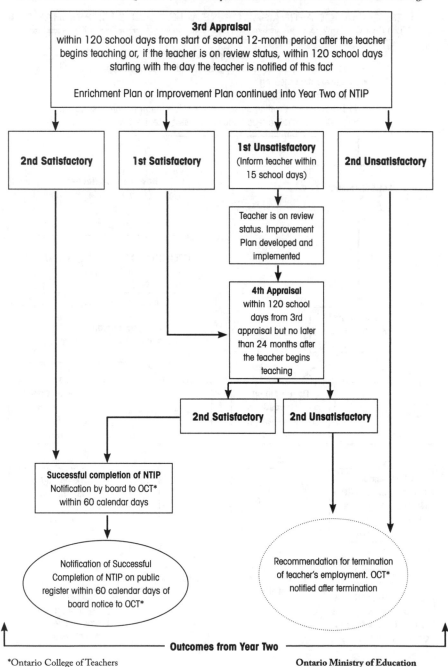

*Ontario College of Teachers   **Ontario Ministry of Education**

Professional dialogue and collaboration are a critical part of the appraisal process and an essential part of a healthy school culture. The performance appraisal process for experienced teachers provides a framework to assess experienced teachers' practices in a manner that reflects their needs for growth and development, and in which both the teacher and the principal take an active role. This includes the engagement of teachers in a professional dialogue that deepens their understanding of what it means to be a teacher as described in the Ontario College of Teachers' *Standards of Practice for the Teaching Profession*. (*Performance Appraisal of Experienced Teachers: Technical Requirements Manual*, 2009, p. 5)

When teachers successfully complete the NTIP, they are placed on the experienced teachers' performance appraisal schedule. This schedule requires that a teacher must have an evaluation year in every five-year period. During the evaluation year, a teacher must receive at least one performance appraisal. Teachers may request appraisals in years other than their evaluation year, and principals may choose to conduct appraisals in other years. The first year in which an experienced teacher is employed by a board is also considered an evaluation year.

Following are the six key components of the appraisal process:

- **Competency Statements**, designed to focus the appraisal on the knowledge, skills, and attitudes that reflect the standards described in the Ontario College of Teachers' Standards of Practice for the Teaching Profession. The sixteen competency statements outline the standards expected of an experienced teacher in Ontario.
- **Annual Learning Plan (ALP)**, intended to help teachers to identify strategies for professional growth during their teaching career. Teachers are required to complete an ALP in consultation with the principal every year. During their evaluation year, the ALP becomes part of the appraisal process. Although boards are no longer required to survey parents and senior students as part of the teacher appraisal process, teachers

are encouraged to consider how they might gather parental and student input when developing their ALP.

- **Appraisal meetings,** which promote professional dialogue between the teacher and the principal, consisting of a pre-observation meeting to prepare for the classroom observation and a post-observation meeting. The meetings are intended to foster the teacher's professional growth and improvement. Note that classroom observation is only one component of the appraisal process. For some competencies, evidence will be gathered by the principal in other ways.

- **Summative report,** which formally documents the appraisal process in Ministry-approved format. This report includes: the principal's comments about those competencies identified by the teacher and principal as the focus of the appraisal (the principal may also comment on other competencies); recommendations for professional growth goals and strategies for the teacher to consider when developing his or her ALP; and an overall rating based on all sixteen competencies. Teachers may also add their own comments to the summative report.

- **Rating scale** to assess the teacher's overall performance. The rating scale for experienced teachers is *Satisfactory* or *Unsatisfactory.*

- **Process for Providing Additional Support,** depending on the outcome of the appraisal. (See Performance Appraisal Process (Overview) below, which is Appendix G of *Performance Appraisal of Experienced Teachers: Technical Requirements Manual* (2009).)

Boards may also identify additional requirements for the performance appraisal of its experienced teachers, such as additional competencies or other material that must be taken into account in the appraisal process, provided that these requirements do not conflict with those set out in the *Education Act.* Teacher federations have also developed resources to help teachers negotiate the performance appraisal process.

Figure 9-3

PERFORMANCE APPRAISAL PROCESS (OVERVIEW)
(from Ontario Ministry of Education (2009), *Performance Appraisal of Experienced Teachers: Technical Requirements Manual*)

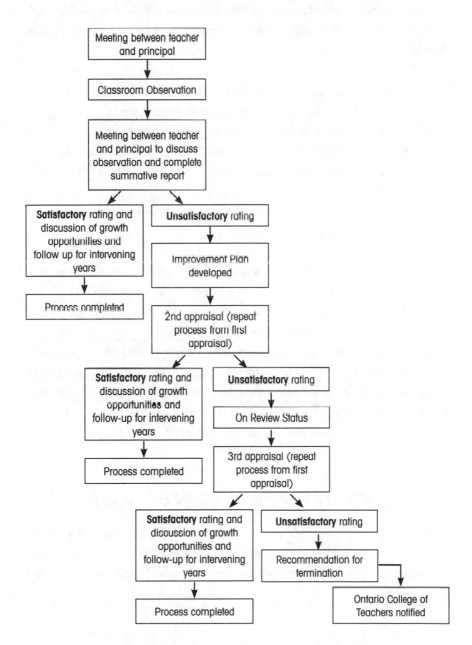

Annual Learning Plan

One recommendation of the Education Partnership Table was to adapt the Annual Learning Plan (ALP) to "provide a more meaningful vehicle for the teacher's professional learning in the intervening years between appraisals" (Ontario Ministry of Education, 2006). This led to *Regulation 98/02*, which came into effect on September 1, 2007. It makes the following changes to the Annual Learning Plans:

- Every experienced teacher shall have a learning plan each year that includes the teacher's professional growth objectives, proposed action plan, and timelines for achieving those objectives.
- Each year after the first year that a teacher has a learning plan, the teacher and the principal shall consult to review and update the plan.
- Both the teacher and principal shall sign and retain copies of the teacher's learning plan for the year.

In this process teachers direct and author their own professional growth in consultation with the principal. The process is also a streamlined one that allows the individual teacher to focus on as few as one professional growth objective. That said, teachers are invited to consider linking their own personal objectives to school board expectations. This appraisal process also provides continuity by allowing the extension of professional development plans across more than one year. Extracurricular activities and community involvement, according to the federations, should not be part of the ALP because they are not among the duties of teachers indicated in the *Education Act* and regulations.

OPERATIONAL ISSUES IN SCHOOLS

Teachers are not responsible for the organization of the school day or the school year. Nonetheless, it is important for them to understand how their classroom teaching situation is shaped by provincial legislation and school board policies.

SCHOOL DAY

According to *Regulation 298*, section 3, the length of the instructional program for pupils of compulsory school age must be not less than five hours, excluding a lunch period, recesses, and travel time between classes. For example, in secondary schools on a semester system, most students are assigned four classes per day of seventy-five minutes each, for a total of three hundred minutes (five hours). The length of the instructional program for kindergarten and junior kindergarten is established by the local school board. Note that the five-hour minimum requirement applies only to students. Teacher workloads, including the number of classes taught and supervisory duties assigned, are a matter of negotiation between local teacher affiliates and school boards. Teachers may be required to assume additional supervisory or administrative duties under the *Education Act* and *Regulation 298* (see chapter 3).

Without special permission of the Minister of Education, the local school board must schedule the instructional program in each of its schools between 8 a.m. and 5 p.m.

When classes actually begin and end, frequently known as "bell times," is a matter for the local school board—or, failing that, the school principal—to decide. In some school boards there is a trend toward starting and ending secondary school classes earlier so buses can then collect elementary school students for their school day, which begins later. This also means that there is more daylight time available at the end of the secondary school day for co-instructional activities.

Co-instructional activities, however, may take place outside the official 8 a.m. to 5 p.m. school day. Sports teams, school bands, and other groups often meet early, before classes begin, or in the late afternoon and early evening; many school events, such as graduation, concerts, plays, and fashion shows, take place in the evening.

Before and After Class

The *Education Act* requires teachers to ensure that their classroom or teaching area is ready to receive pupils at least fifteen minutes before classes begin in the morning and, where applicable, five minutes before they begin in the afternoon. Apart from this, there is nothing in the act that speaks to the time a teacher is expected to arrive in the morning and leave at the end of the day, or come and go during the day. As professionals, teachers are not paid by the hour or even by the day.

The presence of teachers in classrooms and hallways plays an important role in establishing the tone of a school and building relationships with students and colleagues. Teachers have a professional obligation to their students to arrive in the morning early enough to attend to any necessary business or respond to changes of plan before classes begin. They should also consider staying long enough at the end of the day to allow students and colleagues to meet with them informally.

Teachers also have a professional and legal obligation to attend meetings called before or after classes, and a legal obligation to attend parent–teacher meetings, which may be scheduled in the evening. Protocols with regard to whether teachers can leave the school during the school day when they have no assigned classes or duties are usually a matter of school culture. Some schools require teachers to sign out and in at the main office, while others require the teacher to see the principal personally. Teachers should know the expectations and procedures in their schools. (See chapter 3 for administrative duties under education legislation.)

Lunch

Teachers and students are required to have a scheduled lunch break of at least forty consecutive minutes. In many schools, lunch periods are longer than this. Some elementary schools have longer lunches to allow students to return home for lunch. In secondary schools, this may be because there is more than one lunch block, with lunch often being the same length as an instructional period. Schools with large numbers of bused students may schedule two lunch periods, with half of the student body scheduled for lunch break while the other half is still in class.

It may be necessary to assign teachers to supervision duties during lunch periods. When this happens, the teacher will have a scheduled lunch break at a different time of day, to ensure that they still receive the required forty consecutive minutes. Local contracts may sometimes limit the times within which a teacher's lunch break may be scheduled without the mutual consent of principal and teacher. Although it may sometimes be necessary to schedule an emergency meeting during the lunch break, a wise principal is sensitive to the time constraints placed on teachers and the importance for them of having some time during the day for rest and recuperation, meeting informally, and socializing with colleagues, not to mention any last-minute preparation.

OPENING OR CLOSING EXERCISES

Changes to the opening or closing exercises provisions in the *Education Act* illustrate the *ad hoc* way in which the act has been amended over the years in response to the changing nature of Ontario society.

In 1988 the Ontario Court of Appeal struck down section 28(1) of *Regulation 262*, which dealt with religious exercises in public elementary schools. (This subsection did not apply to schools operated by separate school boards.) The court determined that no religion may be given primacy of place in public schools, and that the content of any opening or closing exercises should reflect the multicultural nature of Ontario society. In the wake of the court's decision, the Ministry of Education in 1993 amended the regulation (now renumbered as *Regulation 298*) and published Policy/Program Memorandum 108 in 1993 outlining the new expectations for the exercises:

> The purposes of opening or closing exercises are patriotic and educational. Such exercises are intended to nurture allegiance to Canada and to contribute to the social, moral, and spiritual development of the pupils.
>
> Contributing to the social, moral, and spiritual development of pupils includes reinforcing the positive societal values that, in general, Canadians hold and regard as essential to the well-being of our society. These values transcend cultures and faiths, reinforce democratic rights and responsibilities, and are based on a fundamental belief in the worth of all persons.

Section 4 of *Regulation 298* was amended again, in 2000, to nurture allegiance to Canada. As a result of these changes:

- All public and separate schools in Ontario *must* hold opening or closing exercises.
- These exercises *shall* include the singing of *O Canada*. (Before the revisions of the late 1990s, the requirement was simply that the exercises include *O Canada*.)
- Parents or adult students may request an exemption from the exercises. No reason need be given.

Regulation 435/00 states, in addition:

The principal *may* decide to include a pledge of citizenship. This decision must be consistent with board policy, taken in consultation with the school council, and reviewed annually.

This option to include the pledge was another revision that was made in the late 1990s.

Section 4 of *Regulation 298* also provides further guidance for public schools, as opposed to separate schools, that may wish to extend opening or closing exercises. The exercises *may* include:

- the singing of *God Save the Queen*
- a period of silence, intended for personal reflection or silent prayer
- scriptural writings, including prayers
- secular writings.

Since the social, moral, and spiritual development of Canadians has roots in many religious and philosophical traditions, readings must be drawn from a variety of scriptural and secular sources representative of our multicultural society (PPM 108). Prayers, including the Lord's Prayer, may be included, but only as readings. The courts have ruled that the collective recitation of a specific reading from a particular religious tradition is inconsistent with the *Canadian Charter of Rights and Freedoms*.

It is clear from the above discussion that the question of opening and closing exercises in schools has been the topic of much debate and legislation over the past twenty years. The intensity of debate reflects the seriousness with which society views an activity that has patriotic and religious associations. Schools, then, need to give due weight and consideration to their opening or closing exercises.

One of the key factors in ensuring that students treat opening exercises with the solemnity they deserve is insisting that they arrive in good time, rather than rushing through the school corridors during the singing of *O Canada*. Many schools have pre-recorded programs to encourage students to get to class on time in the morning before the opening exercises begin (including "get to class music" and time checks).

Teachers bear a special responsibility to model the solemnity the exercises deserve and to ensure that their students conduct themselves appropriately. If students elect not to sing *O Canada*, they should at least stand in an attentive manner. Whether students stand or sit during any other components of the exercises is a matter of school culture. Whatever the cultural expectations of the school may be, the classroom teacher should insist that students remain attentive and respectful of the school's expectations.

Where students have been exempted by the principal from participating in the opening or closing exercises (often for religious reasons), the school should make special arrangements so they are not singled out in class.

SCHOOL YEAR

The local school board has the annual responsibility of drawing up a school year calendar to be submitted to the Minister of Education and eventually published for parents and students. In drafting the calendar, the school board must follow the requirements prescribed in *Regulation 304*. This regulation provides an overall framework by stating that the school year must begin on or after September 1 and end on or before June 30, and that between those two dates boards must ensure that a minimum of 194 school days are scheduled. Boards who wish to alter this framework or any of the other requirements in the regulation must have the approval of the minister.

Of the 194 school days, the board must designate *two* professional activity days, and *may* designate an *additional four* such days. "Professional activity" is described in *Regulation 304* as including "evaluation of the progress of pupils, consultation with parents, the counselling of pupils, curriculum and program evaluation and development, professional development of teachers and attendance at educational conferences." It does not include preparation by teachers for classes or instruction.

If the board chooses to designate one or more additional professional activity days, it must ensure that some of the professional activities relate to curriculum development, implementation, and review. When submitting its calendar to the Ministry, the board is required to provide a general outline of the activities that will take place on all professional activity days identified on the calendar. The board must also prepare an agenda for each professional activity day and make it available to teachers and parents at least ten days in advance of the day. It is important to remember that teachers have a legal duty as well as a professional responsibility to attend professional activity days.

Boards may also designate up to ten examination days during the school year. How these days are allocated is left to the discretion of the individual board. A typical configuration in schools on a semester system is to allocate five days at the end of each semester. The regulation also requires teachers to be in school during regular school hours and available to students, unless the board directs otherwise. In many jurisdictions, teachers are permitted to work at home during examination days if they are not supervising an examination, attending meetings, or carrying out other assigned duties. If this is the case in your school, bear in mind that the flexibility to fulfill your school-related obligations elsewhere is a privilege, not a right. Choices should be exercised with professional responsibility. Parents and students are not likely to look favourably on teachers who golf or shop during an examination day.

Regulation 304 also identifies days in the school year that are school holidays, including every Saturday and Sunday, Thanksgiving, the Easter weekend, and Victoria Day. Ten days are designated for a Christmas vacation and five days in March. Remembrance Day is no longer a school holiday but schools are required to hold a Remembrance Day service on November 11, or on the preceding Friday if November 11 falls on a weekend.

Teachers' professional responsibilities do not begin and end with the school day, nor are they limited by the definition of the school year in

Regulation 304. Most teachers have tasks directly associated with their classroom teaching, such as lesson preparation and student assessment, that require them to work evenings and weekends. Similarly, as outlined in chapter 3, teachers have a legal obligation under *Regulation 298* to attend parent–teacher interviews and graduation ceremonies, even if they occur in the evening.

Most teachers also commit themselves to professional development or to helping with co-instructional activities outside the instructional day. Many teachers attend professional workshops or take additional qualification courses during evenings, weekends, or summers in order to upgrade their professional qualifications. Many also devote considerable time to coaching sports, directing arts performances, chaperoning students, or supervising other co-instructional activities. These activities often take place after school in the evening, on the weekend, and sometimes even during school holidays.

Involvement in co-instructional activities can be very rewarding to both students and teachers. These voluntary contributions are integral to school life. Indeed, there is evidence to suggest that students who participate in such programs tend to be more successful in the instructional program. Teachers, however, should be careful to maintain focus on their central role as classroom teacher.

ATTENDANCE REQUIREMENTS FOR STUDENTS

The legislation concerning a person's right to attend school and the requirements concerning compulsory attendance at school were discussed in chapter 7. But what are the obligations of a person already registered at school?

According to section 23 of *Regulation 298*, all students, whatever their age, have a legal duty to attend classes regularly and punctually. Only the principal has the legal authority to excuse a student from attendance at school.

In the case of students under the age of eighteen, the parents are required to give the reason for a student's absence to the principal. They have the obligation to request in writing that the student be excused. Since the *Education Amendment Act (Learning to Age 18)* in 2006, all students under the age of eighteen are also bound by the requirements of section 21 of the *Education Act*, which sets out the legal reasons for non-attendance.

For a person under the age of eighteen already registered as a student in a school, who has not attained an Ontario Secondary School Diploma and has not been suspended or expelled, these reasons effectively come down to sickness or "other unavoidable cause," religious holy days, and a half day a week for music instruction. Parents must have the principal's prior authorization for a student's absence for reasons beyond these.

Adult students are not bound by the compulsory attendance provisions of section 21 of the *Education Act*, but they are still bound by the Requirements for Pupils set out in section 23 of *Regulation 298*. When students register in a school, it is as if they have entered into an unwritten contract with the principal to comply with the *Education Act* and regulations, as well as the school's code of conduct. As adults, these students may write their own request to be excused from attendance. Where persistent lateness and poor attendance patterns develop, the principal may well decide not to accept a reason for absence or grant a request to be excused. If the adult student is unwilling to comply with the principal's expectations, the principal could make it a disciplinary matter.

Although it is the principal who has the legal duty to monitor students' attendance, classroom teachers have an important role to play. The classroom teacher usually has the task of taking attendance at the beginning of the day and reporting the names of absent students to the principal. Where students move from class to class with different teachers, each teacher is usually responsible for checking attendance and reporting the names of students whose absence is unexplained. The classroom teacher may also be responsible for collecting information from students after an absence. Schools have different protocols for handling attendance and contacting parents of students whose absence is unexplained, but the reliability of the whole system is primarily based on the meticulousness of the classroom teacher. Unexplained or frequent absences by younger students should raise overriding concerns about the student's safety and welfare. Teachers who respond early to poor attendance patterns, even with older students, can make the difference between a student's success and failure in school.

CHECKING YOUR UNDERSTANDING

- The principal is the teacher's immediate supervisor in the workplace.

- Teachers have a duty to cooperate with department heads or division leaders in all matters related to classroom instruction.

- Teachers have a duty to teach the classes or subjects assigned by the principal but can be assigned only the classes that they are qualified to teach according to their certificate of qualification.

- Within certain limits, teachers may teach classes for which they do not hold qualifications, provided that both the principal and teacher are in agreement.

- The local affiliates of OTF negotiate collective agreements with individual school boards on behalf of their members and provide teachers with advice and support.

- Discipline of teachers must be substantively and procedurally fair, and should be progressive in nature.

- In most situations, teachers should carry out an order given to them by the principal or vice-principal in the school. Insubordination could lead to dismissal.

- All new teachers hired into permanent contracts are required to participate in the New Teacher Induction Program. Successful completion of the program is evidenced by two satisfactory performance appraisals by the principal.

- Beginning teachers hired on a long-term occasional contract of at least ninety-seven days for the same teacher are required to participate in the induction elements of the NTIP.

- On successful completion of the NTIP, a teacher is placed on the experienced teachers' performance appraisal schedule, in which every fifth year is an evaluation year.

- Experienced teachers are required to develop an Annual Learning Plan each year.

- The instructional program for students of compulsory school age must not be less than five hours, and must be scheduled between 8 a.m. and 5 p.m.

- Teachers have a legal and professional obligation to participate in meetings scheduled outside the limits of the school day.

- Both teachers and students must have a lunch break of forty consecutive minutes.

- All schools are required to hold opening or closing exercises. The exercises must include the singing of *O Canada*, and may include a pledge of citizenship, the singing of *God Save the Queen*, a period of silence, and appropriate readings.

- The school year must contain at least 194 school days, and must begin no earlier than September 1 and finish no later than June 30.

- Every school board must designate two professional activity days, and may designate an additional four. Teachers have a legal duty to attend professional development days.

- A school board may designate up to a maximum of ten examination days per year.

- All students of any age have a duty to attend classes regularly and punctually. Only the principal may excuse a student from attendance at school.

APPLYING YOUR UNDERSTANDING

The Argumentative Teacher

A cloud hung over Mr. Rubens. He had received a written reprimand for insubordination the previous year. In February, Mr. Rubens had been suspended for four days for insubordination. Although he had a short temper, and still felt contempt for his ineffectual principal, he was determined to stay out of trouble.

Mr. Rubens helped chaperone the school dance on Friday, May 13. He had noticed two girls going off with men from outside the school. While he told the girls that he would not tell their parents, Mr. Rubens did inform the principal on Monday morning. The principal informed the parents, who reproved the girls that evening.

The next day, immediately after hearing from the girls, Mr. Rubens encountered the principal in the busy front foyer. An argument ensued. Mr. Rubens then shouted, "Leave them alone! You have done enough damage already!"

The next day, Mr. Rubens was dismissed for insubordination. The school board noted his acts of insubordination in its letter of dismissal.

Mr. Rubens and his federation legal counsel appealed the dismissal to an arbitration panel. Mr. Rubens argued that the principal had acted inappropriately. His lawyer also argued that the punishment was excessive and not consistent with principles of progressive discipline.

(1) Did Mr. Rubens's conduct fulfill his legal and professional duties as a teacher under the *Education Act*, *Regulation 298*, and the *Foundations of Professional Practice*? Explain.
(2) Was Mr. Rubens insubordinate? Were there mitigating factors?
(3) Was dismissal warranted, or should there have been another penalty?
(4) How do you think the arbitration panel would rule in this case?

Offering Advice

At the end of the school day, a colleague steps into your classroom.

"Got a minute?" she asks.

After closing the door and sitting down, she informs you that she received an unsatisfactory report.

"Actually, it is my second unsatisfactory evaluation," she adds.

You are not entirely surprised by the news. She has seemed overwhelmed by classroom management issues this year.

"I am worried that I could lose my job," she says, suppressing a sob.

Then she asks for your advice.

---

(1) What advice would you give her if she is a new teacher (under NTIP)?

(2) What advice would you give her if she is an experienced teacher (under TPA)?

(3) In your answer, consider how to enhance her professional growth and protect her employment rights.

REFERENCES

Note: References do not include legal codes, legal decisions, provincial education documents, and teacher federation or Ontario College of Teachers materials. These are all readily available electronically.

Ainscow, M. (2008). Teaching for diversity: The next big challenge. In Connelly, F., He, M. & Phillion, J. (eds.). *The Sage handbook of curriculum and instruction* (pp. 240–58). Thousand Oaks, CA: Sage Publications.

Bacon, F. (1597; 1965). Of parents and children. *Bacon's essays.* London: Macmillan.

Bennett, S. & Dworet, D. with Weber, K. (2008). *Special education in Ontario schools,* sixth edition. St. Davids, ON: Highland Press.

Bennett, S. & Wynne, K. (2006). *Special education transformation: The report of the co-chairs of the working table on special education.* Toronto: Ontario Ministry of Education.

Bowlby, B., Peters, C. & Mackinnon, M. (2001). *An educator's guide to special education law.* Aurora, ON: Canada Law Books.

Brown, A. (2004). *Legal handbook for educators,* fifth edition. Toronto: ThomsonCarswell.

Brown, A. & Zuker, M. (2002). *Education law,* third edition. Toronto: ThomsonCarswell.

Brown, A. & Zuker, M. (2007). *Education law,* fourth edition. Toronto: ThomsonCarswell.

Browne, L. (2007). 84 per cent of teachers have been cyberbullied. *Professionally Speaking,* September 2007, p. 51.

Bunch, G. & Valeo, N. (2004). Student attitudes towards peers with disabilities in inclusive and special education schools. *Disability and Society* 1(1), 61–78.

Campbell, E. (2003). *The ethical teacher.* Maidenhead, UK: Open University Press.

Coloroso, B. (2003). *The bully, the bullied and the bystander.* New York: HarperCollins.

Cook, K. & Truscott, D. (2007). *Ethics and law for teachers.* Toronto: Thomson Nelson.

Daloz, L.A. (1986). *Effective teaching and mentoring.* San Francisco: Jossey-Bass.

Dewey, J. (1938). *Experience and education.* New York: Collier.

Dickinson, G. (2009). School searches and student rights under the Charter: Old wine in new skins. In Manley-Casimir, M. & Manley-Casimir, K. (eds.). *The courts, the Charter, and the schools: The impact of the Charter of Rights and Freedoms on educational policy and practice, 1982–2007* (pp. 155–80). Toronto: University of Toronto Press.

Epstein, J. & Rodriguez-Jansorn, N. (2004). School, family, and community partnerships link the plan. *Educational Digest* 69(6).

Gersten, R., Baker S., Pugach, M., Scanlon, D. & Chard, D. (2001). Research on teaching in special education, in Richardson, V. (ed.). *The handbook of research on teaching,* fourth edition. Washington: American Educational Research Association.

Guarino, C., Santibanez, L. & Daley, G. (2006). Teacher recruitment and retention: A review of the recent empirical literature. *Review of Educational Research* 76(2), 173–208.

Hansen, D. (2001). Teaching as a moral activity. In Richardson, V. (ed.). *Handbook of research on teaching,* fourth edition (pp. 826–57). Washington, DC: American Educational Research Association.

Howe, M. (1990). *The origins of exceptional abilities.* Oxford: Basil Blackwell.

Keel, R.G. (2001). The spectre of parental and intruder harassment. *Orbit* 32(2), 64.

Kindred, K. (2006). The teacher in dissent: Freedom of expression and the classroom. *Education Law Journal* 15(3), 207–32.

Kindred, K. (2009). The teacher in dissent: Freedom of expression and the classroom. In Manley-Casimir, M. & Manley-Casimir, K. (eds.). *The courts, the Charter, and the schools: The impact of the Charter of Rights and Freedoms on educational policy and practice, 1982–2007* (pp. 135–54). Toronto: University of Toronto Press.

McIntyre, E. & Bloom, D. (2002). *An educator's guide to the Ontario College of Teachers.* Aurora, ON: Aurora Professional Press.

Mackay, W. (2009). The lighthouse of equality: A guide to 'inclusive' schooling. In Manley-Casimir, M. & Manley-Casimir, K. (eds.). *The courts, the Charter, and the schools: The impact of the Charter of Rights and Freedoms on educational policy and practice, 1982–2007* (pp. 39–63). Toronto: University of Toronto Press.

McPhail, J. & Freeman, J. (2005). Beyond prejudice: Thinking toward genuine inclusion. *Learning Disabilities Research and Practice* 20(4), 254–67.

Milner, M., Jr. (2004). *Freaks, geeks and cool kids: American teenagers, schools and the culture of consumption.* New York: Routledge.

National Academy of Education (2005). *A good teacher in every classroom: Preparing the highly qualified teachers our children deserve.* San Francisco: Jossey-Bass.

Noddings, N. (2001). The caring teacher. In Richardson, V. (ed.). *Handbook of research on teaching,* fourth edition (pp. 99–105). Washington, DC: American Educational Research Association.

Nucci, L.P. (2001). *Education in the moral domain.* Cambridge: Cambridge University Press.

Olivierio, C. & Manley-Casimir, M. (2009). The courts and the school: Judicial construction of the school. In Manley-Casimir, M. & Manley-Casimir, K. (eds.). *The courts, the Charter, and the schools: The impact of the Charter of Rights and Freedoms on educational policy and practice, 1982 2007* (pp. 242 62). Toronto: University of Toronto Press.

Ontario College of Teachers (2006). *Foundations of professional practice.* Toronto: Ontario College of Teachers.

Ontario College of Teachers (2006). *Exploring ethical knowledge through inquiry.* Toronto: Ontario College of Teachers.

Ontario College of Teachers (2006). *Teachers' reflections on the standards.* Toronto: Ontario College of Teachers.

Ontario Ministry of Education, 2006, Report to the Partnership Table on a Revised Teacher Performance Appraisal System for Experienced Teachers: Recommendations of the Working Table on Teacher Development, October 23, 2006.

Ontario Ministry of Education (2009). *New teacher induction program: Manual for performance appraisal of new teachers.* Toronto: Ontario College of Teachers.

Ontario Ministry of Education (2009). *Performance appraisal of experienced teachers: technical requirements manual.* Toronto: Ontario College of Teachers.

Ontario Ministry of Education (2001). *Special education: A guide for educators.* Toronto: Ontario College of Teachers.

Ontario Ministry of Education (2004). *The individual education plan (IEP): A resources guide.* Toronto: Queen's Printer of Ontario.

Ontario Ministry of Education (2005). *Education for all: The report of the expert panel on literacy and numeracy instruction for students with special education needs, Kindergarten to Grade 6.* Toronto: Queen's Printer of Ontario.

Ontario Ministry of Education (2007). *Shared solutions: A guide to preventing and resolving conflicts regarding programs and services for students with special education needs.* Toronto: Queen's Printer of Ontario.

Piddocke, S., Magsino, R. & Manley-Casimir, M. (1997). *Teachers in trouble: An exploration of the normative character of teaching.* Toronto: University of Toronto Press.

Praisner, C. (2003). Attitudes of elementary school principals toward the inclusion of students with disabilities. *Exceptional Children* 69(2), 135–45.

Robbins, S. (2000). *Protecting our children: A review to identify and prevent sexual misconduct in Ontario schools.* Toronto: Queen's Printer of Ontario.

Roher, E.M. (1997). *An educator's guide to violence in schools.* Aurora, ON: Aurora Professional Press.

Rouleau, P.S. (2006). Education in transition: A delicate balance. Paper presented at LawWorks, Toronto, August 2006.

Royal Commission on Learning (1994). *For the love of learning.* Toronto: Queen's Printer of Ontario.

Safe Schools Action Team (2005). *Shaping safer schools: A bullying prevention action plan.* Toronto: Queen's Printer of Ontario.

Safe Schools Action Team (2008). *Shaping a culture of respect in our schools: Promoting safe and healthy relationships.* Toronto: Queen's Printer of Ontario.

School Community Safety Advisory Panel (2008). *The road to health: A final report on school safety.* Toronto: Toronto District School Board.

Scott, G.F. (2008). Student privacy and you. *Professionally Speaking,* March 2008, 43–47.

Strike, K. & Ternansky, L. (eds.) (1993). *Ethics for educational professionals: The place of ethics in their preparation and practice.* New York: Teachers College Press.

Task Force on Youth Violent Crime (2000). *Final report.* Toronto: Queen's Printer of Ontario.

Tom, A.(1997). *Redesigning teacher education.* Albany, NY: SUNY Press.

Zuker, M., Hammond, R. & Flynn, R. (2005). *Children's law handbook.* Toronto: Thomson Carswell.

Index of Cases

INDEX